Investor Obligations in International Law

Developments in International Law

VOLUME 86

The titles published in this series are listed at *brill.com/diil*

Investor Obligations in International Law

Edited by

Makane Moïse Mbengue
Jackson Shaw Kern
Mohit Khubchandani

BRILL | NIJHOFF

ISSN 0924-5332
ISBN 978-90-04-76984-7
ISBN 978-90-04-76985-4 (PDF)
DOI https://doi.org/10.1163/9789004769854

Library of Congress Control Number: 2026948196

Brill Nijhoff and Koninklijke Brill BV are part of De Gruyter Brill.
www.degruyterbrill.com

Questions about General Product Safety Regulation: productsafety@degruyterbrill.com

Contents

Introduction: From the Editors' Desks

The true gravity of international law has historically weighed upon the States, and the international law of investment protection presents no exception. Tracing the line from the earliest concepts of a customary minimum standard of treatment and the emergence of treaties expressly codifying State guarantees to the modern era of investor access to arbitration and its subsequent backlash, the force of international law has always fallen upon State conduct. On the other side of the international investment equation, the true control function for regulating *investor conduct* has traditionally found itself relegated to municipal laws and courts, even as the heft of multinational economic actors often rivals that of many States.

The assumptions attending this equation are presently undergoing a re-examination, and the equation itself a consequent rebalancing. While this phenomenon may be gleaned in the natural evolution of international law (as seen increasingly in the jurisprudence of international tribunals), it is also unmistakable in the active workings of the treatymakers. International investment tribunals have begun to openly adjudicate these questions – particularly in the context of host States' counterclaims. In perhaps the most prominent case, one tribunal expressly found that investors are no longer immune from becoming subjects of international law. Meanwhile, emerging bilateral, plurilateral, and multilateral economic treaties establish not only investor protections but also their obligations, thereby directly regulating the conduct of these non-State actors and envisaging a reformed regime that permits a role reversal of stakeholders in investment arbitration.

This volume, the very first entirely dedicated to this topic, results from exemplary collaboration amongst expert contributors.

The immediate concept was born in the 2023 Annual Meeting of the African Society of International Law at the headquarters of the African Union in Addis Ababa, having as its theme *Africa and the Governance of the Global Commons*. Following an intervention regarding international environmental and climate change law obligations under the Protocol on Investment to the Agreement Establishing the African Continental Free Trade Area (AfCFTA), given by Jackson Shaw Kern and Mohit Khubchandani, a conversation ensued in which Professor Makane Moïse Mbengue suggested a dedicated symposium featuring the Protocol's entire suite of investor obligations. Ultimately, the resulting collection, which you now hold in your hands, has reached beyond the African Continent to comprise a contemporary examination of the state of investor obligations in international law. It has nonetheless been guided all the while by the AfCFTA Investment Protocol as perhaps the most ambitious, progressive, and expansive effort towards codification to date.

It cannot be unmentioned that between the time our symposium was convened and the actual publication of this volume, some of the core precepts long characterising international law and international relations have come under renewed and considerable strain. The feeling that we are living in a time of great disruption in the world order is palpable, ever-present, and real. What precisely awaits at the end of this tunnel as we approach a possible point of inflection on the curve of modern human history will only be seen with the benefit of more time. But one may more easily take stock of what is it we are leaving behind. After the Second World War, we experienced a prolonged bipolar era and then, quite abruptly, an essentially unipolar age which – some might say – is now, in its turn, giving way in a reversion to the dominant historical norm. That norm is a more volatile multipolar assortment in which first-tier and lesser-tier powers jockey incessantly for hegemony and influence, whilst a true and durable ordering principle or equilibrium evades us. We may see ongoing flurries of activity in alliance-making and alliance-breaking. As the saying goes, traced to Thucydides, "the strong do what they can, and the weak suffer what they must" – *c'est le droit du plus fort.* The presumption that States, having sovereign forces and allies, are stronger in their bargaining power or position than purportedly weaker investors does not necessarily hold true a quarter into the 21st century. In juxtaposition, investors' turnovers often far exceed the economic output of many States; these investors may additionally be backed by powerful home States. In such a powerplay imbalance, it may not be desirable that acts of investors be left unfettered and unchecked by the norms of international law.

It does seem fair to surmise that we are entering a phase which may see serious and sustained questioning of (and challenge to) the proper place and functioning of international law and legal mechanisms. Some States' purposeful fragmentation of the international legal order may serve to make international investors even more powerful. The incumbent administration in the United States has (again) withdrawn the world's largest economy and largest per-capita emitter of greenhouse gases from the Paris Agreement (and has, as a corollary, lifted moratoriums on non-renewable energy operations by private companies) while taking other measures which strike – from the municipal plane – at the heart of prized internationalist achievements. These include apparently ordering a suspension in enforcement (and a later re-ordering of enforcement priorities) in respect of the nearly-fifty-years-old Foreign Corrupt Practices Act, which has long been a standard-bearer in both national legislations and international treaties, including the nearly universal United Nations

Convention against Corruption. The United States has also announced its withdrawal from key UN organs (while imposing sanctions on other international organisations), and in some instances, other States are following suit. Meanwhile, in Europe, an omnibus package announced in Brussels seems bound to significantly reduce the scope of application of cutting-edge requirements for corporate reporting in the areas of environmental, social, and governance indicators, as well as thoroughness of supply-chain due diligence. Further, various States are reconsidering their commitments under the venerable Energy Charter Treaty. In Africa, the fate of the Dispute Settlement Annex mandated to accompany the AfCFTA Investment Protocol remains uncertain, leaving it unclear precisely how the impressive suite of investor obligations might be effectively enforced.

For those of us in the trade of international lawyering, navigating the waters has never been simple or obvious. This holds true whether one is a generalist international lawyer, an international economic lawyer, a specialist in cross-border mega-transactions, a commercial or investment disputes specialist, a practitioner of international humanitarian or human rights law, or a legal adviser to a multinational enterprise or foreign ministry. Whether or not it is exaggerated or premature to already mourn the demise of the so-called "rules-based international order" – or, put differently, even if it is true that we are fast reverting to a state of greater volatility and uncertainty – one key difference sets this new era apart from all those that have preceded it.

Never before has a disordered "historical norm" sought to re-assert itself against the force of eighty years of dedicated international institution-building. And that is important because the infrastructure that has been assembled during all this time is, and will remain, considerable – it shall not simply be swept away. The forward march of international law cannot be arrested, much less reversed; the diverse instruments, institutions, and fora of international lawyering will not disappear quietly into the night.

Nor will the international lawyers. Indeed – in any age of disjuncture and dislocation, they may be more in demand than ever before.

The Great Debate

The symposium was convened at the University of Geneva in collaboration with ALG LLP and WilmerHale on 16–17 May 2024, opening with a *Great Debate* between Ambassador Mario Oyarzábal and Jackson Shaw Kern in which each was assigned, respectively, to represent the *pro* and *contra* positions regarding investor obligations in the international legal order. The event was moderated by Mārtiņš Paparinskis. Thorough ventilation of the issues via this exercise has resulted in a common position reflected in the essay that the two debaters have now jointly authored. In their essay, the authors trace the traditional arguments and doctrinal constraints historically suggested as hindering an emergence of investor obligations in international law before overviewing the most current trends and discerning a possibly emergent general principle, while indicating the various *fora* that offer themselves for enforcement efforts.

Following this debate, the discussions continued across four panels constituted to consider, first, questions of applicable laws, and thereafter, three independent clusters of affirmative investor obligations.

The Landscape of Laws

The first panel was composed of Anna Kozmenko, Augustin Barrier, and Maria Chiara Malaguti, with moderation by Johannes Fahner.

Anna Kozmenko spoke on Investor Obligations in Relation to State Obligations. In her essay, she addresses three crucial questions while setting the scene for the readers vis-à-vis investors' obligations. She first discusses the driving forces behind the current trend towards more investor obligations. Then, she discusses how widely spread this trend is in doctrine and international practice. Finally, she elaborates on the scope of investors' obligations in current investment agreements. Her discussion of such provisions in "new age" investment treaties helps her derive the conclusion that there is a growing trend of such obligations being crystallised.

Augustin Barrier addressed Compliance with National and International Law. In his essay, he addresses the current imbalance as between State obligations vis-à-vis investors not being commensurate to investors' obligations towards States. He points out that just because States may take actions against investors under domestic law does not, in itself, serve as a potent rationale for investors not bearing obligations towards States on the international plane. In his words, in an international arbitration, the role of national law is often acting as "nothing but a set of facts". He proposes a unique means of adding a *renvoi* to national law in current investment treaties, such that non-compliance with national law may have an international legal effect.

Finally, *Maria Chiara Malaguti* spoke on the Relationship between Investor Obligations and Investment Contracts. In her essay, she previews the progress of UNIDROIT's ongoing project on International Investment Contracts, jointly undertaken with the Institute of World Business Law of the International

Chamber of Commerce. This project "aims at developing guidance to foster the modernisation and standardisation of international investment contracts" and "will explore the interaction between the UNIDROIT Principles of International Commercial Contracts (UPICC) and common provisions in international investment contracts, and it will seek to address a number of recent developments in the area of international investment law, such as the increasing focus on corporate social responsibility and sustainability".

Investor Obligations Cluster I: Global Stewards

The second panel comprised Nilüfer Oral and Won Kidane, with moderation by Sebastian Coulon Bauer.

Nilüfer Oral spoke on the topic of Environmental Protection. In her remarks, she mapped the current regime of international environmental law and how it may be transposable to investors, which issues have now been further explored in an essay on the topic jointly authored by *Jackson Shaw Kern* and *Mohit Khubchandani*. In this essay, the authors offer a view into how the *corpus* of international environmental law and climate change law may be adapted to install obligations upon investors. This includes a discussion of the relevant treaties at play and principles of general and customary international law, such as Environmental Impact Assessments, the Precautionary Principle, the Duty of Due Diligence, the Duty to Cooperate, and the Principle of Preventing Significant Transboundary Harm, as well as the Polluter Pays Principle. The essay also considers the impact of recent Advisory Opinions on Climate Change sought before various international courts and tribunals. Finally, it envisions how an accompanying enforcement mechanism might operate to effectuate the obligations.

Won Kidane addressed the issue of Anti-corruption. His essay, jointly authored with Jackson Shaw Kern, weighs the inherent challenges of pursuing corruption remedies on the international plane with the unique advantages that international law offers where corrupt activities transcend international boundaries. It also flags certain challenges that the implementation of investors' treaty-imposed anti-corruption obligations may pose.

Investor Obligations Cluster II: Human Rights

The third panel comprised Makane Moïse Mbengue, Suzanne Spears, and Mohit Khubchandani, with moderation by Elena Cima.

Makane Moïse Mbengue spoke on the novel conception of investors' socio-political obligations now reflected in his essay "Socio-political Obligations in Investment Treaties".

Suzanne Spears addressed the contemporary topic of Human Rights and Climate Change, which has now equally been examined as part and parcel of the joint essay by Jackson Shaw Kern and Mohit Khubchandani, spanning across international environmental law issues.

Lastly, *Mohit Khubchandani* addressed the enduring issues of Labour Standards and Indigenous Rights. In his essay, he first begins by discussing (and delineating) the soft and hard law instruments in this domain – and their relevance and applicability upon investors' obligations in the context of indigenous communities' rights and labour rights at large. He also discusses relevant recent cases, including those in investment arbitration, that have had an impact on the development of jurisprudence in these subject-matters. He then discusses certain model provisions and standards in recent investment law instruments and considers how they might be strengthened. He concludes by proposing certain key points to drafting stronger clauses relating to investor obligations vis-à-vis labour and indigenous rights.

Investor Obligations Cluster III: The Investor in Focus

The fourth and final panel comprised Mathias Wolkewitz, Steven Finizio, and Vincent Beyer, with moderation by Fuad Zarbiyev.

Mathias Wolkewitz spoke on Corporate Governance. In his essay, he examines the term from the perspective of relevant national laws and proceeds to discuss the relevant definitions and framework, as well as how certain investment treaties (including the AfCFTA Investment Protocol) presently view it.

Steven Finizio spoke on Corporate Social Responsibility. In his essay, he describes how CSR provisions in investment treaties have been drafted and the present evolution of those provisions, including with regard to whether they are mandatory and the specificity of their obligations. He also describes how investors' CSR obligations may be enforced in disputes relating to investment agreements, including through jurisdictional and admissibility objections, defences to claims by investors, and counterclaims. He concludes that, indeed, these obligations have a growing role to play in international investment agreements.

Finally, *Vincent Beyer* spoke on Taxation and Transfer Pricing. In his essay, he discusses the scope of tax-related investor obligations, including in the realm of related-party transactions and base erosion and profit-shifting rules and principles. This contribution also includes a discussion of the "arm's length standard" in investors' dealings and the historical origins of investor obligations on tax. Before concluding, he also confronts potential challenges relating to the inclusion of tax-related investor obligations in international investment instruments.

∴

We thank all the panellists, contributors, moderators, and participants of the symposium. Their crucial support has led to the formulation of this first-of-its-kind book on the subject-matter.

We invite you to enjoy this collection of essays examining the present form and future direction of investor obligations in international law.

Makane Moïse Mbengue
Jackson Shaw Kern
Mohit Khubchandani

Foreword

Why should international lawyers care about the obligations of investors in international law? One response is given in the 2023 Protocol on Investment to the Agreement Establishing the African Continental Free Trade Area (Protocol), a landmark instrument invoked and interrogated throughout this volume.[1] The 17th preambular recital of the Protocol identifies, as one of its purposes, the "*seeking* to achieve an overall balance of the rights and obligations between State Parties and investors under this Protocol".[2] The operative word "balance" introduces the key question, namely whether the striking of an appropriate balance of interests in the field of investment protection law may be improved by adopting or introducing the perspective of the obligations of investors in international law.

The whole volume may be read as a rich and subtle exploration of the answer to this question. In the paragraphs that follow, I will briefly sketch three broader points that seem to me relevant for that inquiry: *first,* the striking of balance in investment law more generally and the way how obligations of investors fit in that endeavour; *secondly,* certain aspects of creative adjudicative engagement with obligations of investors under international law; and, *thirdly,* questions raised by the adoptions of this perspective in international law-making, such as the Protocol.

The search for the appropriate balance of interests in investment law is not new. It goes back to the rubric of the law of State responsibility for the injury caused to aliens familiar from at least the 19th century, then predominantly addressed without procedural involvement of affected individuals, in the inter-State framework of diplomatic protection. Reasonable people have always disagreed on the right interaction between the sovereign, economic, and security interests implicated, and even future Judges of the International Court of Justice (ICJ) published over the years drafts perceived as going too far in deferring to interests of likely respondents or claimants, respectively.[3]

---

1 The official text, as adopted by the African Union's Assembly, has not been released, but the version agreed at the Seventh Extraordinary Session of the Specialized Technical Committee on Justice and Legal Affairs (Experts Meeting) of the AU (16–21 January 2023) is available at <https://www.bilaterals.org/IMG/pdf/en_-_draft_protocol_of_the_afcfta_on_investment.pdf>.

2 Ibid 2.

3 Cf. "Conclusions of the report of the Sub-Committee on State Responsibility, annexed to Questionnaire No. 4 adopted by the League of Nations Committee of Experts for the Progressive Codification of International Law (Geneva, 1926)" in *Yearbook of the International*

Just as in other specialist fields, international law on foreign investment possesses many tools and techniques for striking balance beyond articulating them in terms of obligations, within the rules themselves as well as by drawing upon broader systemic assumptions, such as the permanent sovereignty over natural resources.[4]

There is something undeniably aesthetically pleasing about international legal arrangements that express interests and discuss their interplay in terms of rights and obligations, traceable perhaps to the powerful influence of reciprocity on the foundations of this legal order.[5] It is particularly so in this field, where many States would enthusiastically nod along to Judge Padilla Nervo's words from half a century ago as sound on the realities of power in the 21st-century international economic affairs.[6] But precisely because of this normative pull, it is worth restating the broader point: obligations is *a* technique for drafting satisfactory rules in international law for the benefit of non-State actors, to be read, evaluated, and applied alongside other and alternative drafting approaches.[7] I suspect that the landmark arbitral award in *Urbaser SA and Or v Argentina* (*Urbaser*) will, in the long term, be influential less for its currently much-quoted general pronouncements of principle[8] but rather because of the careful framing of the possible application of international obligations of investors as an important legally relevant consideration to be discussed, among others, in domestic as well as international law.[9]

How, then, should one go about tackling the obligations of investors? Investment protection law is not just about dispute settlement, even if it

---

Law Commission, 1956, vol. II UN doc. A/CN.4/SER.A/1956/Add.1 222; "Draft convention on the international responsibility of States for injuries to aliens, prepared by the Harvard Law School, 1961" in *Yearbook of the International Law Commission, 1969, vol. II* UN doc. A/CN.4/SER.A/1969/Add.1 142.

4 M Paparinskis, "International Investment Law and the European Union: A Reply to Catharine Titi" (2015) 26 EJIL 663, 664–667.

5 A Whelan, *Reciprocity in Public International Law* (CUP, 2023); M Kałduński (ed.), *Reciprocity in International Law* (Palgrave Macmillan, 2024).

6 *Barcelona Traction, Light and Power Company, Limited* (*Belgium v. Spain*) (*New Application: 1962*) [1970] ICJ Rep 3, Separate Opinion of Judge Padilla Nervo 243, particularly 248 ("It is not the shareholders in those huge corporations who are in need of ... protection; it is rather the poorer or weaker States, where the investments take place, who need to be protected against encroachment by powerful financial groups").

7 Cf various approaches to duties in regional human rights law, R Murray, "Articles 27–29: Individual Duties" in R Murray (ed), *The African Charter on Human and Peoples' Rights: A Commentary* (OUP 2019) 576.

8 *Urbaser S.A. and Consorcio de Aguas Bilbao Bizkaia, Bilbao Biskaia Ur Partzuergoa v Argentina,* ICSID Case no ARB/07/26, Award, 8 December 2016, paras 1193–1205.

9 Ibid paras 1206–1210.

may have seemed otherwise during the foundational years of investor-State arbitration around the turn of the century. But it is nevertheless true that arbitration is a key element of the field, and other developments take place predominantly in reaction, or with an eye, to how matters are treated in dispute settlement. The volume skillfully canvasses ways in which the obligations of investors are relevant – expressed in domestic law and investment contracts, invoked through counterclaims – or not legally binding but influential in shaping conduct by corporate actors; or disadvantageous or even fatal for the investor's case on jurisdiction, merits, or compensation, but not articulated as obligations in technical terms. But what one might call the "pure" case, where obligations directly imposed by international law are invoked by the State against the investor and accepted by the tribunal as dispositive in the particular dispute, remains elusive, particularly by contrast with routineness of claims in the other direction. Why is that so, in seeming tension with expectations of equality of parties?

The more obvious response is that the challenge lies not in the realm of international adjudication, where procedural equality may well be upheld,[10] but at the level of substantive obligations. Campbell McLachlan, one of the leading figures in the field (and himself an arbitrator in *Urbaser*), recently made the following carefully worded observation, with the emphasis on the operative verb in the original: "[i]t *may* be possible to recognize that corporations owe particular duties in human rights, as the Tribunal discussed in *Urbaser* v. *Argentina*. But the considerable intellectual effort devoted to constructing a new public international law of human rights remedies against corporations has, so far at least, borne only modest fruit".[11]

Much depends on the quality of reasoning of tribunals engaged with this effort. Consider, by way of example, the following passage of the award in *David R. Aven and Others v. Costa Rica*:

> What about the investor's obligations arising of the investment according to international law? This Tribunal shares the views of *Urbaser* Tribunal that it can no longer be admitted that investors operating internationally are immune from becoming subjects of international law. It is particularly convincing when

10 C McLachlan, *The Institute of International Law's Resolution on the Equality of Parties Before International Investment Tribunals: Introduction, Text and Commentaries* (CUP 2021).

11 C McLachlan, "On the Interface between Public and Private International Law" (2025) 446 Hague Recueil 11, 57 (footnote omitted).

> it comes to rights and obligations that are the concern of all States, as it happens in the protection of the environment. It is pertinent to recall the observation of the International Court of Justice regarding this kind of obligations: "In view of the importance of the rights involved, all States can be held to have a legal interest in their protection; they are obligations *erga omnes*".[12]

Some will find it not entirely easy to follow the Tribunal's reasoning for why *erga omnes* is relevant for answering the question posed in the first sentence quoted. Whether *erga omnes* goes to the legal interest to invoke (and perhaps also implement) responsibility, as *per* the International Law Commission,[13] or to invocation as well as the legal consequences for other actors, as *per* the ICJ,[14] is a debate to be settled elsewhere. But it is tolerably clear that the *erga omnes* or otherwise character of obligations tells us nothing about their scope, including personal scope in relation to investors, which falls to be determined by the traditional analysis of sources of international law. This point is tangential to the broader argument. Still, the modesty of adjudicative harvest noted by McLachlan may well be shaped by the shadow thrown on excessive arbitral creativity by the risk of set-aside, in cases when the identification of obligations under one of the sources of applicable law is found in the review process to have been suboptimal.[15]

If one response to the challenge of international obligations of investors lies in exploring arbitral creativity, the other track tackles them squarely, as the Protocol does in Chapter V (Investor Obligations). Article 32 provides, in general terms, that "[i]nvestors and their investments shall carry out their operations in compliance with ... applicable international law", and other provisions of Chapter V spell out the implications with various degrees of emphasis, also in relation to international law. The Protocol repays careful reading, so I will only say that the application of such treaty rules is likely to give rise to

12 *David R. Aven and Others v. Costa Rica,* ICSID Case no UNCT/15/3, Award of the Tribunal, 18 September 2018 para 738.

13 ILC, "Draft articles on the responsibility of States for internationally wrongful acts" in *Yearbook of the ILC 2001: Volume II Part Two* UN doc. A/CN.4/SER.A/2001/Add.1 (Part 2) 30 paras (6), (8), (9) of the commentary to article 48, article 54.

14 *Legal Consequences Arising from the Policies and Practices of Israel in the Occupied Palestinian Territory, including East Jerusalem* (Advisory Opinion) ICJ Advisory Opinion of 19 July 2024 <https://www.icj-cij.org/sites/default/files/case-related/186/186-20240719-adv-01-00-en.pdf> paras 232, 274, 280.

15 Eg *Venezuela Holdings, BV, and Ors v. Venezuela,* ICSID Case no ARB/07/27, Decision on Annulment, 9 March 2017 Chapter IV(v).

further questions, as international lawyers know well from experience in other fields.[16] By way of a few questions to reflect upon: what is the legal rationale for binding investors by obligations under an instrument that they are not parties to?[17] Do these obligations apply to the investment as an object of protection or the investor as the procedural actor, and what are the implications for the distinction?[18] Is the relevant benchmark for viewing other treaty obligations as relevant to be found in the party status of all the implicated States? [19] Are the secondary rules applicable to the determination of responsibility of the investor (such as attribution and forms of reparation for breach) to be determined by analogy with secondary rules of State responsibility, in general principles of law regarding corporate liability, or in the instrument itself?[20]

The making and implementation of obligations of investors in the field of investment protection law is an important topic that I will certainly follow with the keenest interest, as both technically fascinating and directly touching upon the key pressure points of policy. Some of the issues identified and questions posed in this foreword have more obvious answers than others – and there is valuable guidance to be found in the Protocol itself and other relevant instruments – so my modest point is only that this discussion has high legal and policy stakes and needs to be taken seriously. Whichever path the field ultimately takes, I have no doubt that legal advisers, counsel, arbitrators, scholarly and non-governmental observers, and other participants in the system will greatly benefit from the chapters that follow in navigating through the maze of interlocking rules and institutions.

Mārtiņš Paparinskis

---

16 McLachlan "On the Interface between Public and Private International Law" (n 11) 57–58.

17 See the variety of responses offered over the years to this question in the field of international humanitarian law regarding non-State armed groups, S Sivakumaran, *The Law of Non-International Armed Conflicts* (OUP 2012) 238–242.

18 Notably, Article 32 refers to "[i]nvestors and their investments", (n 1).

19 See instruments discussed regarding obligations of investors, such as the International Covenant on Economic, Social and Cultural Rights, *Urbaser* (n 8) paras 1197, 1209, ratified widely but not universally, including by some States with litigiously inclined investors, < https://treaties.un.org/pages/showDetails.aspx?objid=080000028002b6ed>

20 See the principles on reparations in the International Criminal Court, *The Prosecutor v. Dominic Ongwen,* ICC-02/04-01/15-2074, Reparations Order, 28 February 2024 paras 56–58.

Biographies of Editors and Contributors

Editors' Biographies

Prof. Dr. Makane Moïse Mbengue
Professor of International Law at the Faculty of Law of the University of Geneva, Switzerland

Makane Moïse Mbengue is Professor of International Law at the Faculty of Law of the University of Geneva and Director of the Department of International Law and International Organizations. He is also Affiliate Professor at Sciences Po Paris (School of Law). He holds a PhD in Public International Law from the University of Geneva. Since 2017, he is the President of the African Society of International Law (AfSIL). He is also Associate Member of the *Institut de Droit International* and Member of the Curatorium of The Hague Academy of International Law.

He has acted and continues to act as an expert for the African Union, the Secretary-General of the United Nations, the United Nations Economic Commission for Africa, the United Nations Environment Programme (UNEP), the Office of the High Commissioner for Human Rights, the World Health Organization (WHO), the World Bank, the International Labour Organization (ILO), the Organization of the Islamic Conference (OIC), and the International Institute for Sustainable Development (IISD), among others. He also acts as a Professor for courses in International Law organised by the United Nations Office of Legal Affairs (OLA) and by the United Nations Institute for Training and Research (UNITAR).

He acts as counsel in disputes before international courts and tribunals (in particular, before the International Court of Justice and in investment cases) and as an advisor for governments. He is involved in the negotiations of several International Investment Agreements in Africa. He is a member of the ICSID Panel of Arbitrators.

He is the author of several publications in the field of international law.

Jackson Shaw Kern
Partner, ALG LLP, Dubai, United Arab Emirates

Jackson Shaw Kern is an international lawyer who advises and represents private interests as well as sovereign clients in a diversity of matters. He capably advises in non-contentious settings and has equally delivered successful results in complex international disputes of the highest stakes. He is ALG LLP Partner-in-Charge in Dubai.

He is a frequent guest lecturer and speaker with appearances including the Peking University School of Transnational Law, the Catholic University of Peru, and Addis Ababa University. He is a past visiting fellow of the Lauterpacht Centre for International Law. In addition to numerous articles and book chapters, he is a co-author of the title *Arbitrating the Conduct of International Investors* from Cambridge University Press.

He earned a degree in Economics and Anthropology at McGill University and a Juris Doctor *summa cum laude* at Seattle University where he was inducted into the Alpha Sigma Nu Honor Society.

Mohit Khubchandani
Adjunct Lecturer of International Law, Yerevan State University, Armenia | Public International Law and International Arbitration Consultant | PhD Scholar, Leiden University, The Netherlands

Mohit Khubchandani is an international disputes resolution attorney with more than a decade of experience in public international law and international arbitration. He is currently an Adjunct Lecturer of International Law and Arbitration at Yerevan State University, Armenia. He is also a PhD Scholar at the world-renowned Leiden Law School, The Netherlands, writing on: "*Forum and harm specific metrics of compensation for environmental damages (MCEs) for major international courts and tribunals.*" He regularly teaches and publishes on related and other issues.

He has worked at international arbitration law firms like WilmerHale, London (with Prof. Gary Born), Gaillard Banifatemi Shelbaya Disputes, Paris, and Fietta LLP, London. His diverse experience also includes work at the International Court of Justice, the UN International Law Commission, the UN Office of Coordination of Humanitarian Affairs, New York, the Permanent Mission of India to the UN, and the Office of the Attorney General for India.

He is also a Coordinating Committee Member of the European Society of International Law's Interest Group on Reparations in International Law; South Asia Advisory Board Member of the Foreign Direct Investment Arbitration Moot; Founder and Advisory Board Member of India Very Young Arbitration Practitioners.

He also holds an LLM in International Environmental and Energy Law from Stanford Law School, California, USA.

Contributors' Biographies

Ambassador Mario Oyarzábal

Member, United Nations International Law Commission, Geneva, Switzerland | Former Ambassador of the Argentine Republic to the Kingdom of the Netherlands

Mario J. A. Oyarzábal is the Chief Legal Adviser of the Argentine Foreign Ministry since 2025 (previously also between 2016 and 2020), and member of the

UN International Law Commission. He is also a member of the Permanent Court of Arbitration and an *Associé de l'Institut de Droit International*. He was Deputy Permanent Representative of Argentina before the UN Security Council, and Ambassador to the Netherlands as well as Representative to the international organisations and tribunals in The Hague. He delivered a Special Course at The Hague Academy of International Law and has been invited to deliver the General Course. He is the author of numerous books and scholarly articles on public and private international law.

Dr. Anna Kozmenko
Partner, Curtis, Mallet-Prevost, Colt & Mosle LLP, Geneva, Switzerland

Dr. Anna Kozmenko is a highly experienced disputes lawyer, recognized by leading directories as one of the top international lawyers of her generation. She is a Partner at Curtis, Mallet-Prevost, Colt & Mosle LLP in Geneva and Dubai.

Having practiced in Russia, France, the US, and Switzerland, she has extensive experience in both civil and common law jurisdictions. She represents sovereigns, state, and private entities in high-profile international disputes, including complex litigations, commercial, investment, and sports arbitrations.

Augustin Barrier
Partner, Lalive, Geneva, Switzerland

Augustin Barrier is a Partner at Lalive, Geneva. He specializes in international arbitration, including commercial and investment treaty arbitration in a wide array of business sectors, with particular emphasis on energy, mining, joint ventures, supply and distribution, and foreign investments, notably in Europe and Africa. Augustin regularly publishes content relating to international law, international arbitration, and arbitration law. He also contributes to the preparation of the Revue des revues for the Journal du droit international (Clunet).

Prof. Dr. Maria Chiara Malaguti
President Emeritus, United Nations International Institute for the Unification of Private Law (UNIDROIT) | Professor, Università Cattolica del Sacro Cuore, Milan, Italy

Maria Chiara Malaguti is Full Professor of International Law at Università Cattolica Sacro Cuore (Milan/Rome, Italy). She was appointed President of UNIDROIT (2020–2025) as the first woman to cover such position.

Of Counsel at PedersoliGattai (Milan/Rome), she is also a legal advisor to the Italian Ministry for Foreign Affairs on trade matters and to the World Bank on legal reform of payment systems, financial markets, and governance. An international arbitrator for commercial disputes and foreign direct investments included in various rosters, she supports the General Attorney's Office of Italy in the procedures opened against Italy as for international investment law.

She holds degrees in law and economics, an LLM from Harvard Law School, and a PhD from the European University Institute (EUI) in Florence. She has various publications, mainly focusing on financial markets and sovereign debt, the harmonization of law, and international investment law.

Prof. Dr. Won Kidane
Partner, ALG LLP, Washington, DC, USA | Professor of Law at the Villanova University Charles Widger School of Law, Villanova, Pennsylvania, USA

Won L. Kidane is Professor of Law at Villanova University and the director of its International Entrepreneurship Program, in collaboration with the University of Cape Town. He is a founding partner of ALG LLP and earlier practiced law in Washington, DC, with the firms of Hunton & Williams and Piper Rudnick (now DLA Piper).

His areas of expertise include international arbitration and litigation, comparative law, and the legal aspects of China-Africa economic relations. He is the author and co-author of five books and more than 40 law review articles and book chapters. His most recent comprehensive book is *Africa's International Investment Law Regimes,* now published by Oxford University Press. With extensive practice representing African States, their agencies, and instrumentalities in international commercial and investment arbitration in matters administered by the Permanent Court of Arbitration (PCA), International Chamber of Commerce (ICC), London Court of International Arbitration (LCIA) and sustained scholarly work and teaching, he is globally among the leading experts of international commercial and investment arbitration.

In addition to his teaching, scholarly work, and practice, he is a member of numerous associations, including the Academic Forum for Investor-State Dispute Settlement Reform, the Academic Forum for Institute of Transnational Arbitration (ITA), and the American Society of International Law (ASIL) (past co-chair of the Africa Interest Group). He has also served as an arbitrator and is on the roster of arbitrators of some of the leading arbitral institutions in the Global South, including the Hong Kong International Arbitration Center, (HKIAC) Mauritius International Arbitration Center (MIAC), China International Economic and Trade Arbitration Center (CIETAC), and Saudi Center for Commercial Arbitration (SCCA).

Prof. Dr. Mathias Wolkewitz
General Counsel, Wintershall Dea AG, Germany | Professor, Technical University of Clausthal, Germany

Professor Wolkewitz is the Honorary Professor for the International Law of Natural Resources, Energy and Environment at the Technical University Clausthal, Germany. He is also Managing Director of Professor Wolkewitz & Co. Consulting GmbH – Advocacy & Arbitration · Capacity Building · Human Rights. He was for twenty years the General Counsel, Chief Compliance Officer, and Human Rights Officer at Wintershall Dea GmbH in Kassel, Germany, overseeing legal, compliance, data protection, and insurance matters. He specialises in German and international energy, environmental, investment protection, and corporate law, with extensive experience in leading complex oil and gas transactions across North Africa, South America, Southeastern Europe, and Russia. He has been and is responsible for arbitration proceedings under the rules of the World Bank's dispute resolution mechanism (ICSID), the UNCITRAL, the International Chamber of Commerce (ICC), the SCC, as well as the VIAC. He previously served on the Supervisory Board of VNG Verbundnetz Gas AG and in the German Industry Association's legal committee and is active in the IBA.

Prof. Steven Finizio
Partner, King and Spalding LLP, London, UK | Professor of Practice at SOAS University of London and Deputy Director of the SOAS Arbitration and Dispute Resolution Centre (SADRC), London, UK

Steven Finizio is a partner at King and Spalding LLP, based in London. He serves as an arbitrator and has acted as counsel under the rules of leading international arbitration institutions and in ad hoc proceedings, involving the laws of jurisdictions in Europe, Asia, Africa, South America, and the US, as well as disputes under bilateral and multilateral treaties. He has appeared as counsel in regional and other international courts, and has assisted in drafting national arbitration legislation. He is Professor of Practice at SOAS University of London and Deputy Director of the SOAS Arbitration and Dispute Resolution Centre (SADRC). His publications include *A Practical Guide to International Commercial Arbitration: Assessment, Planning and Strategy* and *International Commercial Arbitration* in The Law of Transnational Business Transactions.

Dr. Vincent Beyer
Expert in Legal Affairs, International Investment Agreements (IIA) Section, UN Trade and Development (UNCTAD), United Nations, Geneva

Vincent Beyer advises governments on international investment policy, investment treaties, and investor–State dispute settlement at UNCTAD's IIA Section since early 2020. He regularly authors and contributes to key UN research publications and provides economic policy advice. In this role, he supports global consensus-building on international investment policy by organizing international conferences and fostering international dialogue and collaboration. He holds degrees in public international law from universities in the Netherlands and Switzerland. Prior to joining UNCTAD, he worked in private practice, litigating WTO disputes. He earned his PhD in international law from the Geneva Graduate Institute, focusing on the interaction among international trade, investment, and tax rules. He has published on international economic law in leading peer-reviewed journals and edited volumes and has taught international investment law at the University of Groningen in the Netherlands. He is a frequent panelist and moderator at international conferences on economic policy.

Foreword by

Prof. Dr. Mārtiņš Paparinskis
Member and Former Chair, United Nations International Law Commission, Geneva, Switzerland | Professor, University College London, Faculty of Laws, UK

Mārtiņš Paparinskis is Professor of Public International Law at UCL Laws. He was the Chair of the 76th Session of the United Nations International Law Commission and is the Special Rapporteur on compensation for the damage caused by internationally wrongful acts of the Commission. He is also an associate member of the Institute of International Law, a member of the Permanent Court of Arbitration, the OSCE Court of Conciliation and Arbitration, and the ICSID Panels of Arbitrators and of Conciliators, and has appeared before the International Tribunal for the Law of the Sea and the International Court of Justice.

CHAPTER 1

On the Obligations of Investors under International Law: Trends and Avenues

Mario J.A. Oyarzábal and Jackson Shaw Kern[1]

1 Introduction

The question of whether international law imposes obligations upon investors is not new. However, the current crisis of legitimacy of investor–State dispute settlement (ISDS) and other related developments have reignited the debate. A lively exchange of views on this important issue took place in a symposium at the Université de Genève on 16–17 May 2024 in the course of which the question was examined from the angle of general international law as well as in relation to special rules, including those concerning environmental protection, human rights, indigenous peoples and local communities, corporate governance, anti-corruption, labour standards, and taxation.

This chapter will examine whether the traditional position – that investors only have *rights* (under investment treaties) but no corresponding *obligations* under international law – continues to hold sway. It argues that international law (IL) not only already imposes obligations upon investors but also that those obligations can be enforced via various mechanisms. It concludes that, although it may be tempting to address the relationship between investment law and IL from a static and binary viewpoint – that IL either does or does not apply across investment law and that it does or does not apply to investors – it may be more realistic to look at such a relationship as a process in which IL is increasingly penetrating the sphere of investment law.

The chapter builds upon the "Great Debate" of the Geneva symposium, during which the co-authors argued the *pro* and *contra* positions for regulating investor conduct at the international level. Like the debate itself, this chapter does not undertake to analyse in depth all sources of investors' obligations but rather aims to provide a general overview of the principal arguments and current trends – as emanating from judicial and arbitral decisions, as well as

1 We are grateful to Professors Mārtiņš Parapinskis and Raúl E Vinuesa for their feedback. Views expressed are strictly those of the authors and do not necessarily reflect the positions of the institutions they are associated with.

HTTPS://DOI.ORG/10.1163/9789004769854-002

international treaty-making – that may be relevant to apprehend the developments presently taking place in the field of investment law and in the diverse areas of the law where investor obligations may arise.

2 Breaking into the Traditional Position

The traditional position holds that IL *cannot, does not,* and indeed *should not* apply to investors or operate directly as a restraint upon their conduct. Such a position tends to be based on two premises. *First,* by nature, IL as a system is directed to States and its other main subjects (notably international organisations). From this perspective, current IL, for the most part, does not directly regulate the conduct of private actors but rather requires the States to regulate such actors in particular ways. *Second* is the notion of investment law as a self-contained regime, under which investment treaties establish special rules (*lex specialis*) that derogate from general IL (*lex generalis*).

The first tenet – that IL *cannot* impose direct obligations upon investors – is largely theoretical and one that cannot be empirically sustained in the present age. In the words of an illustrious commentator, "[t]here is no general rule that the individuals [or corporations, for that matter] cannot be 'subjects of international law', and in particular contexts individuals [as well as corporations] may have rights which they can vindicate by international action, notably in the field of human rights and investment protection".[2] States may, by treaty, confer to individuals or corporations privileges on the international plane and under the national laws of the parties with respect to their activities, such as those provided under ISDS (often including waiver of local remedies, shareholder standing, and enhanced enforcement). If the States, by their agreement, may confer this privileged status, they may equally impose upon investors certain obligations, such as to conform their activities and investments to the requirements of human rights and environmental law.[3]

Nevertheless – turning to the second tenet – IL *does not* currently impose direct obligations upon investors, neither positive nor negative obligations, except as may be provided for in the relevant investment treaty. Those supporting this position stress that individual direct responsibility under (gen-

2 James Crawford, *Brownlie's Principles of Public International Law* (9th edn, OUP 2019) 111.

3 See, particularly, Steven R Ratner, "Corporations and Human Rights: A Theory of Legal Responsibility" (2001) 111(3) Yale Law Journal 443.

eral) IL is circumscribed to serious violations of human rights and international humanitarian law,[4] and that, as a matter of IL, the standard of treatment for investors is to be defined in the terms of investment treaties alone. On the one hand, universal instruments relating to human rights aim at protecting individuals and certain groups from violations *by the State*, which must also supervise compliance by other actors within its territory. At most, the Universal Declaration and the two Covenants on human rights provide that "[n]othing in this [instrument] may be interpreted as implying for any State, group or person any right to engage in any activity or to perform any act aimed at the destruction of any of the rights and freedoms set forth herein".[5] On the other hand, efforts at the international level to confer obligations upon corporations have either fallen short of achieving their intended purpose or have limited scope.

The only normative text endorsed at the multilateral level is the UN Guiding Principles on Business and Human Rights: Implementing the United Nations "Protect, Respect and Remedy" Framework.[6] Adopted (admittedly by unanimity) by the Human Rights Council (a body of universal and yet limited composition) in 2011, the document nonetheless contains no hard investor obligations actionable at law – they are "soft law" principles to *guide* the behaviour of corporations (as their name so indicates). Their immediate antecedent, the so-called "Norms on the Responsibilities of Transnational Corporations"[7] – which purported to be a "*restatement* of the inter-

4 *International Military Tribunal (Nüremberg), Judgement and Sentences* (1947) 41 American Journal of International Law 172, 216–221; UN Security Council, Statute of the International Criminal Tribunal for the Former Yugoslavia (adopted 25 May 1993, as amended 17 May 2002); and UN Security Council, Statute of the International Criminal Tribunal for Rwanda (adopted 8 November 1994, as last amended 13 October 2006); Rome Statute of the International Criminal Court (adopted 17 July 1998, entered into force 1 July 2002) 2187 UNTS 3.

5 Universal Declaration of Human Rights (adopted 10 December 1948) UNGA Res 217 A(III) art 30; International Covenant on Civil and Political Rights (adopted 16 December 1966, entered into force 23 March 1976) 999 UNTS 171 art 5.1; International Covenant on Economic, Social and Cultural Rights (adopted 16 December 1966, entered into force 3 January 1976) 993 UNTS 3 art 5.1.

6 UNHRC "Human Rights and Transnational Corporations and Other Business Enterprises" (6 July 2011), UN Doc A/HRC/RES/17/4, adopted without a vote (UN Guiding Principles). See also UNHRC "Report of the Special Representative of the Secretary-General on the Issue of Human Rights and Transnational Corporations and Other Business Enterprises, John Ruggie" (21 March 2011), UN Doc A/HRC/17/31.

7 UNCHR (Sub-Commission), "Norms on the Responsibilities of Transnational Corporations and Other Business Enterprises with Regard to Human Rights (Draft)" (26 August 2003) UN Doc E/CN.4/Sub.2/2003/12/Rev.2. The document is believed to have been principally

national legal principles *applicable* to businesses with regard to human rights, humanitarian law, international labour law, environmental law, consumer law, anticorruption law, and so forth"[8] and to contain both primary (general) obligations and secondary (implementation) rules[9] – were rejected by the then-UN Commission on Human Rights (the Human Rights Council's predecessor) as having "no legal standing".[10] A current initiative to draft a binding instrument on business and human rights – launched by Ecuador in 2014 at the Human Rights Council and though alive and well[11] – does not seem directed to "provide for the establishment of effective remedies for victims in cases where domestic jurisdiction is clearly unable to prosecute effectively those companies" as was originally envisaged,[12] but rather to undertake corporate compliance through the lens of State obligations (including obligations to enact and enforce positive law).[13] The future treaty would not (in its current form) *internationalise* investor (mis)conduct. Instead, the traditionalist might suggest, it represents another instance demonstrating that IL more naturally acts upon non-State actors via the intermediation of the States. It would operate in the municipal and transnational space (in a manner akin to, for

---

authored by the late Professor David Weissbrodt, who reportedly suggested that it was "designed to be controversial" (cf Bernadette Hearne, "Proposed UN Norms on Human Rights: Is Business Opposition Justified?", Ethical Corporation, 22 March 2004, cited by Carlos M Vázquez, "Direct vs. Indirect Obligations of Corporations Under International Law" (2005) 43 Columbia Journal of Transnational Law 927, 928–929).

8 David Weissbrodt and Muria Kruger, "Norms on the Responsibilities of Transnational Corporations and Other Business Enterprises with Regard to Human Rights" (2003) 97 American Journal of International Law 901 (emphasis added).

9 Ibid., 912–913.

10 UNCHR, Responsibilities of Transnational Corporations and Related Business Enterprises with Regard to Human Rights, UNCHR Res 116 (2004) UN Doc E/CN.4/2004/L.11/Add.7.

11 UNHRC "Open-Ended Intergovernmental Working Group on Transnational Corporations and Other Business Enterprises with Respect to Human Rights" <https://www.ohchr.org/en/hr-bodies/hrc/wg-trans-corp/igwg-on-tnc> accessed 12 September 2024 (containing information on the history and progress of the process and relevant documents) (OEIGWG).

12 See Statement on behalf of a Group of Countries at the 24th Session of the Human Rights Council (September 2013) <https://media.business-humanrights.org/media/documents/files/media/documents/statement-unhrc-legally-binding.pdf> accessed 12 September 2024.

13 UNHRC "Text of the Updated Draft Legally Binding Instrument with the Textual Proposals Submitted by States During the Ninth Session of the Open-Ended Intergovernmental Working Group on Transnational Corporations and Other Business Enterprises with Respect to Human Rights" (13 February 2024), UN Doc A/HRC/55/59/Add.1.

example, the nearly universal UN Convention against Corruption[14]) by relying upon the States parties for its implementation.[15]

Only in Africa have the States moved toward creating a regional system of investor liability at the international level, with the most recent adoption of the Protocol on Investment to the Agreement Establishing the African Continental Free Trade Area (the AfCFTA Investment Protocol) by the Assembly of the Heads of State and Government of the African Union in February 2023.[16] Still, once the Protocol enters into force, it would only apply to intra-African investments where the home State of the investor and the host State of the investment are both amongst the States parties to the Protocol, leaving the plethora of international investment agreements (IIAs) concluded by them with third States unaffected. Moreover, the adoption of Rules and Procedures governing Dispute Prevention, Management and Resolution of disputes between an investor and a host State under the AfCFTA Investment Protocol remains pending.[17]

Notwithstanding the African exception, there remains a reluctance by States to impose direct obligations upon investors at the international level, precluding the emergence of obligations of general application to investors under IL (either in the form of custom or general principles).[18] According to

14 United Nations Convention against Corruption (31 October 2003, entered into force 14 December 2005) 2225 UNTS 209.

15 See Jose Daniel Amado, Jackson Shaw Kern, and Martin Doe Rodriguez, "Elevating Corruption to an International Tort", in Jean Ho and Mavluda Sattorova, *Investors' International Law* (Hart Publishing 2021) 352.

16 At the time of writing the official text as adopted by the AU Assembly had not been released while the version agreed at the Seventh Extraordinary Session of the Specialized Technical Committee on Justice and Legal Affairs (Experts Meeting) of the AU (16–21 January 2023) was available at <https://www.bilaterals.org/IMG/pdf/en_-_draft_protocol_of_the_afcfta_on_investment.pdf> accessed 12 September 2024. The official text has since been published and is available at <https://au.int/sites/default/files/treaties/45078-treaty-EN_AfCFTA_Protocol_on_Investment.pdf> accessed 3 July 2026.

17 Appropriate "Rules and Procedures" must be put in place in an annex forming an integral part of the AfCFTA Investment Protocol that was to be negotiated and adopted within twelve months of the adoption of the Protocol, i.e., by February 2024 (cf. AfCFTA Investment Protocol art 46.3).

18 See the discussion in José Alvarez, "A Bit on Custom" (2009) 42 International Law and Politics 17. The question of whether customary international law imposes obligations upon investors is distinct, while not completely separate, from the question of whether the process of contemporary jurisprudence by investment tribunals has given rise to certain international standards regarding the treatment of investors. See Campbell McLachlan, "Investment Treaties and General International Law" (2008) 57 International and Comparative Law Quarterly 361, 391–401. See also Mārtiņš Paparinskis, "Investment treaty interpretation and customary investment law: Preliminary remarks" in Chester Brown and Kate Miles (eds), *Evolution in Investment Treaty Law and Arbitra-*

this view, investor obligations are to be determined exclusively by reference to the applicable investment treaty – which *may* or *may not* provide for the application of other written or unwritten rules of IL – as observed in much of the investment treaty arbitration jurisprudence. While acknowledging the potential influence of the *Urbaser* award[19] – which found that investors currently have certain *negative* direct obligations under IL – the traditionalists point at the exceptionality of its findings, which were treaty-specific (the Spain–Argentina treaty includes as components of the applicable law "other agreements in force between the Parties" and "the universally recognized principles of international law"[20]) as well as sector-specific (in the context of the right of access to water, although the tribunal's findings have wider implications) and contingent on the arbitral tribunal's acceptance that it has jurisdiction to entertain counterclaims. Moreover, the *Urbaser* standard may be too high for those seeking to attach human rights obligations to investors, as it requires only that they do not engage in activity *aimed at destroying* human rights,[21] and that they abstain from activity prohibited under IL[22] (thus not imposing any positive obligation to perform, which the Covenants impose only upon States[23]).

Finally, it is claimed that IL *should not* move in the direction of directly imposing obligations on investors. If international legal norms were extended to corporations and backed by effective enforcement mechanisms, States would lose control over compliance with the norms, which is likely to be resisted by States (as the outcome of normative initiatives at the international level has so far shown). Conversely, if not accompanied by an effective enforcement mechanism, the norms would likely be widely disregarded, which would do little for the interests to be protected and may trivialise IL.[24]

Another string of arguments holds that more recent decisions of arbitral tribunals already show a shift in the decried expansive standards of protection

---

tion (Cambridge University Press 2011); Andreas Kulick and Michael Waibel (eds), *General International Law in International Investment Law: A Commentary* (OUP 2024).

19 *Urbaser SA and Consorcio de Aguas Bilbao Bizkaia, Bilbao Biskaia Ur Partzuergoa v. The Argentine Republic,* ICSID Case No ARB/07/26, Award (8 December 2016).

20 Acuerdo para la promoción y protección recíproca de inversiones entre el Reino de España y la República Argentina y Protocolo anejo (1991) art IX.5.

21 *Urbaser* Award (n 19) para 1199.

22 Ibid., 1210.

23 Ibid., 1208 and 1210. See Kevin Crow and Lina Lorenzoni Escobar, "International Corporate Obligations, Human Rights, and the *Urbaser* Standard: Breaking New Ground?" (2018) 36 Boston University International Law Journal 87.

24 See Vázquez (n 7) 927.

provided to investors under IIAs,[25] demonstrating the ability of investment tribunals to prioritise public policy issues, such as public health and the environment.[26] One might argue that the addition of certain investor obligations in new-generation IIAs entails that investment protection in the future may be limited by ensuring that investors meet the obligations prescribed, thus serving as mitigating factors against (or perhaps entirely offsetting) those reliefs sought by investors before investment tribunals.[27] This argument points at the capacity of ISDS to address human rights, environmental, and other related concerns, and also claims that instead of reinforcing human and victims' rights, a wider system of international legal norms upon investors may provide an excuse or escape valve for States not to "do their job", thus weakening the current level of protection. For this position, tackling corruption and strengthening domestic institutions should be the proper focus of international efforts, which will ensure individual and collective rights protections without discouraging the foreign investment that is necessary for development.

The second premise on which the classical position lies is the *sui generis* nature and origins of ISDS. It argues that IIAs are self-regulating arrangements conferring substantive rights to investors and imposing obligations to States (primary rules) alongside an (arbitral) mechanism to ensure compliance by States (secondary rules). Such arrangements are perfectly in accordance with general IL, including Article 33(1) of the UN Charter[28] (calling for pacific settlement of international disputes) and the Vienna Convention on the Law of Treaties.[29] Although this position is rarely fully elaborated, it maintains that other rules of IL – such as human rights – do not intrude upon ISDS, concededly except as the application of other rules of IL is provided for in the IIA, or

25 *Philip Morris Brands Sarl v. Oriental Republic of Uruguay*, ICSID Case No ARB/10/07, Award (8 July 2016).

26 Babatunde Fagbohunlu and Inyene Robert, "Standards of Protection and the Obligations of the Investor" (*Global Arbitration Review*, 17 October 2023), is available at <https://globalarbitrationreview.com/guide/the-guide-telecoms-arbitrations/second-edition/article/standards-of-protection-and-the-obligations-of-the-investor> accessed 12 September 2024. However, in one notable award, a tribunal majority interpreted an environmental carve-out provision within the applicable treaty to mean that it did not remove the State's obligation to compensate. See *Eco Oro Minerals Corp. v. Republic of Colombia*, ICSID Case No ARB/16/41, Decision on Jurisdiction, Liability and Directions on Quantum (9 September 2021) 367.

27 Fagbohunlu and Robert (n 26).

28 United Nations (UN), "Charter of the United Nations" (signed 26 June 1945, entered into force 24 October 1945), available at <https://www.un.org/en/about-us/un-charter/full-text> accessed 12 September 2024.

29 Vienna Convention on the Law of Treaties (adopted 23 May 1969, entered into force 27 January 1980) 1155 UNTS 331.

reference is made to the applicable domestic law which incorporates international standards, or perhaps where a treaty-based or non-treaty-based rule has the character of *ius cogens*. This thesis weighed heavily in earlier arbitral decisions[30] but it is since losing its favour.[31]

It is not the object of this chapter to rebut all arguments raised as favouring the traditional position – neither as a matter of theory nor to address them in further detail. The purpose is rather to evoke recent developments and draw any observable general conclusions that may indicate a change of trend, which task we will next undertake.

3 International Law Already Imposes Obligations on Investors

The common impression that IL does not impose obligations upon investors stems largely from the fact that bilateral investment treaties only or mostly impose obligations upon States, and only or mostly confer rights to investors. Overreliance on investment treaties, in turn, obscures the other sources of investor obligations.[32] As explained by Professor Viñuales, "[t]he sources of foreign investment regulation are not merely treaties, but also a wide array of domestic norms, contractual arrangements, and an evolving body of customary and treaty-based international norms concerning matters such as corruption, social rights, human (including collective) rights and environmental protection".[33]

For decades, there have been initiatives to subject multinational enterprises and financial institutions to some standards of conduct, giving rise to a body of international standards for "corporate social responsibility" (CSR) and "socially responsible investment" (SRI).[34] The Guidelines for Multinational Enterprises of the Organisation for Economic Cooperation and Development

30 E.g., *CMS Gas Transmission Co v. Republic of Argentina*, Case No ARB/01/8, Jurisdiction (17 July 2003) para 48; *AES Corp v. Argentine Republic*, ICSID Case No ARB/02/17, Jurisdiction (26 April 2005) para 30.

31 See *Urbaser* Award (n 19). For an early decision, see *Asian Agricultural Products Ltd v. Republic of Sri Lanka*, ICSID Case No ARB/87/3, Award (27 June 1990) 21.

32 See Jorge E. Viñuales, "Investor Diligence in Investment Arbitration: Sources and Arguments" (2017) 32–3 ICSID Review - Foreign Investment Law Journal 346, 367.

33 Ibid., 367. See also Jorge E Viñuales, "The Sources of International Investment Law: Conceptual Foundations of Unruly Practices", in Samantha Besson and Jean d'Aspremont (eds), *The Oxford Handbook of the Sources of International Law* (Oxford University Press, 2016).

34 Viñuales (n 32) 346–347.

(OECD) – adopted in 1976 and updated most recently in June 2023[35] – and the United Nations Principles for Responsible Investment[36] are prominent examples of CSR and SRI instruments. Requiring a certain level of "diligence" from foreign investors, these instruments are, in most cases, of a soft law nature. However, a standard can become legally binding if incorporated by treaty or contract[37] or pursuant to the applicable domestic law, and also where it evolves into an international custom or general principle of law.

More recently, the negative impact that investor activities may have on the societies where they operate, together with perceived pitfalls of the investor–State arbitration regime, have led to initiatives for the creation of norms providing for investor obligations and their enforcement at the international level.

First, the trend is seen via IIAs of the latest generation and other investment-related agreements, which contain references to CSR standards. According to UN Trade and Development (UNCTAD), this trend is on the increase – the vast majority of investment agreements concluded in the last decade and a half and many model bilateral investment treaties (BITs) include investors' duties in the form of endorsing sustainable development goals while also giving a broader leeway for host States to regulate and providing for exceptions to treaty protection.[38] By tailoring the definition of protected investment – that investment must significantly contribute to the development of the host State economy[39] – and including a legality requirement – that only investments made in accordance with the law are protected under the treaty, thereby

35 OECD, Guidelines for Multinational Enterprises: Recommendations for Responsible Business Conduct in a Global Context, Annex I to the Declaration on International Investment and Multinational Enterprises, OECD/LEGAL/0144, 8 June 2023 (OECD Guidelines).

36 UN Principles of Responsible Investment <https://www.unpri.org/about-us/what-are-the-principles-for-responsible-investment> accessed 12 September 2024.

37 See Viñuales (n 32) 348, 350, 354–355. See also UNIDROIT's ongoing project on International Investment Contracts (IICs), which aims at developing guidance to foster the modernisation and standardisation of international investment contracts <https://www.unidroit.org/work-in-progress/investment-contracts-upicc/#1637156948432-1d041 68e-7a08> accessed 12 September 2024. See, in this regard, Chapter 6 in this volume.

38 UNCTAD, "International Investment Agreements Reform Accelerator 2020" <https://unctad.org/system/files/official-document/diaepcbinf2020d8_en.pdf> accessed 12 September 2024; and "Trends in the Investment Treaty Regime and a Reform Toolbox for the Energy Transition" (August 2023) <https://unctad.org/system/files/official-document/diaepcbinf2023d4_en.pdf> accessed 12 September 2024.

39 E.g., Burkina Faso–Turkey BIT (2019) art 1.1; Congo–Morocco BIT (2018) art 1.1; Egypt–Mauritius BIT (2014) art 1.1; Morocco–Nigeria BIT (2016) art 1.

excluding investments made through corruption or fraud, for example[40] – the new IIAs introduce requirements on investors to promote international CSR standards in order to preserve their own investment protections. Moreover, the inclusion of human rights and environmental provisions in IIAs, even if they are preambulatory clauses or are addressed to the States – e.g., not to seek to attract investment by lowering human rights, environmental, and labour standards[41] or offering to waive or derogate from environmental or labour laws where it would be inconsistent with related human rights,[42] or to reinforce the State's right to regulate to protect legitimate welfare objectives such as human rights, health, public order and safety, labour rights, and the environment[43] – also effectively creates obligations for investors. Ultimately, these and other prospective procedural reforms – such as excluding certain areas from the application of ISDS, narrowing the scope of (if not simply eliminating) stabilisation clauses, or allowing States to file counterclaims against investors[44] as well as providing for possible intervention by impacted parties within the host State[45] – establish a fairer equilibrium in the State–investor relationship.

Second, as noted, inter-governmental negotiations are ongoing since 2014 for a legally binding instrument on transnational corporations and other business enterprises and human rights.[46] It is noteworthy that the developed countries – which initially opposed the initiative – now are joining the nego-

40 E.g., Burkina Faso–Turkey BIT (2019) art 1.1 and 2; Canada–EU CETA (2016) art 8.1; Congo–Morocco BIT (2018) art 1; EU–Singapore Investment Protection Agreement (2018) art 2.1.1; EU–Vietnam Investment Protection Agreement (2019) art 1.2(q); Iran–Nicaragua BIT (2019) art 1.1; Japan–Jordan BIT (2018) art 1(a); Morocco–Nigeria BIT (2016) art 1; United Arab Emirates–Uruguay BIT (2018) art 1.2. Investments established by corruption have routinely been found to be barred by generic legality clauses featuring in earlier-generation IIAs, or even in their absence. See *Plama Consortium Limited v. Bulgaria*, ICSID Case No ARB/03/24, Award (27 August 2008). Newer-generation treaties have made the prohibition more explicit.

41 E.g., US Model BIT (2012) art 12.2 and 12.3; Norway Model BIT (2015), art 11.1.

42 E.g., US Model BIT (2012) art 12.2 and 13.2 and 13.3.

43 E.g., Colombia Model BIT (2017) preamble. See Carolina Olarte-Bácares, Enrique Prieto-Rios, Juan P Pontón Serra, "The 2017 BIT Model of Colombia: A Human Rights Assessment from Investments Disputes Against the State", in Nitish Monebhurrun, Carolina Olarte-Bácares, Marco A Velazquez-Ruiz (eds), *International Investment Law and Arbitration from a Latin American Perspective* (Springer 2024).

44 Africa Arbitration Academy Model Bilateral Investment Treaty (2022) art 22 G; India Model BIT (2015).

45 See Jose Daniel Amado, Jackson Shaw Kern and Martin Doe Rodriguez, *Arbitrating the Conduct of International Investors* (Cambridge University Press 2018) chap 5.

46 OEIGWG (n 11).

tiation table including the United States, the United Kingdom, and most European Union members as well as China. Two issues remained particularly contentious at the ninth session of the intergovernmental working group in 2023.[47] First is the scope of the future instrument – with developing States seeking to limit the treaty to transnational corporations, while developed States insist that it should apply to all "business enterprises" (at least those of a certain size).[48] Second is the object of the regulation – victim-centred rules and the establishment of mandatory mechanisms for the protection of human rights in the context of business activity, as favoured by developing States (e.g., Brazil[49]); or European-style due diligence rules mirroring due diligence laws recently adopted by France, Germany, and other European countries[50] or as seen in the newly adopted EU Corporate Sustainability Due Diligence Directive (CSDDD 2024).[51] Other differences concern the definition of human rights abuses – with Russia opposing and the United Kingdom seeking to clarify the term "internationally recognized" human rights[52] as well as references to environmental rights[53] and the relationship of the future instru-

---

47 See OEIGWG "General Statements from States and non-State stakeholders" <https://www.ohchr.org/sites/default/files/documents/hrbodies/hrcouncil/igwg-transcorp/session9/igwg-9th-compilation-general-statements.pdf> accessed 12 September 2024; "Statements delivered by States during the State-led negotiations" <https://www.ohchr.org/sites/default/files/documents/hrbodies/hrcouncil/igwg-transcorp/session9/igwg-9th-compilation-state-statements.pdf> accessed 12 September 2024.

48 For the Latin American perspectives, see Humberto Cantú Rivera (ed.), *El tratado sobre las empresas y los derechos humanos: Perspectivas latinoamericanas* (Tirant Lo Blanch 2022).

49 See the statements of Brazil (n 47).

50 Loi 2017–399 du 27 mars 2017 relative au devoir de vigilance des sociétés mères et des entreprises donneuses d'ordre, France, ELI: https://www.legifrance.gouv.fr/eli/loi/2017/3/27/ECFX1509096L/jo/texte; Dutch Child Labour Due Diligence Act, published in the Federal Law Gazette on 13 November 2019, <https://zoek.officielebekendmakingen.nl/stb-2019-401.html> accessed 12 September 2024; German Act on Corporate Due Diligence Obligations in Supply Chains (Gesetz über die unternehmerischen Sorgfaltspflichten in Lieferketten), published in the Federal Law Gazette on 22 July 2021 <https://www.bgbl.de/xaver/bgbl/startxav?startbk=Bundesanzeiger_BGBl&jumpTo=bgbl121s2959.pdf#__bgbl__%2F%2F*%5B%40attr_id%3D%27bgbl121s2959.pdf%27%5D__1720818462615> accessed 12 September 2024; The Transparency Act, Norway, published on 29 August 2023 <https://www.forbrukertilsynet.no/vi-jobber-med/apenhetsloven/the-transparency-act> accessed 12 September 2024.

51 EU Directive 2024/1760 on corporate sustainability due diligence [2024] OJ L2024/1760 (Due Diligence Directive).

52 See the statements of Russia and the United Kingdom, respectively (n 47).

53 See the statements of Iran and the EU (n 47).

ment with investment treaties.[54] Despite these differences, the decision to appoint legal experts to assist with intersessional, interregional thematic consultations to discuss the draft legally binding instrument,[55] together with the growing participation and express support for a treaty by previously reluctant States (e.g., France[56]), shows that consensus is building toward holding corporations accountable at the international level through an international treaty, even though the possibility of it establishing direct obligations to corporations (as opposed to indirect obligations to be enacted and/or enforced by the States) remains in doubt.

Third, the adoption in 2023 of the AfCFTA Investment Protocol – which provides numerous positive investor obligations – constitutes a significant development. Upon its entry into force, the Protocol mandates that *investors and their investments* shall, in carrying out their business activities, respect and protect the environment and, in particular: respect the right to a clean, healthy, and sustainable environment; comply with the principles of prevention and precaution; carry out environmental impact assessments in accordance with the best international standards and practices; apply the precautionary principle to their environmental impact assessments and decisions related to a proposed investment; take steps to mitigate and to restore impacted sites where their business activities cause environmental harm; and not exploit or use natural resources to the detriment of the rights and interests of the host State or its local communities.[57] The obligations set out in Article 34 of the Protocol evoke other environmental standards existing in IL: the duty of due diligence, the duty to cooperate, the obligation to prevent significant trans-boundary harm, and the polluter-pays principle.[58] Another originality of the Protocol is the relation it establishes between the ecological imperative and human rights by suggesting that the environment may be the object of a human right – the right to a clean environment, for example – and institutionalising said relationship through the concept of "human rights

54 See the statements of Brazil, Colombia, Honduras and the United Kingdom (n 47).

55 UNHRC "Report on the Ninth Session of the Open-Ended Intergovernmental Working Group on Transnational Corporations and Other Business Enterprises with Respect to Human Rights", para 31(e) (26 December 2023) UN Doc A/HRC/55/59.

56 See the statement of France (n 47).

57 AfCFTA Investment Protocol (n 16) chap 5. The Protocol also prescribes positive investor obligations in the areas of human rights, indigenous peoples and local communities, corporate governance, anti-corruption, labour standards, and taxation. See other chapters in this book.

58 See in this book Chapter 5 by Jackson Shaw Kern and Mohit Khubchandani, "Enforcing International Environmental and Climate Change Law on Investors: Reflections on the Investment Protocol to the African Continental Free Trade Area and Beyond".

linked to environment".[59] It is notable that even prior to the Protocol, regional instruments within Africa included investor obligations, as did the 2016 Draft Pan-African Investment Code.[60] The Protocol may be said to represent a consolidation of the position in favour of investor obligations on the African continent.

The decisions of some investment arbitral tribunals have not been oblivious to these inter-State developments and to the preoccupations voiced by affected States and civil society on the need to make investors fully accountable for the harmful impacts of their activities. The tribunal in *Urbaser v. Argentina*[61] affirmed in its much commented 2016 decision, arguably for the first time, that investors do have obligations under IL, at least an obligation not to engage in activity aimed at destroying human rights,[62] as well as to abstain from activity prohibited under general IL.[63] This conclusion was reaffirmed in the 2018 decision in the case of *Aven v. Costa Rica* in which the tribunal accepted that investors are bound by international *erga omnes* obligations particularly in the field of environmental law.[64] While these findings have not always been echoed by other tribunals, and they do not constitute legally binding precedent, they assist with the determination of the existence and content of rules of IL, as indicated in the International Law Commission's Draft Conclusions on Subsidiary Means for the Determination of Rules of International Law.[65]

What emerges from this *tour d'horizon* is that IL already imposes legal and quasi-legal obligations to investors at the international level, with recent developments showing a certain tendency to impose upon investors *direct negative obligations* – as recognised in *Urbaser* – but also *direct positive obligations* as in latest generation IIAs including the AfCFTA Investment Protocol.

---

59 Alioune Sall, "L'impératif du développement durable dans le nouveau droit africain des investissements" (Colloque Le Mans Université, September 2023).

60 See Southern African Development Community Protocol on Finance and Investment (2006) art 10; Investment Agreement for the Common Market for Eastern and Southern Africa (2007) art 13; Supplementary Act of the Economic Community of West African States (2008) art 14; see also Draft Pan-African Investment Code (2016) chap 4.

61 *Urbaser* Award (n 19).

62 Ibid., para 1199.

63 Ibid., 1210. See Crow and Lorenzoni Escobar (n 23).

64 *David R Aven and Others v. Republic of Costa Rica*, ICSID Case No UNCT/15/3, Award (18 September 2018) para 739.

65 Draft conclusions 6 and 7 and commentary 7 to draft conclusión 2 as adopted by the International Law Commission (ILC) on first reading. See ILC, "Draft Report of the International Law Commission on the Work of its 75th Session" (28 May 2024) UN Doc A/CN.4/L.999.

Those obligations can be framed in terms of an *obligation to act diligently* to avoid the deprivation of human and other rights that may be due to the affected individuals and groups and also, arguably, to positively ensure their enjoyment; an obligation that is reflected in the increasing number of instances in domestic and international practice where such diligent conduct has been demanded from and enforced upon investors. There is support for the view that due diligence has arisen as a general principle of law in the sense of Article 38(1)(c) of the Statute of the International Court of Justice – and as such, as a source of IL – as a standard of conduct applicable in different areas of IL, generating specific obligations not only from States and international organisations but also for multinational corporations, business operators, private investors, and other non-State actors in those areas where the principle operates.[66] There is a multiplicity of fields in which commentators have sought to use due diligence. These include standards emerging from international environmental and criminal law in particular, but also in relation to labour and communities' rights[67] and the control of corporations – including foreign investors – in line with the 2011 UN Guiding Principles on Business and Human Rights.[68] A determination of the applicability of the due diligence principle to foreign investors would require a comparative analysis to show that the principle exists in the different legal systems and regions of the world and that it is transposable to the international legal system,[69] or alternatively, that the principle has been formed *within* the international legal system.[70] The content and scope of the principle must also be discerned – for example, what is the degree of care or vigilance, or the absence of negligence, that may be required from the obligated subjects. Nevertheless, it may be argued that a

66 See Penelope Ridings, "Due Diligence in International Law" in ILC, "Report of the International Law Commission on the Work of Its 75th Session" Annex II paras 3 and 21 (2024) UN Doc A/79/10.

67 See Alessandra Mistura, "Foreign Investor Diligence: An Actionable Cartography for Sustainable Investment" (DPhil thesis, Geneva Graduate Institute 2023) 173–190.

68 UN Guiding Principles (n 6); see also the discussion in Jonathan Bonnitcha and Robert McCorquodale, "The Concept of 'Due Diligence' in the UN Guiding Principles on Business and Human Rights" (2017) 28(3) European Journal of International Law 899; John Gerard Ruggie and John F Sherman III, "The Concept of 'Due Diligence' in the UN Guiding Principles on Business and Human Rights: A Reply to Jonathan Bonnitcha and Robert McCorquodale" (2017) 28(3) European Journal of International Law 921.

69 Draft conclusions 3(a) and 4 to 6 as adopted by the International Law Commission on first reading. See ILC, "Report of the International Law Commission on the Work of its 74th Session" (19 May 2023) UN Doc A/CN.4/L.982.

70 Ibid., draft conclusions 3(b) and 7.

certain level of due diligence is already required by international law from foreign investors.

The manners in which investors' obligations can be enforced will be the subject of the following section.

4 Investor Obligations Can Be Enforced via Different Mechanisms

Investors not only have international legal obligations incumbent upon them, but those obligations can also be enforced via different mechanisms.[71]

Investment arbitration is the more obvious forum for enforcement of investor obligations, even when the failure of certain arbitral tribunals to fully recognise the State's right to regulate or to hold investors to account for illegal practices and resultant harms incurred is amongst the origins of the current process for investment system reform.[72] Nevertheless, the illegality of the proffered investment, fraud, corruption, or breach of host State law may naturally become relevant as jurisdictional or admissibility issues in an investment proceeding.[73] Investor negligence can also act as a host State defence, excluding or limiting its responsibility for breach of investment protection or leading to a reduction in the amount of compensation awarded.[74] Moreover, tribunals are increasingly addressing counterclaims based on the

71 See generally Mistura (n 67); Viñuales (n 32).

72 Several initiatives are ongoing for the reform of the ISDS mechanism at regional and multilateral levels, in the latter case at the United Nations Commission on International Trade Law (UNCITRAL), where intergovernmental negotiations have led to the recent agreement on the establishment of a Multilateral Advisory Centre <https://uncitral.un.org/en/working_groups/3/investor-state> accessed 12 September 2024.

73 E.g., *World Duty Free Company Limited v. Republic of Kenya*, ICSID Case No ARB/00/7, Award (4 October 2006) (contracts obtained by bribery are deemed to be unenforceable under applicable Kenyan and English law, as well as international law – relying on the concept of *ordre public*); *Plama* Award (n 40) paras 138–9 (the legality requirement must be read as an implicit term of the contract – even if the tribunal had jurisdiction, *quod non*, the claim would be inadmissible); *Alasdair Ross Anderson and Others v. Costa Rica*, ICSID Case No ARB(AF)/07/3, Award (19 May 2010) paras 51–61 (the illegality of the "Ponzi" scheme in which the investors invested barred jurisdiction).

74 E.g., *Robert Azinian, Kenneth Davitian, & Ellen Baca v. The United Mexican States*, ICSID Case No ARB (AF)/97/2, Award (1 November 1999) paras 103–5 (negligent conduct of investor justified intervention by the State); *MTD Equity Sdn Bhd and MTD Chile SA v. Republic of Chile*, ICSID Case No ARB/01/7, Award (25 May 2004) paras 242–3 (investor must bear part of the damages it suffered where it acted negligently in assessing the regulatory risks).

investor's breach of international and domestic law; in so doing, they are recognising that investment arbitration is not a "closed system" that exists in isolation.[75]

There are several examples that reveal the potential of the legal mechanisms that are inherent in ISDS to enforce investors' compliance with human rights, environmental, and other standards developed at the international level, even in the absence of an express clause in the relevant IIA.[76] On the other hand, there may also be structural challenges for the ISDS to unravel its full potential for the protection of international standards in the absence of a comprehensive reform of the ISDS system.[77] This merits consideration of – and explains the resort to – additional and alternative mechanisms to seek enforcement of investor diligence as well.

One such alternative is litigation before the domestic tribunals of the host State for breach of international standards that may be applicable to the investment or investor by virtue of contract, by their incorporation into national law, by the relevant IIA, or by other rules of IL. Some IIAs expressly provide for the application of the treaty itself and IL,[78] while others may produce the same effect when the application of the law of the host State is provided for in the investment treaty[79] and even in the absence thereof, in relation with those rules of IL which have been incorporated into the domestic legislation of the State via treaty or custom in accordance with its own constitutional law. Article 42(1) of the Convention on the Settlement of Investment Disputes between States and Nationals of Other States (commonly known as the ICSID Convention) expressly provides that "[i]n the absence of [...] agreement, the Tribunal shall apply the law of the Contracting State party to the dispute (including its rules on the conflict of laws) and such rules of inter-

75 *Urbaser* Award (n 19) (counterclaim was permitted under the applicable treaty and justified by the "manifest" connection between the investor's and the State's claims); *Burlington Resources Inc v. Republic of Ecuador*, ICSID Case No ARB/08/5, Decision on Ecuador's Counterclaims (7 February 2017) (based on the breach of domestic law); *Aven* Award (n 64) (18 September 2018) (based on treaty passage regarding the environment).

76 See generally Viñuales (n 32) 346, 355–366; Mistura (n 67) 261–291.

77 For proposals to overcome these challenges, see generally Amado, Kern, and Doe Rodriguez (n 45).

78 E.g., Energy Charter Treaty (ECT) art 26(6); North American Free Trade Agreement (NAFTA) art 1131; Singapore–US Free Trade Agreement (2003) art 15.21 of the investment chapter; AfCFTA Investment Protocol (n 15) art 32.

79 This clause is sometimes called the "Sri Lanka clause" because it is found mainly in Sri Lanka BIT practice, e.g., Korea–Sri Lanka (1980) art 9, and Finland–Sri Lanka (1985) art 8; see also AfCFTA Investment Protocol (n 15) art 32.

national law as may be applicable".[80] There should be little doubt that the law of the host State is always applicable to an investment except as it may have been validly excluded by the parties. While it is true that domestic or contract-based litigation of IIA standards has been uncommon, such may provide a venue for States as well as affected individuals and communities – who may not readily enjoy access to ISDS – to enforce international standards vis-à-vis investors.[81]

For employees and local communities, transnational civil litigation may also be an appropriate avenue for the actionability of foreign investor diligence. Key jurisdictions (including the United States, United Kingdom, Canada, Netherlands, France, and Italy) have admitted claims against the parent company for adverse consequences of its subsidiaries' activities abroad.[82] Moreover, recent national vigilance laws and the new EU Due Diligence Directive – which adopts a CSR approach to global value chains – also stand to increase legal liability for businesses operating in the European Union.

Based on due care considerations under general tort law principles, these developments stand for the proposition that multinational companies may be held liable for failure to implement group policies which are sufficiently concrete and targeted to ensure compliance with international human rights, environmental, and other standards worldwide. Such may include potential liability for the failure to disclose information relating to the investment activities, as required under non-financial disclosure laws.[83] Moreover, climate-related litigation before domestic courts and tribunals is growing rapidly in parallel with the worsening of the climate crisis, providing a venue for compensation of damage caused by climate change or for the coercive curbing of

80 Convention on the Settlement of Investment Disputes Between States and Nationals of Other States (18 March 1965, entered into force 14 October 1966) 575 UNTS 159 art 42(1).

81 For an exploration of models conferring such access in ISDS, see Amado, Kern, and Doe Rodriguez (n 45) chap 2.

82 E.g., *Vedanta Resources Plc v. Lungowe* [2019] UKSC 20, [2019] 2 WLR 1051 in the United Kingdom; *Four Nigerian Farmers and Stichting Milieudefensie v. Royal Dutch Shell PLC* [2021] ECLI:NL:GHDHA:2021:132 (*Oruma Case*), ECLI:NL:GHDHA:2021:133 (*Goi Case*), and ECLI:NL:GHDHA:2021:134 (*Ikot Ada Udo Case*) in the Netherlands. See generally Mistura (n 67) 294–317.

83 E.g., EU Directive 2014/95/EU on the disclosure of non-financial and diversity information [2014] OJ L330 (Non-financial Reporting Directive) ("large" companies and groups with more than 500 employees are required to disclose group-level information on environmental protection, human rights, social and employment issues, and anti-corruption).

CO_2 emissions by a subsidiary abroad.[84] While the actionability of investor due diligence before foreign national courts is not without any hindrance – as litigation costs and enforcement actions may present insurmountable challenges for impacted individuals and local communities – foreign direct litigation nonetheless provides a promising avenue for enforcing investor diligence and corporate accountability beyond borders.

Finally, a range of soft international mechanisms exists to aid in ensuring foreign investor diligence, such as the implementation procedure of the OECD Guidelines and the Compliance Advisor Ombudsman (CAO) Procedure of the International Finance Corporation (IFC). While the OECD Guidelines provide for a three-phase procedure – assessment of the complaint, mediation, and recommendations, determinations, and follow-up – to be conducted by the "national contact point" with the participation of interested parties (including the business community, workers' unions, and non-governmental organisations), the CAO performs dispute resolution and compliance functions which may lead to the imposition of sanctions under the IFC's own framework – e.g., in the form of exclusion from future loans for non-compliant clients. Although non-judicial grievance mechanisms have not been shielded from criticism and face limits of their power, in limited instances they can and do play an essential role as part of the toolkit in ensuring corporate accountability.

Last but not least, and in addition to the arguments and defences used in ISDS and non-ISDS litigation, one avenue often overlooked – by both the literature and (interestingly enough) also by States – for giving effect to business responsibilities concerns the application of the rules of general IL, particularly when related to treaty interpretation and the content of State responsibility.[85]

---

84 E.g., the decision of the District Court of The Hague in *Milieudefensie et al v. Royal Dutch Shell PLC* [2021] ECLI:NL:RBDHA:2021:5339 (English version), paras 4.4.2, 4.4.55, and 5.3 (the court concluded that Royal Dutch Shell is obliged to reduce the CO_2 emissions of the Shell group's activities by a net 45% by the end of 2030, the reduction obligation being an obligation of result; in its interpretation of the unwritten standard of care, the court included the UN Guiding Principles and the responsibility of States and society). The decision was reversed by The Hague Court of Appeal [2024] ECLI:NL:GHDHA:2024:2100 (English version), paras 7.17–7.27 and 7.111 (the court ruled that Shell is obliged to reduce its CO_2 emissions but that it was unable to determine which percentage should apply; that this obligation is based on the human right to protection against dangerous climate change; and that it is first and foremost up to governments to ensure the protection of human rights, but indirectly those rights do also have a bearing on the social standard of care which companies like Shell must observe).

85 See Mārtiņš Paparinskis, "Comments to OECD Public Consultation on Business Responsibilities and Investment Treaties" (15 May 2020) 77 <https://discovery.ucl.ac.uk/

In investment proceedings, it has been suggested that the host State to the investment could do well to invoke the customary rules on State responsibility for the mitigation of loss, as reflected in Article 39 of the ILC's 2001 Articles on Responsibility of States for Internationally Wrongful Acts.[86] Outside investment proceedings, the host State may, in certain circumstances, invoke the international responsibility of the State of origin of the investment if the harmful (otherwise "private" conduct) can be attributed to that State – for example, if the head office in State X bears responsibility for the activity of the branch in State Y, and a claim may be raised under IL by the latter State against the former[87] – and take non-forcible counter-measures in order to procure its cessation and to achieve reparation for the injury.[88] A State may also suspend the advantages granted to the investors of the other contracting State to the IIA on the basis of the *exceptio non adimplenti contractus* in accordance with Article 60 of the Vienna Convention on the Law of Treaties.[89]

This summary, far from providing a comprehensive analysis of how due diligence may operate on investment matters, supports the proposition that the due diligence standard may be applied and the international obligations of investors can be enforced in investment proceedings and other legal mechanisms. Referred to in some literature as "entry points", the different mechanisms in investment arbitration and foreign and domestic judicial litigation increasingly provide avenues through which the international sources of investor obligations can be grounded.

5 Concluding Observations

The preceding analysis allows for certain concluding observations.

First, though it may be tempting to view the relationship between investment law and IL from a static and binary viewpoint – that general IL either *does* or *does not* apply to investment law – it may be more accurate to consider

id/eprint/10106342/7/Paparinskis_OECD-Investment-treaties-Public-consultation-2020_extracted.pdf> accessed 12 September 2024.

86 Draft Articles on Responsibility of States for Internationally Wrongful Acts, with commentaries, *Yearbook of the International Law Commission*, 2001, vol II (Part Two) 109 (2001 Draft Articles). Cf. Paparinskis, Ibid., 78.

87 Ibid., arts 8 and 11.

88 Ibid., 22.

89 Viñuales (n 32) 367.

such a relationship as a process in which IL is increasingly penetrating investment law.[90]

Second, both analytically and in practice, the idea of the investment arbitration system as a "self-contained regime," which originally occupied the investment field discourse, has given way to certain decisions[91] and a rich literature holding the (correct) understanding of IL as a "legal system" in which specialised regimes – like the one for investment – do not and should not erode the systematisation of IL.[92] Meanwhile, the application of the rules and principles that support the necessary compatibility between investment law and other – e.g., human rights and environmental – rules of IL continues to depend on the discretion of arbitral tribunals, which may be reluctant to interpret the rules in IIAs within the context of other general rules of IL.[93]

Third, over-reliance on earlier investment treaties may have contributed to a misimpression that investors do not have obligations derived from IL.[94] It also obscures the potentials of other avenues available to victims of foreign investors' abuses of international human rights and environmental standards. More still, it may have inadvertently contributed to the artificial isolation of the investment regime from general IL, making ISDS more vulnerable to the

---

90 A prominent case in point is the judicial finding that arbitral tribunals do not have jurisdiction in intra-European Union investment disputes. See Case 284/16 *Slowakische Republik v. Achmea BV* [GC] [2018] ECLI:EU:C:2018:158 paras 32 (art 344 of the Treaty on the Functioning of the European Union (TFEU) forbids Member States to "submit a dispute concerning the interpretation or application of the Treaties to any method of settlement other than those provided for" in the EU Treaties) and 49 (a tribunal established under an intra-EU BIT does not qualify as a "court or tribunal" of a Member State under art 267 of the TFEU).

91 *Urbaser* Award (n 19); *Bear Creek Mining Corporation v. Republic of Peru*, ICSID Case No ARB/14/22, Award (30 November 2017) (Partial Dissenting Opinion of Professor Philippe Sands).

92 Raúl E Vinuesa, "La fragmentación del derecho internacional y su impacto en el derecho internacional de los derechos humanos" in Departamento de Derecho Internacional, Facultad de Derecho, Universidad de Chile (ed), *Estudios de derecho internacional contemporáneo: Homenaje al Profesor Edmundo Vargas Carreño* (Thomson Reuters 2024) 319 (discussing the question of complementarity versus compatibility of human rights law and investment law, including in the context of the right of access to water and indigenous rights); see also Eyal Benvenisti, "The Conception of International Law as a Legal System" (2008) 83 Tel Aviv University Law Faculty Papers <http://law.bepress.com/taulwps/art83> accessed 12 September 2024; James Crawford, "Change, Order, Change: The Course of International Law. General Course on Public International Law" (2013) 365 Recueil des Cours de l'Académie de Droit International 9, 205–229.

93 Vinuesa, Ibid.

94 See Viñuales (n 32) 367.

criticisms and challenges which have themselves spawned the current process of IIA and multilateral investment system reform.

The overall conclusion is that IL imposes legal obligations to investors at the international level. Further, there is evidence that due diligence may be establishing itself as an overarching standard of conduct required by international law of foreign investors, either as anchored and provided for in the municipal laws or independently under IL.

Whether the best way to enforce the due diligence standard is through the ISDS system, an alternative international mechanism, or various other venues currently available, and whether an international system establishing direct obligations to investors will ultimately serve the end of ensuring corporate compliance and effective protection of human rights and other international standards, are matters for another time.

CHAPTER 2

Investor Obligations in Relation to State Obligations

Anna Kozmenko[1]

1 Introduction

Investment treaties concluded in the late 20th and early 21st centuries were aimed at providing protections to foreign-owned investments. This approach was shaped by certain historical and economic developments of that era. These agreements largely granted protected investors recourse against unlawful State interference with their investments, while imposing no corresponding obligations on investors towards the host States. As those treaties have been interpreted over time, this has created a regulatory imbalance.

Today, this approach is being replaced by a new trend of placing more emphasis on investor obligations. In essence, while these agreements continue to protect investor interests, they now also recognize or impose certain responsibilities on investors with respect to their activities in their host States.

This shift raises several key issues, which this paper outlines:

1) What are the driving forces behind the current trend towards more investor obligations?
2) How widespread is this trend in doctrine and international practice?
3) What is the scope of investors' obligations in current investment agreements?

2 A Brief Doctrinal Overview of the Trend

There is now a significant body of work on the history and development of investment protection treaties, discussing their origins and evolution at national and international levels, and situating them within broader trends. Some of this commentary addresses specifically the issue of imbalance – the traditional lack of direct investor obligations in investment treaties. Viache-

1 This paper was prepared with the assistance of Igor Voskoboynik, a trainee lawyer at Curtis Mallet Prevost Colt Mosle LLP.

slav Semenko contends, for example, that the reason for the existing imbalance lies in the desire of developing countries to attract foreign capital, accelerating the adoption of BITs that largely served the interests of investors from capital-exporting nations. Little attention was given to the obligations of multinational corporations towards the host States and their communities.[2]

Invoking often vaguely worded standards of treatment in treaties, which came to be interpreted by many arbitral tribunals as offering broad protections, investors increasingly turned to international arbitration to resolve disputes. This trend resulted in unpredictable legal outcomes, as investors were able to bypass domestic courts and invoke often novel arguments about the scope of States' international obligations under investment treaties.

Frank J. Garcia and his co-authors observe the roots of the previously existing trend from a different angle. They note that the process of concluding treaties coincided with the decolonisation period. Newly independent States, eager to break free from the political and economic control of their former colonisers, sought to assert the power of their own laws. This shift created anxiety among foreign investors, many of whom were nationals of the former colonial powers.[3]

To address these concerns, countries introduced BITs, offering foreign investors fair and equitable treatment, along with national and most-favoured-nation status. They also established rules governing expropriation. During this time, when former colonisers were the primary exporters of foreign direct investment, BITs served as a one-way protection programme, primarily benefiting the investors from these powerful nations.[4]

Today, this trend is changing. There is a growing body of publications suggesting that international investment law needs to be more balanced and shift current regulation away from pro-investor protection towards a more balanced approach that takes into account the interests of States. These authors see differently how this trend should be implemented.

As Peter Muchlinski notes, the preamble of a treaty can play a crucial role in its interpretation, outlining the key goals and guiding how governments and tribunals will understand its provisions. In so-called "old-generation BITs", preambles were typically brief, focusing on the primary goals of investment stability and creating favourable conditions for investment and cooperation.

---

2 Viacheslav Semenko, 'Duties of investors in international investment law: analysis of model BITs of the latest generation' (Ghent University, Faculty of Law Academic Year 2017–18) 7.

3 Frank J. Garcia and J. Jeffrey, 'Reforming the international investment regime: lessons from international trade law' (2015) 18(4) Journal of International Economic Law 866.

4 Ibid., 867.

These early agreements rarely addressed broader goals like sustainable development, instead generally assuming that an increase in foreign investment naturally equated to development.[5]

In this light, Suzanne Spears notes that preambles of older investment treaties were typically focused on creating favourable conditions for investments, while non-economic goals, such as the State's right to regulate, sustainable development, or rights of workers, were barely addressed.[6] That focus, she argues, led to investment tribunals interpreting gaps or ambiguities in the investment treaties in favour of investor rights.[7]

She further noted that in the current days there is a shift towards the new liberalism, which is based on the idea that development must be sustainable, addressing not only economic growth but also social and environmental dimensions. Moreover, the ideas of economic development, though playing an important role, should not overshadow these non-economic concerns.[8] Hence, the author suggests that the preambles of new-generation BITs should incorporate language that reflects the principles of sustainable development. This approach would serve as a tool for more balanced interpretation, ensuring that the treaties do not solely favour investors' interests but also consider the interests of States and other non-economic values.[9]

Muthucumaraswamy Sornarajah notes that there has been "little movement towards the recognition of obligations of multinational corporations towards the host States and the communities in which these corporations operate".[10] He attributes this lack of movement primarily to the fact that the need for "firm rules" regulating multinational corporations is a recent development in international law. He concurs that investment treaties have traditionally focused on the interests of multinational corporations, not addressing the harm they cause and the vulnerabilities of developing States.[11] Professor Sornarajah notes that reforms of new-generation BITs can begin to shift away from a focus on investment protection to incorporate "valid con-

5 Peter Muchlinski, 'Negotiating new generation international investment agreements' in Steffen Hindelang and Markus Krajewski (eds), *Shifting Paradigms in International Investment Law: More Balanced, Less Isolated, Increasingly Diversified* (OUP 2016) 46.

6 She notes that the NAFTA was an unusual example among the older investment treaties which expressly preserved the State's right to regulate.

7 Suzanne A. Spears, 'The quest for policy space in a new generation of international investment agreements' (2010) 13(4) Journal of International Economic Law 1037.

8 Ibid., 1067.

9 Ibid., 1071.

10 M Sornarajah, *The International Law on Foreign Investment* (4th edn, Cambridge University Press 2017) 174.

11 Ibid., 172.

cerns of those arguing the case for environmental protection, human rights and economic development".[12]

Another commentator Professor Zeng Huqun, asserts: "the adoption, interpretation and related practice of provisions on broad definition of investment, broad definition of investors, right of establishment, extensive application of F&E [fair and equitable] treatment, extensive adoption of Hull formula, and the direct right for investors in ISDS reflect particularly the general trend, the continuous approach and the firm stance of developed capital-exporting States, and the increasing imbalance and/or un-equality between developed States and developing States in international investment activities".[13] He suggests that reforming the current system should be based on three key concepts: "balance", "sustainable development", and "integration". Any reform of future BITs, he suggests, should be grounded in these principles.[14]

Thus, after reviewing some of the relevant commentary, we can identify various calls for more balanced approaches in the practice of drafting BITs, approaches that focus not only on reaffirming the inherent rights and even duties of States to regulate, but also on the obligations of investors. Are these calls a fundamental shift in the approach to international investment, or a continuation of past trends? Let us turn to these questions.

3 The History of Attempts to Balance the State–Investor Relationship by International Organisations

Efforts to ensure that investors contribute positively to sustainable development outcomes in their host States are not new. The bulk of these efforts occurs at the national level through environmental, labour, tax, consumer protection, and other legislation. But, due to some of the unique opportunities and challenges arising in connection with multinational enterprises – i.e., international investments by corporations – there have also been efforts at the international level to address investor conduct and obligations. This section sketches some of those.

12 Ibid., 267–268.

13 Zeng Huaqun, 'Balance, sustainable development, and integration: Innovative path for BIT practice' (2014) 17(2) Journal of International Economic Law 308.

14 Ibid., 329.

3.1 Declaration on the Establishment of a New International Economic Order

In 1974, the United Nations took a significant step towards balancing the relationship between States and investors. The UN General Assembly adopted the Declaration on the Establishment of a New International Economic Order, a groundbreaking effort to place investors, particularly transnational corporations (TNCs), under stricter control.[15] This move was driven by capital-importing countries, which sought to recognise the rights of host States to control the activities of TNCs operating within their borders. The declaration also aimed to establish a code of conduct for these corporations, preventing the economic exploitation of host countries.

The declaration was a bold call for a new economic order based on equity, sovereign equality, interdependence, and cooperation among all States, regardless of their economic or social systems. It sought to correct global inequalities, address existing injustices, and bridge gaps between developed and developing countries. By promoting steady economic and social development, the UN hoped to ensure peace and justice for both present and future generations.

3.2 Code of Conduct on Transnational Corporations

To implement certain provisions of the 1974 Declaration on the Establishment of a New International Economic Order, the United Nations made a determined effort to bring transnational corporations under a stricter regulatory framework. To achieve this, the United Nations Centre on Transnational Corporations initiated negotiations for a Draft Code of Conduct on Transnational Corporations (the UNCCTC).[16] These talks began in the late 1970s, driven by the desire to create a fairer global economic system that protected the interests of host States.

However, as the global landscape began to shift in the early 1990s, with a growing trend towards liberalising foreign direct investment regulations to attract capital, the negotiations faced significant challenges. Ultimately, despite years of discussions, the negotiations ended without producing a final,

---

15 Declaration on the Establishment of a New International Economic Order (1 May 1974) UNGA Res 3201 (S-VI)-EN.

16 Draft United Nations Code of Conduct on Transnational Corporations (1983) <https://investmentpolicy.unctad.org/international-investment-agreements/treaty-files/2891/download> accessed 20 August 2024.

signed document.[17] The changing macro-economic and political circumstances of the time contributed to this outcome.

Despite this setback, the UNCCTC's efforts were not in vain. The negotiations brought to light critical issues that highlighted the concerns of host States and the areas that required additional protection from the influence of powerful transnational corporations. The discussions underscored the need for a balanced relationship between investors and host States, even if a formal code of conduct was never realised.[18]

The primary idea of the UNCCTC was rooted in respect for national sovereignty. Transnational corporations were expected to honour the laws, regulations, and administrative practices of the countries in which they operated. Each State retained its right to regulate and oversee the activities of foreign entities within its borders, particularly in the management of its natural resources.[19]

The UNCCTC also emphasised that TNCs should align their activities with the economic goals and development objectives set by the governments of their host countries.[20] This alignment extended beyond mere economic engagement, as TNCs were also urged to respect the social and cultural values of these nations. They were cautioned against introducing products, services, or practices that could harm the cultural fabric of the societies in which they operated.[21]

Human rights and fundamental freedoms were non-negotiable under the UNCCTC. Transnational corporations were required to uphold these rights, avoiding any form of discrimination based on race, colour, sex, religion, or political opinion. They were expected to comply with government policies aimed at promoting equality and fair treatment.[22]

Furthermore, the UNCCTC strictly prohibited corrupt practices. TNCs were instructed to abstain from offering bribes or gifts to public officials and to maintain accurate records of all their financial transactions. These records were to be made available to authorities upon request, ensuring transparency and accountability.[23]

---

17 P. Sauvant, 'The negotiations of the United Nations code of conduct on transnational corporations: experience and lessons learned' (2015) 16(1) Journal of World Investment and Trade 35.

18 UNCCTC (n 16).

19 Ibid., arts 6–8.

20 Ibid., arts 9–10.

21 Ibid., art 12.

22 Ibid., art 13.

23 Ibid., art 20.

In the realm of employment, the UNCCTC drew from the principles of the International Labour Organization and its texts, suggesting that TNCs adhere to fair employment practices, training programmes, and decent working conditions. The goal was to promote not just economic growth but also social well-being through improved labour standards.[24]

TNCs were also encouraged to engage with host governments in addressing balance-of-payments issues, ensuring that their operations did not contribute to financial instability in the countries where they were based. Restrictions on the transfer of goods, services, or funds that could exacerbate these financial issues were discouraged.[25]

Taxation was another critical area addressed by the UNCCTC. TNCs were warned against manipulating their corporate structures or intra-corporate pricing practices to evade taxes in host countries. They were expected to operate in good faith, complying with local tax laws and contributing their fair share to the economies they benefited from.[26]

Environmental protection was an important concern as well. The UNCCTC required TNCs to adhere to national environmental regulations and to take proactive steps to protect and rehabilitate the environment. The development and application of environmentally friendly technologies were also encouraged.[27]

States were given the right to regulate the presence of TNCs within their borders, determining the role these corporations could play in national development. This included the right to limit or prohibit their operations in certain sectors. Additionally, States were acknowledged as having the authority to nationalise or expropriate the assets of TNCs, provided that appropriate compensation was given in accordance with legal principles.[28]

To ensure the effective implementation of the UNCCTC, States were called upon to take action at the national level. This included publicising the UNCCTC, monitoring its application, and reporting back to the United Nations Commission on Transnational Corporations. The goal was to embed the principles of the UNCCTC into national laws and administrative practices, fostering a more equitable and just global economic system.[29]

---

24 Ibid., art 46.
25 Ibid., art 30.
26 Ibid., art 34.
27 Ibid., art 41.
28 Ibid., art 54.
29 Ibid., art 66.

3.3 OECD Guidelines for Multinational Enterprises

Although efforts to conclude the UNCCTC failed, similar initiatives were pursued and concluded in other forums. One important output was the OECD Guidelines for Multinational Enterprises, which were introduced in 1976, adopted in a revised form in 2011, and subsequently revised and broadened in 2023 (the Guidelines).[30]

The Guidelines serve as a set of recommendations jointly addressed by governments to multinational enterprises. They set forth "voluntary principles and standards for responsible business conduct consistent with applicable laws and internationally recognised standards" that may "go beyond what enterprises are legally required to comply with", but that are "intended to encourage responsible trade and investment and thereby multiply the benefits of" those cross-border economic activities.[31] The Guidelines emphasise that multinational enterprises are expected to obey local laws, but that responsible business conduct may also require more than mere compliance with the host State's legal mandates.[32]

The Guidelines set out a range of responsibilities, including contributing to economic, environmental, and social progress in pursuit of sustainable development. Companies are expected to respect internationally recognised human rights and work towards building local capacity by engaging with local communities and developing their activities in both domestic and foreign markets.[33]

The Guidelines also emphasise the importance of good corporate governance, effective self-regulation, and management practices that foster trust between businesses and the societies they operate in.[34] Multinational enterprises are encouraged to promote awareness and compliance among their workers and to avoid discriminatory actions against employees who report legal or policy violations in good faith.[35]

In addition, companies are urged to engage with stakeholders to consider their views, especially when planning projects that could significantly impact

30 All citations herein are to the 2023 version. See OECD, OECD Guidelines for Multinational Enterprises 2023 Edition <https://www.oecd-ilibrary.org/governance/oecd-guidelines-for-multinational-enterprises_9789264115415> accessed 20 August 2024.

31 Ibid., Preface, paras 3, 5; see generally Ibid., Preface.

32 Ibid., ch I, paras 1–2.

33 Ibid., ch II (A) (setting forth these and other responsibilities).

34 Ibid., ch II (A), paras 6–7.

35 Ibid., ch II (A), paras 8–10.

local communities.[36] The Guidelines call for enterprises to refrain from improper involvement in local political activities, further promoting responsible and ethical business practices.[37]

All States adhering to the Guidelines are also required to create and operate "National Contact Points", non-judicial grievance mechanisms that claimants can use to allege that a company has failed to comply with the MNE Guidelines' norms.[38]

There have been other international and regional efforts at addressing similar issues. The UN Guiding Principles on Business and Human Rights, which have also been incorporated into the Guidelines, is one particularly significant text.[39] Recent EU initiatives on sustainability reporting and due diligence are additional examples of this ongoing pattern of intergovernmental attempts to regulate investor obligations in their international activities.[40] These efforts have focused on recognising investor responsibilities in diverse areas relating, for instance, to environmental protection, labour and human rights, anti-corruption, and due diligence and disclosures regarding the same.

4 The "New-Generation Bit" Practice

Let us now turn to how the concepts described above have been implemented in investment treaties. It has long been common for treaties to include express legality clauses in their provisions, indicating that the treaty only protects investments established or acquired in accordance with the host State's law. There are also examples, such as in the 1981 investment agreement among the Member States of the Organisation of the Islamic Conference,[41] that impose obligations upon investors with respect to the operation of their invest-

36 Ibid., ch II (A), paras 15, (B), 28; Ibid., ch III, paras 30, 32; Ibid., ch IV, para 45; Ibid., ch VI, para 72.

37 Ibid., ch II (A), para 16; ch VII.

38 Ibid., ch I, para 11. See also Decision of the Council on the Guidelines for Multinational Enterprises on Responsible Business Conduct (adopted 27 June 2000, amended 8 June 2023).

39 United Nations Guiding Principles on Business and Human Rights (annexed to A/HRC/17/31, endorsed by the Human Rights Council 16 June 2011).

40 See, e.g., the Corporate Sustainability Reporting Directive, which entered into force 5 January 2023; Corporate Sustainability Due Diligence Directive, which entered into force 25 July 2024.

41 Agreement on Promotion, Protection and Guarantee of Investments among Member States of the Organisation of Islamic Cooperation, art 4.

ments.[42] Even absent such express legality clauses, tribunals have interpreted treaties as implicitly excluding from their protections any investments established or obtained through fraud, corruption, or other similarly severe illegalities occurring at the time of investment. Thus, the notion that investors have obligations and that non-compliance with them can carry consequences under investment treaties is not new. However, a number of more recent models and agreements have gone further, adopting additional approaches to recognising, imposing, encouraging compliance with, and even enforcing investor obligations. Practice is increasingly extensive and diverse. Some highlights and themes may here be noted.

These modern texts stand in contrast to the "old generation" ones, which have been controversially interpreted as prioritising investor protection, even at the expense of a State's right to regulate.[43]

Working in chronological order through some of the examples, the Investment Agreement for the COMESA Common Investment Area, signed in 2007, is one relevant text.[44] It provides that "investors and their investments shall comply with all applicable domestic measures of the Member State in which their investment is made"[45] and that a respondent State in an ISDS proceeding "may assert as a … counterclaim … that the COMESA investor bringing the claim has not fulfilled its obligations under this Agreement, including the obligations to comply with all applicable domestic measures…".[46]

The Southern African Development Community's Model BIT Template (the SADC Model BIT), adopted in 2012, illustrates another approach. It sets forth in the treaty itself certain investor obligations, as opposed to merely referring to and incorporating obligations under the law of the host State.[47] With respect to enforcement, and like the COMESA Agreement, it contemplates counterclaims against investors, stating that a "Host State may initiate a counterclaim against the Investor before any tribunal established pursuant to this agreement for damages or other relief resulting from an alleged breach of the

42 Ibid., art 9 ("The investor shall be bound by the laws and regulations in force in the host state and shall refrain from all acts that may disturb public order or morals or that may be prejudicial to the public interest. He is also to refrain from exercising restrictive practices and from trying to achieve gains through unlawful means.").

43 Polina Christodoulou and Marina K Vassiliou, *Investor-State Arbitration and the Next Generation of Investment Treaties* (extract from Lexology In-Depth: Investment Treaty Arbitration - Edition 9) <https://gzg.com.cy/insights/insights/investment-treaty-arbitration/> accessed 17 April 2025.

44 COMESA is the Common Market for Easter and Southern Africa.

45 COMESA Investment Agreement, art 13.

46 Ibid., art 28(9).

47 See SADC Model BIT, part 3, arts 10–19.

Agreement."[48] Yet, it goes further in that it also provides for claims against the investor in the investor's home State[49] and imposes obligations on home States to help ensure that the home State's law enables civil actions for harms caused by investors and their investments in the host State when conduct leading to those harms occurred in the home State, and that the home State's courts will take jurisdiction over such claims.[50]

These two agreements can be contrasted with the approaches taken in other models developed and agreements concluded around that time that, although they refer to issues like the importance of environmental protection, labour rights, and the prevention of corruption and bribery, they do so by focusing on the States' obligations to address appropriate investor performance on those issues, not investors' own obligations.[51] Of course, States' compliance with obligations will necessitate the imposition and enforcement of obligations on investors; however, the obligations set forth in the treaties only apply directly to the States.[52]

The 2016 India Model BIT was another notable development. That text specifies that an enterprise is required to have "significance for the development of the Party in whose territory the investment is made" in order to be an

---

48 Ibid., art 19.2.

49 Ibid., art 19.4.

50 Ibid., art 17 ("17.1. Investors and Investments shall be subject to civil actions for liability in the judicial process of their Home State for the acts, decisions or omissions made in the Home State in relation to the Investment where such acts, decisions or omissions lead to significant damage, personal injuries or loss of life in the Host State. 17.2. Home States shall ensure that their legal systems and rules allow for, or do not prevent or unduly restrict, the bringing of court actions on their merits before domestic courts relating to the civil liability of Investors and Investments for damages resulting from alleged acts, decisions or omissions made by Investors in relation to their Investments in the territory of the Host State.").

51 See, e.g., Dominican Republic–Central America–United States Free Trade Agreement (signed 5 August 2004, entered into force 1 March 2006) [CAFTA-DR]; Canada and the Republic of Peru Free Trade Agreement (signed 29 May 2008, entered into force 1 August 2009) [Canada–Peru FTA]; S Department of State, 2012 US Model Bilateral Investment Treaty (April 2012).

52 One example of this approach can be seen in the 2012 US Model BIT, Articles 12 and 13. These provisions emphasise the importance of effective implementation of environmental and labour laws, instructing States not to waive or derogate from those laws in order to attract or keep investment. See, e.g., Canada–Peru FTA, arts 809–810. Many treaties containing this language have specified that a breach of these provisions is not actionable through ISDS and/or State–State dispute settlement. See, e.g., Canada–Peru FTA, art 819 (stating that an investor cannot bring an ISDS claim for an alleged breach of Articles 809 or 810).

"investment" under the treaty.[53] It then contains a specific chapter, Chapter III, dedicated to and entitled "Investor obligations". In that chapter, the State parties reaffirm that investors and investments must "comply with all laws, regulations, administrative guidelines and policies of a Party concerning the establishment, acquisition, management, operation and disposition of investments"[54] and highlight specifically the duties of investors and investments to comply with tax law and timely pay their tax liabilities.[55] The Model also reiterates that investors and their investments are not to offer or promise (or be complicit in inciting, aiding, abetting, or conspiring to offer or promise) any improper financial benefit, either directly or indirectly, to public officials as an inducement to take, or refrain from taking, any action.[56]

Additionally, investors are required to provide relevant information about their investments, corporate history, and practices as needed by the host countries, either for decision-making purposes or purely for statistical reasons.[57]

Finally, the Model instructs that investors "shall endeavour to voluntarily incorporate internationally recognised standards of corporate social responsibility in their practices and internal policies, such as statements of principle that have been endorsed or are supported by the Parties".[58] There are no provisions directly addressing the issue of enforcement, such as whether and under what circumstances a respondent State may be able to initiate a counterclaim against an investor for breach of its treaty obligations. The approach reflected in this text has been incorporated by India in BITs it has subsequently negotiated, such as the BIT it signed with Belarus in 2018.

Another marker was set by the Draft Pan-African Investment Code of 2016 (the PAIC). In its article on "Definitions", the PAIC, like the Indian Model BIT, indicates that an enterprise must make a "significant contribution to the host State's economic development" in order to constitute a covered "investment".[59] It also contains a separate chapter, Chapter 4, that is specifically dedicated to investors' obligations and is more extensive than the Indian Model BIT.

---

53 Model Text for the Indian Bilateral Investment Treaty 2015 (Government of India, Ministry of Finance, 28 December 2015), art 1.4.

54 Ibid., art 11(i).

55 Ibid., art 11(iii).

56 Ibid., art 11(ii).

57 Ibid., art 11(iv).

58 Ibid., art 12.

59 PAIC, art 4.

Chapter 4 of the PAIC starts with Article 19, which establishes the framework for corporate governance. It mandates that investments adhere to both national and internationally accepted standards of corporate governance, particularly in areas like transparency and accounting practices. Investors are expected to treat all shareholders equitably, foster cooperation between corporations and stakeholders, and disclose all relevant information about the corporation, including financial performance, governance, and environmental liabilities. Furthermore, human resource policies, including programmes for development, must be adequately communicated.

Article 20 deals with the socio-political obligations of investors. They are required to respect national sovereignty, comply with local laws, honour socio-cultural values, and avoid interference in political and intergovernmental affairs. Investors must also respect labour rights and avoid influencing political appointments or financing political parties. Additionally, they are to refrain from engaging in unlawful or restrictive practices in pursuit of their goals.

Bribery is explicitly prohibited under Article 21. Investors must not offer or give any form of unlawful advantage to public officials or their associates in exchange for favourable actions or decisions. Moreover, investors are forbidden from "aid[ing] or abet[ting] a conspiracy to commit or authorise acts of bribery".[60]

Corporate social responsibility is addressed in Article 22. Investors are expected to comply with the laws and regulations of the host State and ensure that their economic objectives align with the host State's social and economic development goals. They are mandated to contribute positively to the economic, social, and environmental progress of the host State, with the broader aim of sustainable development.

Article 23 focuses on the responsible use of natural resources. Investors are required to avoid exploiting local resources in a way that harms the rights and interests of the host State. They must also respect the rights of local populations and avoid practices such as land grabbing which could negatively impact local communities.

Finally, Article 24 outlines principles governing business ethics and human rights. Investors are instructed that they should support and respect internationally recognised human rights, avoid complicity in human rights abuses, work to eliminate forced labour and child labour, eliminate discrimination in employment, and ensure that the wealth generated from investments is shared equitably.

---

60 Ibid., art 21(2).

As we can see, the PAIC identifies key areas of concern and outlines specific expectations for investors within those domains. It goes beyond simply establishing general dos and don'ts, or mandating compliance with domestic law, and outlines a range of obligations and standards that the investors must meet under the treaty.

Skipping ahead chronologically, it is important to note here that the PAIC served as an important foundation for the subsequent negotiation of the Investment Protocol of the African Continental Free Trade Agreement (the AfCFTA Investment Protocol), which was adopted in 2023. That text incorporates elements of the PAIC, such as the requirement that an enterprise make a significant contribution to the sustainable development of the host State in order to constitute an "investment', and a dedicated chapter, Chapter 5, on investor obligations. The content of the AfCFTA Investment Protocol's chapter on investor obligations, however, is more detailed than the PAIC's. It groups the obligations into nine categories: compliance with national and international law (Article 32); business ethics, human rights, and labour standards (Article 33); environmental protection (Article 34); indigenous peoples and local communities (Article 35); socio-political obligations (Article 36); anti-corruption (Article 37); corporate-social responsibility (Article 38); corporate governance (Article 39); and taxation and transfer pricing (Article 40). With respect to those obligations, it contains a mix of mandates, including compliance with relevant domestic law, international standards, and new AfCFTA mandates, as well as treaty obligations to "endeavour to" take (and refrain from) other actions in order to promote (or avoid) certain sustainable-development-related outcomes in the host State.

Returning to 2016, the Morocco–Nigeria BIT of that year has also been widely recognised as an important text on these issues, setting forth what were among the most, if not the most, detailed and comprehensive regulations regarding investor obligations compared to other concluded agreements at that time.

The BIT requires investors to conduct environmental impact assessment processes in accordance with the law of the host State or home State, whichever is more rigorous, and also requires them to conduct social impact assessments in accordance with standards developed under the treaty.[61] The BIT also dictates that "investors, their investment and the host state authorities"

61 Reciprocal Investment Promotion and Protection Agreement between the Government of the Kingdom of Morocco and the Government of the Federal Republic of Nigeria (signed 3 December 2016) art 14.

are to apply the precautionary principle in connection with their environmental impact assessments.[62]

The BIT also imposes specific prohibitions on investors and their investments regarding corruption and bribery, rather than referring to and incorporating domestic law or other international standards. It specifies that if the investor breaches these treaty obligations, it will be treated as a breach of domestic law concerning the establishment and operation of an investment which, in turn, may require that the investor will not be able to access ISDS (in addition to other penalties it might face under applicable domestic law).[63]

The BIT sets standards for corporate governance, requiring investments to meet or exceed national and international standards, including those related to transparency and accounting practices. It further mandates investments to "establish and maintain, where appropriate" community liaison processes, again in accordance with international standards.[64] To the extent relevant international standards have not yet been developed, or were developed without the participation of developing countries, the treaty provides that a committee it establishes can craft them.[65] It further emphasises corporate social responsibility, reiterating investors' obligations to comply with the host State's law and the BIT's mandates, and encouraging investors to contribute to the sustainable development of host States and local communities through socially responsible practices. Investors are advised to follow high standards of responsibility and international guidelines, including those set by the ILO Tripartite Declaration on Multinational Investments and Social Policy, as well as specific or sectoral standards of responsible practice where these exist.[66] The host States are entitled to request information about investors' corporate governance practices, with safeguards for protecting confidential business information.[67]

With respect to enforcement, like the SADC Model BIT, the Morocco–Nigeria BIT imposes obligations on the home State to facilitate efforts to hold investors accountable in the home State for harms caused in the host

62 Ibid., art 14.
63 Ibid., art 17.
64 Ibid., art 19(1)(b).
65 Ibid., art 19(1)(c).
66 Ibid., art 24.
67 Ibid., art 21.

State.[68] It does not, however, expressly enable the respondent State to seek to enforce investor obligations under the BIT through counterclaims.[69]

In 2017, Colombia made a contribution to this issue through the release of its Model BIT. In a different approach than the texts previously discussed, the model specifies that a State can deny benefits of the treaty to an investor if the latter has engaged in certain categories of wrongful conduct in the host State (e.g., activity causing serious environmental harm, tax fraud, corruption, grave violations of labour laws). It can even deny the investor benefits based on wrongful activity engaged in by the investor irrespective of where that activity occurred (e.g., commission of serious human rights violations, sponsorship of terrorist organisations, engagement in money laundering activities).[70] The model also separately requires investors to "respect" the obligations either State party has entered into relating to human rights and the environment, and it requires any claimant pursuing an ISDS claim to have treated such obligations as mandatory throughout the making and operation of its investment.[71]

Moreover, the BIT requires that, to bring an ISDS claim, the investor must consent to the respondent State bringing a counterclaim against it,[72] which, as the model further specifies, may relate to allegations that the claimant has breached applicable international law or the law of the host State in connection with the establishment or operation of its investment.[73]

Another important development occurred in 2018 in connection with renegotiation of the North American Free Trade Agreement (with the renegotiated text being referred to herein as the United States–Mexico–Canada Agreement or USMCA). As part of the renegotiation, the USMCA's dispute settlement chapter now contains an annex providing for a "Facility-Specific Rapid Response Labour Mechanism" (RRLM).[74] Pursuant to the RRLM, whenever a State party to the treaty has a "good faith belief" that workers in a "covered facility" located in another State party are being denied the rights of free association and collective bargaining, that State may request that a labour panel review the allegations regarding that facility. The USMCA also

68 Ibid., art 20.

69 The treaty does not seem to contemplate that the State can initiate an ISDS case. See Morocco–Nigeria BIT of 2016, art 27(1).

70 Colombia Model Bilateral Investment Treaty (2017), art [], Denial of Benefits, para 1(d).

71 Ibid., art [], Investors' Social Responsibility.

72 Ibid., art []. Submission of a Claim before a Court of Law or Arbitral Tribunal, para 6(a).

73 Ibid., art [], Scope of Application of Investor–State Dispute Settlement, para 2.

74 USMCA (2018), Annex 31, with Annex 31-A being for US–Mexico and 31-B being for Canada–Mexico. This mechanism does not apply as between the US and Canada.

contemplates that private individuals and entities can submit petitions alleging denials of rights through domestic processes and request that the State pursue action against a covered facility in another State through the RRLM. If the panel finds a breach of relevant labour rights at the covered facility, possible remedies include suspension of preferential treatment for goods manufactured at that facility, imposition of penalties on the facility, and denial of entry for goods produced by the facility. Thus, this is an example of an economic treaty providing for penalties to be directly imposed on multinational enterprises for breaches of specified labour laws at specific enterprise locations.

A final example to note is the 2019 Dutch Model BIT, which, among other things, directs that an ISDS tribunal, "in deciding on the amount of compensation [to be awarded to an investor claimant], is expected to take into account noncompliance by the investor with its commitments under the UN Guiding Principles on Business and Human Rights, and the OECD Guidelines for Multinational Enterprises".[75] Although the text is not explicit on this point, it appears at least arguable that, based on this provision, the damages can be reduced even if the investor claimant's non-compliance with the Guidelines was not a contributing factor to, and did not have a causal link with, the harm the investor suffered (as reduction of the amount of compensation due would otherwise already be appropriate if the investor's wrongful conduct had caused or contributed to the harm suffered). According to such a reading, this provision in the Dutch Model can operate akin to a penalty or fine for non-compliance with the investor's responsibilities.

As these examples illustrate, there are growing instances of investment treaties adopting a "more balanced" approach in terms of restating or even directly imposing investor obligations, encouraging compliance with those obligations by specifying penalties (such as losing treaty protection or access to ISDS) for non-compliance, and also strengthening mechanisms for direct enforcement of investor obligations in the home State, through claims or counterclaims by the host State, or even, as in the USMCA, through treaty-specific rules that provide processes for investigation and sanctions for breach.

75 Dutch Model Bilateral Investment Treaty (2019), art 23.

5 Conclusion

Based on the existing trends, commentary, and BIT practice, there is an apparent trend towards shifting the approach in investment protection agreements from one that is too often interpreted as primarily safeguarding and favouring investors to one that also respects the rights and duties of States, including with respect to the regulation of investors and investments subject to their jurisdiction. One way this is evidenced is by States using their investment treaties to reaffirm, impose, encourage compliance with, and even support enforcement of investor obligations.

As reflected by other initiatives at intergovernmental levels – which include work on the UNCCTC, the adoption and subsequent revisions to the OECD's MNE Guidelines, the development and adoption of the UN Guiding Principles, and similar initiatives within the EU – these efforts to use international agreements so as to improve the contributions that multinational enterprises can make to sustainable development outcomes, while also preventing and remedying harms, are not new. But they are now being made more express in investment treaties. This shift will likely continue, expanding the scope of investor responsibilities in agreements while more clearly affirming the regulatory rights of States.

Bibliography

Legislation

Declaration on the Establishment of a New International Economic Order dated 1 May 1974, № A_RES_3201(S-VI)-EN

Draft United Nations Code of Conduct On Transnational Corporations, 1983 version <https://investmentpolicy.unctad.org/international-investment-agreements/treaty-files/2891/download> accessed 20 August 2024.

OECD Guidelines for Multinational Enterprises, 2011 Edition <https://www.oecd-ilibrary.org/governance/oecd-guidelines-for-multinational-enterprises_9789264115415-en;#:~:text=The%20updated%20Guidelines%20include%20new,country%20in%20which%20they%20operate> accessed 20 August 2024.

US-DR-CAFTA of 2007

COMESA Investment Agreement of 2007

Canada-Peru FTA of 2008

USA Model BIT of 2012

SADC Model BIT Template of 2012

India Model BIT of 2015
The Draft Pan-Africa Investment Code of 2016
Morocco-Nigeria BIT of 2016
Colombia Model BIT of 2017
Belarus-India BIT of 2018
USMCA of 2018
Dutch Model BIT of 2019
AfCFTA Investment Protocol of 2023

Articles

Polina Christodoulou, Marina K Vassiliou, *Investor-State Arbitration and the Next Generation of Investment Treaties* (extract from Lexology In-Depth: Investment Treaty Arbitration – Edition 9).

Frank J. Garcia, *Reforming the international investment regime: lessons from international trade law*. Journal of International Economic Law 18.4 (2015).

Zeng Huaqun, *Balance, sustainable development, and integration: Innovative path for BIT practice*. Journal of International Economic Law 17.2 (2014).

Peter Muchlinski, *Negotiating New Generation International Investment Agreements*. in: Steffen Hindelang, Markus Krajewski, (Eds.). Shifting Paradigms in International Investment Law: More Balanced, Less Isolated, Increasingly Diversified. OUP.

Karl P. Sauvant, *The negotiations of the United Nations code of conduct on transnational corporations: experience and lessons learned*. The Journal of World Investment and Trade 16.1 (2015) 35.

Viacheslav Semenko, *Duties of investors in international investment law: analysis of model BITs of the latest generation*. Ghent University, Faculty of Law Academic Year (2017–2018).

Muthucumaraswamy Sornarajah, *The international law on foreign investment*, fourth edition, Cambridge University Press 2017.

Suzanne A. Spears, The quest for policy space in a new generation of international investment agreements. *Journal of International Economic Law* 13.4 (2010).

CHAPTER 3

Compliance with National Law and International Law

Augustin Barrier[1]

1 Introduction

A recurrent theme in the ongoing conversation about investor–State dispute settlement is the lack of reciprocity, or even the imbalance, between States' and investors' obligations in bilateral or multilateral investment treaties or investment codes.

Critics argue that States undertake a myriad of commitments vis-à-vis foreign investors, including to treat them and their investments fairly and equitably, grant them full protection and security, protect them against illegal expropriation, ensure the free transfer of capital by investors outside the country, and treat foreign investors like their own nationals, or no less favourably than other foreign investors. The list is long and not exhaustive.

By contrast, investors are perceived as having no obligations under the various treaties or codes. Their only obligation is that they must comply with the host State's domestic law. Indeed, a breach of the host State's domestic law is the only threshold obligation to access international protection that is exclusively attributable to the investors' conduct prior to the dispute.

However, some argue that even this requirement is a fiction for two reasons.

First, at a national level, the threat of arbitration may have a chilling effect on a State's duty to ensure that investors comply with domestic law. States often refrain from sanctioning illegal conduct by investors out of fear of arbitration. States may also consider a project favourably and be willing to tolerate some corners being cut for the sake of benefiting from a foreign investment. Either way, when States invoke breaches of their domestic law left unsanc-

1 The author wishes to thank Ms Jaimee Salgado for her assistance in the preparation of this article.

 | HTTPS://DOI.ORG/10.1163/9789004769854-004

tioned at the time in a subsequent arbitration, their conduct may appear opportunistic, leading to these defences being rejected.[2]

Second, on an international law plane, national law is nothing but a set of facts, not directly enforceable, so a breach of domestic law may not necessarily impact the State's obligation to afford its protection. Thus, unless the treaty or the investment code provides otherwise, only breaches of national law in the process of making the investment may be invoked by States to challenge a tribunal's jurisdiction or the admissibility of the investor's claims. Even then, only breaches of national law of a particular gravity may be invoked. States cannot invoke minor breaches or breaches of which the State was or should have been aware.

This raises the question of the interplay between investors' obligations under national law and international law. More specifically, the question is whether there really are remedies available under international law to sanction the conduct of an investor that is contrary to the host State's domestic law.

The truth is that the line between investors' obligations on the national law level and the international law level are sometimes blurred in two main respects.

On the one hand, treaties or international instruments can proceed by *renvoi* to national law, so that noncompliance with national law may have an international legal effect.

On the other hand, there are instances where an investor's compliance with national law becomes an international obligation that can be directly sanctioned on an international law plane, on a standalone basis.

This article examines both of the aforementioned instances.

2 Compliance with National Law as a Requirement to Access International Protection

The following sections analyse circumstances where compliance with domestic law is not an obligation that is directly enforceable against investors (i.e., by way of counterclaims) but indirectly through express and implied language in treaties and agreements between the parties. While not a directly enforceable obligation, non-compliance still has an impact on the investor's ability to

2 See, e.g., *Ioannis Kardassopoulos v. Georgia*, ICSID Case No. ARB/05/18, Decision on Jurisdiction (6 July 2007), paras 185–194.

access the protections afforded by the treaty and can potentially affect their right to compensation.

2.1 Jurisdiction and Admissibility: "In Accordance with Law" Clauses

The most common aspect of requirements to comply with domestic law can be found in the so-called "in accordance with law" clauses, which provide that the investment must have been made in accordance with national law.

These "in accordance with law" clauses are quite common in bilateral investment treaties, or BITs. Article II(1) of the Spain–El Salvador BIT states that "[e]ach Contracting Party shall promote investments in its territory by investors of the Contracting Party and shall accept such investments *in accordance with its laws*".[3] Likewise, the Germany–Ghana BIT Article 2(1), relays: "[e]ach Contracting Party shall promote investments in its territory by investors of the Contracting Party and shall accept such investments *in accordance with its laws*".[4] Other similar clauses are found in the Ecuador–France BIT,[5] the Argentina–Spain BIT,[6] and the India–Lithuania BIT,[7] just to name a few.

3 Agreement between the Kingdom of Spain and the Republic of El Salvador on the Reciprocal Promotion and Protection of Investments (Spain–El Salvador) (adopted 14 February 1995, entered into force 20 February 1996) 1933 UNTS 363 art II(1) (emphasis added).

4 Treaty between the Federal Republic of Germany and the Republic of Ghana concerning the Encouragement and Reciprocal Protection of Investments (Germany–Ghana) (adopted 24 February 1995, entered into force 23 November 1998) BGBl II 1997, 2055 art 2(1) (emphasis added).

5 "Each Contracting Party shall permit, promote, and facilitate, *in accordance with its legislation* and with the provisions of this Agreement, investments made by nationals and companies of the other Contracting Party." France and Ecuador Agreement on the Reciprocal Promotion and Protection of Investments (France–Ecuador) (adopted 7 September 1994, entered into force 10 June 1996) 1980 UNTS 167 art 3 (emphasis added).

6 "Each Party shall, to the extent possible, promote investments made in its territory by investors of the other Party and shall accept those investments *in accordance with its legislation.*" Agreement between the Argentine Republic and the Kingdom of Spain on the Reciprocal Promotion and Protection of Investments (Argentina–Spain) (adopted 3 October 1991, entered into force 28 September 1992) 1699 UNTS 187 art II(1) (emphasis added).

7 "This Agreement shall apply to all the investments made by the investors of either Contracting Party in the territory of the other Contracting Party, accepted as such, *in accordance with its laws and regulations* prior to as well as after the entry into force of this Agreement, but shall not apply to any dispute concerning an investment which arose or could have arisen, or any claim which was settled before its entry into force." Agreement between the Government of the Republic of India and the Government of the Republic of Lithuania for the promotion and protection of investments (adopted 31 March 2011, entered into force 1 December 2011) 3105 UNTS 77 art 2 (emphasis added).

These clauses constitute a *renvoi* to national law, where a failure to comply with a domestic law requirement at the stage of making the investment will have the international legal effect of restricting access to the treaty, and thus a tribunal's jurisdiction, to investments having not been made in accordance with domestic law.

An example of not abiding by domestic law when making the investment, and therefore being stripped of a BIT's protection, is the case *Inceysa v. El Salavador*.[8] While in the bidding process for government contracts, Inceysa submitted false financial statements and forged documents, while misrepresenting the identity of its strategic partner and that partner's experience, thus making false representations in relation to what it knew were crucial considerations when awarding the bid.

El Salvador submitted an objection to the tribunal's jurisdiction, claiming the BIT application to the dispute only extended protection under the treaty to investments made in accordance with Salvadorian law, and not to investments procured by fraud, forgery, and corruption.[9] In response, Inceysa took the position that the Supreme Court of El Salvador had sustained the legality of the bidding and adjudication process, that the allegations made by El Salvador were irrelevant, and that, in any case, the tribunal should not consider these allegations from a procedural perspective because they involved alleged defects of the underlying investment, which was an issue relevant to the merits.[10]

After analysing the language of the BIT (the "in accordance with law" clauses) and acknowledging the consent of the parties, as expressed by signing the BIT, the tribunal determined that the only correct interpretation was that any investment made in breach of Salvadorian law was outside of the BIT's protection.[11] Therefore, the tribunal found that it lacked jurisdiction. Interestingly, the tribunal found comfort in the fact that the claimant's breach of national law had its own equivalent on an international law plane with the principle of good faith, so that the breach invoked by the State was not exclusively a breach of national law.[12]

In addition to *Inceysa*, *Metal-Tech v. Uzbekistan* provides another illustration of the protection from the BIT being stripped from an investor for breaching domestic law in the process of making the original investment. The

8 *Inceysa Vallisoletanan S.L. v. Republic of El Salvador*, ICSID Case No. ARB/03/26, Award (02 August 2006) [hereinafter *Inceysa*].

9 Ibid., para 45.

10 Ibid., para 63.

11 Ibid., para 203.

12 Ibid., paras 207, 234.

respondent State alleged that Metal-Tech violated the Uzbek Criminal Code at the time of investing into a joint venture formed to build and operate a molybdenum production plant because it had bribed a government official.[13] Metal-Tech claimed that the alleged conduct did not amount to bribery under Uzbek law and that the respondent had based its arguments on academic works and not authoritative interpretations of Uzbek law.[14]

The tribunal analysed Article 1(1) of the BIT, which contained the relevant language, examined the anti-bribery and corruption legislation of Uzbekistan, and determined that corruption had been found at a level sufficient to violate Uzbek law, that Metal-Tech therefore did not have a qualifying investment under the BIT, and could thus not benefit from the jurisdiction of the tribunal.[15] The tribunal eventually rejected both the claims and counterclaims for lack of jurisdiction.[16]

The importance of compliance with national law is even more stringent in investment arbitration based on investment contracts. For instance, in *World Duty Free v. Kenya*, the respondent State argued that the claimant's investment for the construction, maintenance, and operation of duty-free complexes at the Nairobi and Mombasa airports was tainted with corruption.[17] Indeed, the claimant had admitted that it had been required to pay a "personal donation" to the then-President of Kenya to do business with the Kenyan government, which the claimant presented as a form of local custom.[18] After the making of the investment, the claimant alleged they had been unwittingly involved in a fraud scheme to obtain illegal funds for the President's re-election campaign, and that the government had expropriated the claimant's investment in order to destroy vital evidence to prosecute said corruption.[19] The respondent claimed that the accusations regarding the fraud were time-barred. However, the respondent argued that the initial "personal donation" by the claimant to the President constituted a bribe, and thus a criminal act under Kenyan and international law, and therefore deprived the underlying contract of any legal force.[20]

---

13 *Metal-Tech Ltd. v. Republic of Uzbekistan*, ICSID Case No. ARB/10/3, Award (4 October 2013), paras 278–280.

14 Ibid., para 281.

15 Ibid., paras 372–374.

16 Ibid., para 423.

17 *World Duty Free Company v. Republic of Kenya*, ICSID Case No. ARB/00/7, Award (4 October 2006).

18 Ibid., para 66.

19 Ibid., paras 68, 70, 74.

20 Ibid., paras 81, 105.

The parties had agreed that the law governing the agreement was Kenyan law, which the tribunal applied according to Article 42(1) of the ICSID Convention, while English law would apply as the law of the procedure.[21] After reviewing both English and Kenyan law, the tribunal found that the payment to the President was not a personal donation, but was considered a bribe under both legal systems because it was made to gain audience with the President with a goal of concluding the contract in question. The tribunal considered, as a result, that the claimant could not seek international protection as it had violated the law of the contract, i.e., the domestic law chosen by the parties.[22]

These cases helped pave the way for some tribunals to consider that, even without an "in accordance with law" clause, investments made in breach of national law could not benefit from other treaties, such as the Energy Charter Treaty, or ECT.

2.2 Jurisdiction and Admissibility: Implied Language and Unlawful Conduct

A tribunal need not always have the express language of the "in accordance with law" clauses to find that an investor has broken domestic law and is, thus, not protected on an international level.

The tribunal in *Plama v. Bulgaria*[23] considered that an investment made in complete disregard for Bulgarian law could not benefit from the protection of the Energy Charter Treaty, despite the lack of express language to that effect in the treaty. In *Plama*, Plama Consortium Limited was found to have misrepresented itself during negotiations for shares in Nova Plama, an oil refinery, which amounted to fraud under Bulgarian law as well as violations of international law principles, such as the good faith requirement. The tribunal agreed with Bulgaria and added that even if Plama had received protection under the ECT, its claims would, in any case, have failed on the merits.

Likewise, in *Hamester v. Ghana*, the tribunal found that "an investment will not be protected if it has been created in violation of national or international principles of good faith; by way of corruption, fraud, or deceitful conduct" and

---

21 Ibid., para 158.

22 Ibid., paras 136, 179, 188.

23 *Plama Consortium Limited v. Republic of Bulgaria*, ICSID Case No. ARB/03/24, Award (27 August 2008).

"[The investment] will also not be protected if it is made in violation of the host State's law".[24]

Worley v. Ecuador involved a dispute surrounding several agreements for the development of oil and gas infrastructure projects in Ecuador.[25] In April 2016, the Panama Papers were released triggering investigations into potential acts of corruption by the claimant, and the respondent ceased all payments to the claimant, leading to the arbitration.[26] The tribunal found that the claimant had been on the receiving end of insider information, allowing it to procure more favourable terms for one of the agreements in dispute, and that it deliberately misrepresented its intentions to comply with the 30% subcontracting requirement for several other agreements, knowing it would not have been awarded the contracts otherwise.[27]

The tribunal found that it consequently lacked jurisdiction, and the claimant's claims were inadmissible due to the acts of corruption that tainted the making of the investment. Faced with the lack of express language in the treaty regarding an investor's compliance with national law, the tribunal stated:

> In the Tribunal's view, the crucial question is not whether it should read a legality requirement into the Treaty, but rather whether a tribunal should assume that a State would have given its consent to arbitration to protect investments that breached its own law. This question must clearly be answered in the negative: There is no doubt that the requirement of the conformity with law is important in respect of the access to the substantive provisions on the protection of the investor under the BIT.[28]

The tribunal went on to say:

> Accordingly, the Tribunal concludes that the absence of an express legality clause in the Treaty does not preclude an enquiry into whether the Claimant's alleged investment complied with the law. Any such illegality may impact the adjudication of this dispute in several ways. In particular, existing illegalities may deprive the Claimant's alleged investment from the substantive protec-

24 *Gustav F W Hamester GmbH & Co KG v. Republic of Ghana*, ICSID Case No. ARB/07/24, Award (18 June 2010) para 123.

25 *Worley International Services Inc. v. Republic of Ecuador*, PCA Case No. 2019-15, Final Award (22 December 2023).

26 Ibid., paras 108–111.

27 Ibid., paras 355, 400.

28 Ibid., para 304.

> tions of the Treaty or ... bar the jurisdiction of the Tribunal or the admissibility of the Claimant's claims.[29]

However, while many tribunals considered that express language was not required to hold that violating domestic law is a ground for depriving an investor from international protection in case of a serious breach of national law, many other tribunals made an opposite finding. For instance, in *Bear Creek Mining v. Peru*, the tribunal stated that an investor's good faith was not an implicit prerequisite to establishing its jurisdiction:

> [U]nder international law, the Tribunal may not import a requirement that limits its jurisdiction when such a limit is not specified by the parties ... the Tribunal does not consider that the alleged good faith of the investor is a further condition under the [domestic law] for the jurisdiction of the Tribunal.[30]

The tribunal did, however, clarify that the above conclusion did not exclude the potential relevance of illegal activity or lack of good faith in the merits analysis.[31]

Other tribunals have expressed a similar reasoning in *Stati v. Kazakhstan (I)*,[32] *Malicorp v. Egypt*,[33] and *Khan Resources v. Mongolia*.[34]

Whether the language is express or implied, all the above cases suggest an approach where one must look at two criteria to determine whether a jurisdictional or admissibility objection can be brought based on non-compliance with domestic law: 1) did the investor breach a domestic law obligation?, and 2) does this breach constitute a breach of an international law obligation?

Corruption, in all forms, will arguably violate both domestic law and be sufficient to also violate international standards. However, breaches of environmental obligations or human rights violations, for instance, are not as clear-cut.

29 Ibid., para 307.

30 *Bear Creek Mining Corporation v. Republic of Peru*, ICSID Case No. ARB/14/21, Award (30 November 2017) paras 320–321.

31 Ibid., para 324.

32 *Ascom Group S.A., Anatolie Stati, Gabriel Stati and Terra Raf Trans Trading Ltd. v. Republic of Kazakhstan (I)*, SCC Case No. 116/2010, Award (19 December 2013) para 806.

33 *Malicorp Limited v. Arab Republic of Egypt*, ICSID Case No. ARB/08/18, Award (7 February 2011) para 806.

34 *Khan Resources Inc., Khan Resources B.V. and Cauc Holding Company Ltd. v. The Government of Mongolia and Monatom Co., Ltd.*, PCA Case No. 2011-09, Decision on Jurisdiction (2 March 2015) paras 384–385.

The tribunal in *Kim and Others v. Uzbekistan* set a test to clarify when a violation of domestic law reaches the level of severity required to also preclude an investor from benefiting from rights under a BIT.[35] In *Kim*, regulatory and judicial measures taken by the Uzbek government allegedly led to the unlawful nationalisation of two cement companies that the claimant had invested in. One of the respondent's objections was that the claimant made the investment in violation of Uzbek law. While the tribunal majority denied this objection, they developed the so-called "*Kim* Test" in the process.

The *Kim* Test is a proportionality test that aims at balancing the seriousness of an investor's conduct on the one hand and, on the other hand, the significance of the domestic law obligation it allegedly breached. On a case-by-case basis, this test helps ensure that the harshness of removing an investor's protection under the BIT is a proportionate consequence for the violating conduct.[36]

The test consists of three steps:

1. ***Assessment of the significance of the obligation with which the investor failed to comply.*** This prong of the test is meant to probe the level of importance accorded by the domestic law system to the alleged breach by examining the sanction provided for such breach. The significance of the breach will not be the same depending on whether the sanction of that breach is a low-level fine or imprisonment. Likewise, the tribunal may inquire whether the State actively enforces the obligation in question, how often similar breaches are investigated or prosecuted, or if there is widespread non-compliance with the law.[37]
2. ***Assessment of the seriousness of the investor's conduct.*** This prong analyses whether the investor genuinely and/or willingly violated the law or regulation in question. The tribunal may thus assess the investor's intent, as it transpires from the evidence, whether the investor exercised due diligence, the clarity of the rule, whether the law was stable or constantly evolving, and whether it was coherent or not. The State's conduct, once it was made aware of the alleged breach, may also be taken into account.[38]
3. ***Assessment of whether the combination of the investor's conduct, the significance of the breach, and the resulting impact on the State's inter-***

35 *Vladislav Kim and others v. Republic of Uzbekistan*, ICSID Case No. ARB/13/6, Decision on Jurisdiction (8 March 2017).

36 Ibid., para 404.

37 Ibid., para 406.

38 Ibid., para 407.

> ***est is sufficient to justify stripping the investor of international protection.***[39] This is the balancing step where the tribunal must take into consideration the above (non-exhaustive) factors and determine whether the investor can bring its claim.

Interestingly, the tribunal in *Cortec Mining v. Kenya* made use of the *Kim* Test in circumstances that did not involve a case of fraud, corruption, or deceitful conduct. In *Cortec*, the claimants argued that their investment in a mining project had been illegally expropriated in breach of the BIT. The State's defence was that the claimants should not have access to the BIT because they had violated its national law by skirting environmental approvals and circumventing legal requirements through political lobbying.[40]

The tribunal accepted the State's position and found that the regulatory obligations that the claimants had violated were "of fundamental importance in an environmentally vulnerable area"[41] and that the claimants' attempt to by-pass requirements to obtain a mining licence violated the State's fundamental public policies and constituted a breach of their obligations.[42] The combination of these factors led the tribunal to conclude that the claimants' actions not only violated Kenyan law but, "in terms of international law, warrant[ed] the proportionate response of a denial of treaty protection under the BIT and the ICSID Convention".[43]

This reasoning confirms that serious breaches of national law may be invoked by States to deny investors the benefit of a treaty. In any case, if a tribunal finds an investor has breached domestic law, that violation may very well affect the level of compensation awarded if the claim progresses to the merits phase, even if it does not qualify as a bar to the tribunal's jurisdiction.

2.3 Substantive Requirements

Non-compliance with national law may also have an impact on an investor's ability to seek compensation.

The international law concept of contributory fault (i.e., to what extent an investor's conduct, and notably compliance with domestic law, had an impact on the damage claimed) must be considered.

---

39 Ibid., para 408.

40 *Cortec Mining Kenya Limited, Cortec (Pty) Limited and Stirling Capital Limited v. Republic of Kenya*, ICSID Case No. ARB/15/29, Final Award (22 October 2018).

41 Ibid., para 346.

42 Ibid., paras 349, 351.

43 Ibid., para 365.

Article 39 of the Responsibility of States for Internationally Wrongful Acts (ARSIWA) says the following:

> Contribution to the injury
>
> In the determination of reparation, account shall be taken of the contribution to the injury by wilful or negligent action or omission of the injured State or any person or entity in relation to whom reparation is sought.[44]

An example of contributory fault is *Copper Mesa v. Ecuador.*[45] *Copper Mesa* violated domestic law by hiring private militias to face local populations coming onto the property. The tribunal considered that this action constituted a "reckless escalation of violence" and further considered "the Claimant's own contributory negligent acts and omissions and unclean hands". This led the tribunal to order a 30% reduction of the claimant's compensation.[46]

Likewise, in *Yukos v. Russia,*[47] the tribunal stated that Yukos' tax avoidance scheme "risked adverse reaction from Russian authorities" and found that there was a "sufficient causal link between Yukos' abuse of the system in some of the low-tax regions and its demise which triggers a finding of contributory fault on the part of Yukos".[48] The tribunal then determined that Yukos contributed to 25% of the claimed damages and thus reduced compensation by that amount.[49]

Occidental v. Ecuador (II) sets out another example of contributory fault based on unlawful actions.[50] Occidental had entered into an agreement with Ecuador for oil exploration. Ecuador terminated this agreement, claiming Occidental had wrongly transferred certain rights under the agreement without government approval. The tribunal found that while Ecuador ultimately violated the fair and equitable treatment standard, committed expropriation, and failed to compensate the claimant under the BIT, as well as various violations of Ecuadorian law, Occidental had contributed to its own loss by unlaw-

44 Responsibility of States for Internationally Wrongful Acts, UNGA Res 56/83 (annex) art 39 (12 December 2001) art 39.

45 *Copper Mesa Mining Corporation v. Republic of Ecuador*, PCA Case No. 2012-02, Award (15 March 2016).

46 Ibid., paras 4.265, 6.97.

47 *Yukos Universal Limited (Isle of Man) v. The Russian Federation*, PCA Case No. 2005-04/AA227, Final Award (18 July 2014).

48 Ibid., paras 1578, 1615.

49 Ibid., para 1637.

50 *Occidental Petroleum Corporation and Occidental Exploration and Production Company v. Republic of Ecuador (II)*, ICSID Case No. ARB/06/11, Award (5 October 2012).

fully transferring certain rights to its concession.[51] The tribunal thus reduced the claimant's damages by 25%.[52]

The assessment of contributory fault is, of course, highly fact-driven and dependent on individual cases, and sometimes painstaking for the tribunal to analyse.[53] Yet, tribunals do not shy away from using the contributory fault tool when they determine an investor has acted recklessly or unlawfully under domestic legislation.

3 Compliance with National Law as a Direct International Obligation

Compliance with domestic law can also come in the form of a direct international obligation applicable to the investment under the international instrument. Following domestic law can be material as a direct international obligation in two ways.

First, in case there is an express specification in the treaty to that effect. For example, Article 42(1) of the ICSID Convention provides that, in the absence of an agreement between the parties, the tribunal is free to apply the law of the State party to the dispute:

> The Tribunal shall decide a dispute in accordance with such rules of law as may be agreed by the parties. In the absence of such agreement, the Tribunal shall apply the law of the Contracting State party to the dispute (including its rules on the conflict of laws) and such rules of international law as may be applicable.[54]

Second, the arbitration clause may be broad enough to include any dispute arising in connection with the investment, including disputes arising from the breach of national law obligations.

It must be noted, however, that the application of national law in these circumstances applies only as a result of procedural rules. It does not amount to elevating domestic rules to an international plane. This process is best

51 Ibid., para 680.
52 Ibid., para 687.
53 Markus Burgstaller and Dmytro Galagan, "Contributory Fault in International Investment Arbitration" (2024) J of Intl Arbitration 397, 435.
54 Convention on the Settlement of Investment Disputes between States and Nationals of Other States (entered into force 14 October 1965) 575 UNTS 159 art 42(1) [hereinafter ICSID Convention].

exemplified by the host State's ability to bring counterclaims based on its own national law.

3.1 Counterclaims as Sanction of the Violation of Direct International Obligations

Examples of both express treaty specifications and broad arbitration clauses, where domestic law can create a direct international obligation, are found in *Burlington v. Ecuador*[55] and *Perenco v. Ecuador56.*[56]

In both proceedings, Ecuador filed counterclaims against the claimants for soil and groundwater pollution.[57] The tribunals in both arbitrations considered that these counterclaims were admissible because Ecuadorian law was applicable.[58] In *Burlington*, the tribunal used the second leg of Article 42 of the ICSID Convention (using the law of the host State party) in combination with the broad arbitration clause in the Ecuador–United States BIT to justify the applicability of Ecuadorian law. In *Perenco*, the reasoning was less clear, but the arbitration clause was also very broad. Both tribunals determined that the companies had violated Ecuadorian environmental law, admitted the respondent's counterclaims, and awarded the State damages.

However, it bears mentioning that, in these two cases, the investor had accepted to arbitrate the State's counterclaims, possibly to mitigate the risk that they be otherwise litigated in other fora. Successful counterclaims based on national law are limited by the language of most bilateral investment treaties. Despite the increase in respondent States asserting counterclaims, the majority of these fail for lack of jurisdiction, specifically the key requirement of the investors' consent to arbitrate in relation to these counterclaims.[59]

The tribunal in *Roussalis v. Romania* aptly summarised the issue:

55 *Burlington Resources, Inc. v. Republic of Ecuador*, ICSID Case No. ARB/08/5, Decision on Counterclaims (7 February 2017) [hereinafter *Burlington*].

56 *Perenco Ecuador Limited v. Republic of Ecuador*, ICSID Case No. ARB/08/6, Award (27 September 2019) [hereinafter *Perenco*].

57 *Burlington* (n 55) para 52; *Perenco* (n 56) para 481.

58 *Burlington* (n 55) paras 74–75; *Perenco Ecuador Limited v Republic of Ecuador*, ICSID Case No. ARB/08/6, Interim Decision on the Environmental Counterclaim (11 August 2015) para 611(1).

59 Mark A. Clodfelter and Diana Tsutieva, "Counterclaims in Investment Treaty Arbitration", Arbitration Under International Investment Agreements: A Guide to the Key Issues (2nd ed Oxford University Press 2018) paras 17.03–17.04.

> [T]he BIT imposes no obligations on investors, only on contracting States. Therefore, where the BIT does specify that the applicable law is the BIT itself, counterclaims fall outside the tribunal's jurisdiction.[60]

The tribunal then went on to find that the parties did not consent to arbitrate the respondent's counterclaims and that, thus, the counterclaims fell beyond its jurisdiction.

Likewise, in *Oxus Gold v. Uzbekistan*, the tribunal declined jurisdiction on the ground that "[t]he wording of Article 8(1) of the BIT is, for this Arbitral Tribunal, a clear indication that the Parties' consent to arbitration under the BIT only cover claims from investors against the host State, but not claims from the host State against the investors …".[61]

A possible avenue for the expansion of counterclaims, or the application of domestic law principles at an international level, is the instances where international law principles tend to mirror national law requirements, so that domestic law requirements may be enforced at an international level through their international proxy. The example of environmental and human rights obligations is particularly interesting in this regard, even though the few decisions in this area have been severely criticised.

3.2 Holding Investors Accountable to Principles of International Law

The key decision in relation to environmental obligations is the award in *Urbaser v. Argentina*.[62] In *Urbaser*, the claimants had brought a claim against Argentina for breach of the Spain–Argentina BIT, alleging that the respondent had breached the treaty in relation to an investment in water concessions. The respondent then brought a counterclaim, stating that the claimant had violated its international obligations relating to the human right to water. While the tribunal found the claimant's adherence with the negative obligation (i.e., to refrain from violating the human right to water) was not of concern in the current case and rejected the counterclaim,[63] it acknowledged that investors

60 *Spyridon Roussalis v. Romania*, ICSID Case No. ARB/06/1, Award (7 December 2011) para 871.

61 *Oxus Gold plc v. Republic of Uzbekistan, the State Committee of Uzbekistan for Geology & Mineral Resources, and Navoi Mining & Metallurgical Kombinat*, ad hoc arbitration, Final Award (17 December 2015) para 948.

62 *Urbaser S.A. and Consorcio de Aguas Bilbao Biskaia, Bilbao Biskaia UR Partzuergoa v. Argentine Republic*, ICSID Case No. ARB/07/26, Award (8 December 2016) [hereinafter *Urbaser*].

63 Ibid., para 1210.

have human rights obligations, especially not to engage in conduct that is contrary to human rights.[64]

This requirement may be strengthened with the increasing reference in investment treaties and investment codes to investors' obligations to comply with requirements that States accepted to uphold as part of their international obligations.

As an example, Article 13 of the ECOWAS investment rules states that investors are obligated not to engage in acts of corruption contrary to the conventions that member States have committed to enforce. Along the same lines, Article 14 says that investors have the same obligations as the host State in relation to human rights, labour standards, and regional environmental and social obligations.[65]

Similar provisions to ECOWAS Articles 13 and 14 are found in Articles 10 and 15 of the SADC Model BIT, with Article 10 outlining the negative obligation to not bribe a number of different parties, whether with money or information, and Article 15 affirming the duty to respect human rights,[66] and in Article 11 of India's Model BIT, stating that all investors shall comply with the host State's laws, shall not bribe, and shall comply with tax provisions.[67]

While not strictly tied to the State's obligations, other BITs are starting to incorporate general principles of international law, like anti-corruption provisions, as well. The Iraq–Japan BIT, Article 9 states "[e]ach Contracting Party shall ensure that measures and efforts are undertaken to prevent and combat corruption regarding matters covered by this Agreement in accordance with its laws and regulations".[68] At least 14 other Japanese BITs contain the same language.[69]

Article 16 of the Burkina Faso–Canada BIT also contains a provision stating:

> Each Party should encourage enterprises operating within its territory or subject to its jurisdiction to incorporate internationally recognized standards of

64 Ibid., paras 1189–1199.

65 ECOWAS Supplementary Act on Investments (2008) arts. 13, 14.

66 SADC Model Bilateral Investment Treaty Template with Commentary (Southern African Development Community 2012) arts. 10, 15.

67 Model Text for the Indian Bilateral Investment Treaty (2015) art 11.

68 Agreement between Japan and the Republic of Iraq for the Promotion and Protection of Investment (adopted 7 June 2012, entered into force 25 February 2014) 3056 UNTS 337 art 9.

69 Charles N Brower and Jawad Ahmad, "The State's Corruption Defence, Prosecutorial Efforts, and Anti-corruption Norms in Investment Treaty Arbitration", in Katia Yannaca-Small (ed), *Arbitration Under International Investment Agreements: A Guide to the Key Issues* (2nd edn, Oxford University Press 2018) para 18.89.

> corporate social responsibility in their practices and internal policies, such as statements of principle that have been endorsed or are supported by the Parties. These principles address issues such as labour, the environment, human rights, community relations and anti-corruption.[70]

The anti-corruption and social responsibility provisions above have been a product of the last two decades, and it is likely that States will continue to add and update these types of rules.

3.3 The Reverse Umbrella Clause: A Theoretical Tool to Guarantee Investors' Adherence to National Law?

Another possible avenue for treaty drafters to hold investors accountable for general principles of international law derives from the work of Professor Crenguta Leaua,[71] Gustavo Laborde,[72] and others who have suggested the incorporation in treaties of reverse umbrella clauses.

An Umbrella Clause is a generic term used to describe provisions of investment treaties relating to the requirements of a State to observe all their obligations under the applicable municipal law, including contractual obligations.[73] For instance, Article 10(1) of the ECT states that "[e]ach Contracting Party shall observe any obligations it has entered into with an Investor or an Investment of an Investor of any other Contracting Party".[74]

A Reverse Umbrella Clause may have two different meanings.

First, a reverse umbrella may characterise provisions inserting public international law obligations into private law contracts.[75] Within this meaning, a reverse umbrella clause creates a contractual obligation to comply with certain municipal or international law provisions for both parties who agree to

70 Agreement between the Government of Canada and the Government of Burkina Faso for the Promotion and Protection of Investments (adopted 20 April 2015, entered into force 11 October 2017) 3313 UNTS 1 art 16.

71 Crenguta Leaua, "The Reverse Umbrella Clause: A Note in the Quest for the Conceptualization of Another Elephant in the Room" in Julie Bédard and Patrick W. Pearsall (ed), *Reflections on International Arbitration: Essays in Honour of Professor George Bermann* (Juris Publishing 2022).

72 Gustavo Laborde, "The Case for Host State Claims in Investment Arbitration" (2010) 1 J of Intl Dispute Settlement 97.

73 Leaua (n 71) 901.

74 The Energy Charter Treaty (adopted 17 December 1994, entered into force 16 April 1998) 2080 UNTS 95 art 10(1).

75 Leaua (n 71) 902.

the contract, including the investor.[76] A reverse umbrella clause may thus provide for obligations to comply with domestic and international law aspects concerning human rights, environmental law, and other social responsibilities that are typically harder to enforce vis-à-vis investors or private parties due to their broad nature and their general applicability to States.[77] These provisions in an investment contract ensure an investor's consent to be bound by a certain set of obligations, making counterclaims based on a breach of these obligations admissible in subsequent disputes.[78]

Second, a Reverse Umbrella Clause could be construed as a provision to be inserted in international agreements, including bilateral and multilateral investment treaties. Such clauses would include a number of domestic law or international law obligations with which investors seeking to benefit from the protection of the treaty must comply. Such clauses could be used to enforce domestic law obligations on an international level, notably by enabling States to object to tribunals' jurisdiction by arguing that an investor has failed to meet its domestic law obligations, but also to raise counterclaims on the basis of the obligations contained in the Reverse Umbrella Clause.

The main hurdle with this conception of Reverse Umbrella Clauses is the same as for counterclaims by host States: the issue of the investor's consent to arbitrate domestic law issues based on a treaty providing exclusively for obligations by the State. However, this issue may be overcome by the use of appropriate language in the treaty, for instance, by making it clear that, to benefit from the protections of the treaty, investors must have met the conditions set by the Reverse Umbrella Clause and consented in advance to having these obligations enforced against them by way of counterclaims.[79]

76 Ibid.

77 Ibid.

78 Ibid., 903.

79 See, e.g., Jose Amado, Jackson Kern, Martin Rodriguez, *Arbitrating the Conduct of International Investors* (CUP 2018) 14, 87–90; 180–184, proposing treaty language for a similar provision, whereby the investor consents in advance to the tribunal's jurisdiction to adjudicate counterclaims by the State or nationals of that State, as a precondition for accessing the treaty.

CHAPTER 4

The Debate on Investor Obligations in International Investment Law and the Role of Investment Contracts

Maria Chiara Malaguti

1 The Context

International Investment Agreements (IIAs) were classically built as a tool that leans towards investors' interests and protection. IIAs typically provide for States' obligations to protect foreign investment mainly from political and economic risk (change of policy, or other regulatory changes affecting the economics of an investment up to full deprivation), with no or few commitments on the side of investors.

The underlying premise is that investment protection is granted to foreign companies in exchange for their commitment to invest. Indeed, only a certain degree of protection, which guarantees stability, would attract significant investment flows in the medium and the long term. No surprise if, in such a classical setting, the obligations are all or mostly "on the side" of the State, while no obligation is generally imposed on foreign investors. This rationale takes one to the so-called "one sidedness" of international investment law (IIL).

However, transformation is on the way. Mainly in what we generally call "third generation IIAs" (or new-generation IIAs), a still limited but growing number of solutions are emerging, together with (although still scarce) arbitral decisions that may pave the way to a significant change or revision of traditional legal categories. A certain number of third generation IIAs, indeed, deviate from the classical structure and provide for an increasing number of investors' commitments, particularly as regards sustainable development, climate change, environmental protection, contribution to local growth, respect of social and labour standards and human rights, or good governance.[1]

1 Maria Chiara Malaguti, 'The New Italian Model Bit Between Current and Future Trends' (2021) 1 The Italian Review of International and Comparative Law, 113–131; A. Petrangeli, M. Silvi, M.C. Malaguti, 'Why and how to upgrade the Italian Model BIT' (2017) 2 Riv. Comm. Int., 389–395.

HTTPS://DOI.ORG/10.1163/9789004769854-005

The language appears to be of different intensity, sometimes formulated as a best effort, sometimes more peremptory. However, in some of the new IIAs, it may be the case that these commitments are characterised as a condition for protection (within the given definition of covered investment or in special clauses requiring the national and/or international legality of the investment), which may be raised as a bar to jurisdiction or admissibility if a procedure is initiated by the investor. Alternatively, these provisions may be characterised as a trigger for a denial of benefits (in the dispute settlement clause) or, finally, as grounds for counterclaims, which States seem increasingly willing to introduce in arbitration, in the attempt to have protections of investors' rights as well as their obligations toward the host State be heard simultaneously in a single procedure (where the behaviour of the investor would thus matter on liability, beyond the mere possibility of contributory fault).[2]

This process seems to have now found momentum and possibly a systematisation with the 2023 Protocol on Investment to the Agreement Establishing the African Continental Free Trade Area (the "AfCFTA Protocol"), and, as long as it spreads in the years to come, it may reverse the traditional "one sidedness" of IIL.[3]

There is, however, heated debate over how investors' obligations might be best articulated in an IIA, as well as their scope, the appropriate legal basis (national or international), and their enforceability.

Furthermore, the appropriateness of investment treaty arbitration is challenged when dealing with matters such as sustainability, climate change, or human rights. Classically, investment arbitration is not shaped to assess investor liability (there are no adequate provisions for the gathering and assessing of evidence, which strongly differ from those for assessing the State's violation of IIL, nor appropriate specific rules on remedies and the calculation of damages fitting the context). The proper place to adjudicate private liability (corruption, environmental damages, and human rights violations) would rather seem to be domestic courts, where this would be judged in tort, or even

---

2 Maxi Scherer, Stuart Bruce, Juliane Reschke, 'Environmental Counterclaims in Investment Treaty Arbitration' (2021) 36(2), ICSID Review, 413–440.

3 Edit, 'AFCFTA Protocol on Investment (2023)' Electronic Database of Investment Treaties (EDIT) <https://edit.wti.org/document/show/e5d51824-c467-4e24-922b-3fb376d89550> accessed 24 October 2024 (see, in particular, Chapters 4 – Sustainable Development-Related Issues and 5 – Investor obligations). See also Makane Moïse Mbengue and Stefanie Schacherber, 'The "Africanization" of international investment law: The Pan-African Investment Code and the reform of the international investment regime' (2017) 18(3), Journal of World Investment and Trade, 414–448.

under criminal law. This would mainly occur in the host State, but sometimes also in the home State, if this is permitted by the relevant home State law.

At the same time, social alarm was often raised by certain arbitral awards seen to lead to unreasonable results, with foreign investors being awarded significant compensation of damages, although significant elements had emerged to deem them responsible either for corruption, violation of health and safety, environmental standards, workers' rights, poor management, or violence against locals (including cases where the challenged States' measures were claimed to be meant to remedy investors' abuses).[4] It is thus more and more perceived as fair and ethical to require investors to abide by certain principles in the establishment and management of an investment and that compensation not be deserved when those principles are not respected. Consequently, the examination of both States' and investors' conducts in one single proceeding is increasingly perceived as a rule that might prevent conflicting decisions and cases of manifest injustice.

Within such context, how could investment contracts help attain the goal of embodying investor obligations in IIL, or better respond to some of the criticalities emerged in relation to IIAs and investment treaty arbitration?

Contracts, by implication, can provide a degree of relativity based on the circumstances and flexibility produced by negotiation. They could, therefore, introduce the possibility of balancing different interests.

Of course, the values that the provisions on investor obligations aim to guarantee are of general (global) interest and thus absolute. They therefore deserve maximum protection. Any mechanism that is adequate to prevent regulatory chilling in these matters and to ensure enforcement when a State exercises its powers related to public policy should be welcomed, to avoid that the policies protecting these values be put at risk. However, the cooperation that is asked of the investor for the realisation of these objectives, and which inevitably compresses its rights, must be achieved by seeking to protect the latter's prerogatives and reasonably safeguard its economic results. What the general rules of a treaty cannot resolve, by their very nature, can instead be resolved based on the balancing mechanisms specific to the contract. Contracts are a precious instrument to cater protection and liability rules to the specific circumstances of the case.

4 See, for instance, the issues addressed and the debate surrounding cases such as: *Burlington v. Ecuador*, ICSID Case No. ARB/08/5; *Aven v. Costa Rica*, ICSID Case No. UNCT/15/3; *Al Tamimi v. Oman*, ICSID Case No. ARB/11/33; *Silver Limited v. Bolivia*, PCA Case No. 2013–2015; *Copper Mesa v. Ecuador*, PCA Case No. 2012-2.

2 Can Investment Contracts Help to Reach Public Policy Goals through the Balancing of Investor Obligations and Investor Protections?

Investment contracts can help in many ways, providing the necessary amount of flexibility that IIAs may lack. In principle, and if allowed by the legal context, they can clarify the options that parties decide to adopt, providing them with the necessary space to establish responsibilities in line with national standards or the highest international standards (if this is the case), or even establishing the set of investor obligations that should take precedence, depending on the specific circumstances of the case and the interests at stake.

Contracts could complement the applicable IIA and clarify the scope and legal effects of the investor obligations included in new-generation IIAs. On the other side, looking at the many examples of best efforts and the generic language used in many of such new-generation IIAs, contracts could be useful not only to give more specific content to the obligations of investors in the interest of legal certainty, but also to tighten the commitments of investors still couched in endeavour language in IIAs.

Especially if the parties choose to refer to international law standards, contracts may identify more specifically investor obligations and their scope, the concrete rules applicable to the case (including on procedures, evidence and compensation), and the legal consequences of their violations as regards dispute settlement, as well as possibly providing a legal basis for States' contractual claims to be brought before arbitral tribunals. In this case, contracts would be a legal means to expressly turn into legally enforceable obligations those investor commitments that usually States try to enforce through counterclaims in investment treaty arbitration and that, in a contractual setting, may be enforced as an ordinary (unilateral) claim.

Investment contracts may even become relevant when an IIA protection is not in place. This may occur when an IIA is not in force, or is in force but lacks ISDS arbitration provisions, or there is a (valid) waiver of treaty protection under the same IIA, or if treaty arbitration is not available in a certain legal context (for instance, in intra-EU disputes following the "*Achmea/Komstroy jurisprudence*"[5]). In these cases, contracts could work as a substitute for treaty

5 Judgment of the European Court of Justice (Grand Chamber) of 6 March 2018, *Slowakische Republik v. Achmea BV*, Case C-284/16, ECLI:EU:C:2018:158; Judgment of the European Court of Justice (Grand Chamber) of 2 September 2021, *République de Moldavie v. Komstroy LLC*, Case C-741/19, ECLI:EU:C:2021:655.

protection while trying to keep a balance with an optimised set of investor obligations.

In particular, investment contracts may lay down a balanced set of States' obligations to protect the foreign investment/investor (ensuring regulatory stability and the security of the investment) while also striking a balance between investor protective standards, on the one side, and common standards concerning investor obligations on the other. These are still to be fully identified but may revolve around those established in the 2011 UN Guiding Principles on Business and Human Rights,[6] the OECD Guidelines for Multinational Enterprises on Responsible Business Conduct,[7] and the recent AfCFTA Protocol. Such standards may provide more clarity on the scope of the existing investors' obligations, but also on the limits of their protection, and be adapted to parties' interests in the specific case.

Since one of the intrinsic limits of contracts is fragmentation, in the sense that each contract has its own negotiation history and life and, in principle, only applies to its signatories, the establishment of some common rules and principles is recommendable. In this way, not only consistency is favoured, but rules can also be established based on a common understanding and taking into account, as far as possible (and advisable), all industries, sectors, and dimensions of investors and States.

This is the objective that the UNIDROIT Working Group on Investment Contracts, established in 2023, is trying to achieve.[8]

UNIDROIT's Project on International Investment Contracts (IICs) aims at developing guidance to foster the modernisation and standardisation of international investment contracts. It explores the interaction between the UNIDROIT Principles of International Commercial Contracts (UPICC) and common provisions in IICs and seeks to address recent developments in IIL, with a special eye on investor obligations.

The Project is jointly undertaken by UNIDROIT and the International Chamber of Commerce's Institute of World Business Law (ICC Institute). This partnership is meant to combine UNIDROIT's expertise in developing international law instruments in the field of private law with the ICC Insti-

6 UN OHCHR (2011), *UN Guiding Principles on Business and Human Rights* < https://www.ohchr.org/sites/default/files/documents/publications/guidingprinciplesbusinesshr_en.pdf> accessed 29 October 2024.

7 OECD (2023), *OECD Guidelines for Multinational Enterprises on Responsible Business Conduct* <https://doi.org/10.1787/81f92357-en> accessed 29 October 2024.

8 UNIDROIT, *Study L-IIC, International Investment Contracts* <https://www.unidroit.org/work-in-progress/investment-contracts-upicc> accessed 6 January 2025.

tute's expertise on investment arbitration and the development of model clauses.

There are presently few findings to be publicly shared, and many decisions on the substance are still in progress. The horizon of its work is, however, that of looking into whether the UPICC may be adapted to the needs of IICs, what adaptations would be needed, and which principles coming from international practice should be included in the final instrument. The final aim is to adopt an instrument that would provide guidance in the form of guidelines and/or a list of principles that, if accepted and used by prospective users (States and private investors), may update IIC rules and adapt them to the needs of the new millennium.

3 Scope of Investor Obligations: What Practice Teaches Us

The debate on investor obligations in IIL mainly turns around the (loose) concept of sustainable development, usually understood in the debate in quite wide terms, as including economic and social development, environmental protection, climate change mitigation and transition economy, as well as good governance and protection of human rights.

Without entering this debate or assuming to give definitions for general purposes, a task force that was established to work on existing investment contracts to support the UNIDROIT Working Group elaborated findings over approximately 100 publicly available contracts, mainly in the extractive industry, from all regions of the world.[9] This kind of exercise was also attempted by individual scholars independent from the UNIDROIT works[10] and leads to the conclusion that, in more recent experience, some obligations are indeed inserted in investment contracts, although there is a difference among regions, and articulation strongly differs according to the type of clause. A word of caution is needed since, as said, the subject contracts come, for the most part, from

9 The Task Force is embedded in the Roma3-UNIDROIT Centre for Transnational Commercial Law and International Arbitration. For more information on the Task Force, see <https://www.roma3unidroitcentre.org/> accessed 6 January 2025.

10 See, for instance, Chapter 16 – Marco Pertile and Sondra Faccio, 'Extractive industry for sustainable development? Some reflections on the role of investment contracts in ensuring benefit sharing and community participation in natural resource governance' in Daniëlla Dam-de Jong and Britta Sjöstedt (eds), *Research Handbook on International Law and Environmental Peacebuilding* (Edward Elgar 2023), 355–380.

the extractive industry, while differences across industries surely exist.[11] Moreover, any statistic provides limited evidence, as it always covers only a tiny percentage of existing agreements due to most of the contracts in this area falling under restricted standards of access because of language issues or confidentiality rules. There is thus no pretence of drawing determinative conclusions from this research but rather only the benefit of an informational exercise for the UNIDROIT Working Group.

The study by the Task Force has already produced some results that deserve attention.[12] In the very first place, a discretionary (and thus challengeable) categorisation was chosen that needs to be made explicit to understand the results:[13]

> i. *Economic development clauses* would include, for the purposes of the survey, contractual obligations of the investor that materially contribute to the economy and production or enable the capacity of the host State and its citizens (e.g., local sourcing, preference for local contractors, hiring programmes, training programmes) during the duration of the contract (irrespective of whether they presuppose material enforceability, or a violation of the obligations concerned can constitute a ground of termination or may determine liability under the contract).
> ii. *Environmental protection clauses* have been delimited to include contractual obligations of the investor that reference substantive or procedural standards (national law, international best practices, and treaty or customary international law) and reinforce accountability under statutes (domestic) or for environmental concerns (e.g., due diligence, risk assessment, planning and mitigation measures, standards for regulated activities, monitoring, liabilities). This includes any duty to abstain from certain activities (specific or not) as well as the specific reservations taken by States to ensure enforceability of their regulatory powers.

11 Note that the documents analysed are not model contracts, but rather actual contractual texts, each concerning an autonomous investment and thus subject to circumstances.

12 Results as described are preliminary and reflect an interim memorandum presented by the Task Force to the members of the Working Group in October 2024. Special thanks go to Dr. Argha Kumar Jena, who elaborated the final version of such memorandum under the supervision of Dr. Rocco Palma, UNIDROIT. Many more researchers contributed to the previous versions of this memorandum (which is one of the many provided by the Task Force on various topics relevant to IICs but going beyond the scope of this contribution).

13 For a full understanding, it should be noticed that the angle of analysis was on public policy goals as reflected in contractual clauses rather than specifically on articulation of investor obligations.

iii. *Social clauses* have been significantly delimited to include only those contractual obligations of the investor *vis-à-vis* workers of the parties to the contract (e.g., adherence to safety and health standards, social security, resulting liabilities, and indemnification) based on national and/or international standards, depending on the regional area (domestic law or standards of the industry).

iv. *Intellectual property and proprietary information clauses* have been construed broadly to include contractual obligations that refer to the maintaining of records or collection of data that concern execution of the contract in any manner as well as any reporting obligation flowing therefrom, transfer of any information collected or held during the period of the contract's duration, and the use or transfer of intellectual property that relates to the execution of the contract.

v. *Community development clauses* have been construed broadly to accommodate overarching policy objectives that may have been reflected in the covenants and relate to the mitigation or amelioration of living conditions as preventative or compensatory measures for those communities that could not avoid the impact of investment operations deriving from the execution of the contract (contribution to national, local, or indigenous development; social programmes; capacity creation; participation rights; resettlement plans; protection of cultural or religious heritage; access rights; profit sharing), to the extent they do not overlap with other categories and have thus been included under the previous ones.

Throughout the assessment of clauses as categorised, four types were, in turn, identified: a) a due diligence standard, substantive and/or procedural, concerning activities and/or performances to be carried out under the contract (DDS); b) a standard of protection in favour of the State derived from specific obligations, compensatory measures, and/or allocation of liabilities (SPS); c) a standard of protection in favour of third parties/non-parties to the contract derived from specific obligations, guarantees, and/or allocation of liabilities (SPT); and d) a corporate social responsibility clause (self-imposed or statutory) (CSR).

Recurring features in relation to economic development clauses were as follows: reference was often found to accepted or prevalent industry standards, as well as to domestic legislation, although in some cases, only reference to domestic law was found. Mandatory procurement of goods and services from local sources was also found, as well as mandatory engagement and training of local human resources, and stringent reporting requirements to ensure compliance.

For environmental protection, reference was often found to domestic legislations of the host State, while no direct reference to international soft law standards was identified, although specifically researched for. On the other side, specific allocation of liabilities was found, also when third parties were affected, and indemnification of the host State for costs incurred in protection of the environment and/or the requisite of holding an insurance. Pre-operational and periodic due diligence (e.g., Environmental Impact Assessment) and reporting requirements are often established, including with a high level of detail and by reference to special testing per area of activity (disposal and waste management, metal value recovery, environmental baseline assessment, hazardous waste transport).

In social clauses, prevailing references to domestic legislations of the host State concerning labour and to underlying principles of law (e.g., equal labour conditions, equal pay) were found as well, but also some references to international soft law.

Of interest in intellectual property and proprietary information clauses, there is a frequently established right of inspection by host State personnel and the acknowledgement that data and other proprietary information are deemed property of the State, requiring the State's authorisation before dissemination to third parties, as well as data surrender conditions.

Finally, overarching obligations that favour development of local non-parties to the contract may be found in community development clauses, with the inclusion – in only one contract among those analysed – of reference to policy objectives to develop local communities. More frequent are provisions for mandatory participation in community development programmes, to increase awareness of potential health hazards or to protect local history and culture.

Absent the possibility of quoting or illustrating all clauses found in this exercise, and reiterating that extreme caution must be used to draw any possible conclusion in the light of the limitations described above, a sample pertaining to the category of community development clauses is reproduced to communicate at least a flavour of the possible articulation of such clauses. In the clause reproduced, an institutional mechanism is provided to ensure participatory rights and an adequate focus on a comprehensive local development strategy in the investment area:

CHAPTER FOUR: Regional Development

4.1 The Government will establish the "Southern Gobi Regional Development Council" (the "Council") and shall lead its activities. [DDS][14]

4.2 The Council will be governed by a board, which shall include representatives of the Government, local governance organisations, private sector entities, civil society organisations and donor and international financial institutions with activities directed towards the Southern Gobi region. [DDS]

4.3 The Investor will be a member of the Council's governing board, and shall support the Council and its activities. [DDS]

4.4 The Council will assist the Government in the following areas in terms of preparation, financing, organising and implementation of the Southern Gobi local and regional development strategy, plans and budgets: 4.4.1. support to local and regional development and encouraging transparent and responsible governance; 4.4.2. coordination of in-migration influx; 4.4.3. resolving matters of urban planning and development, including power, roads, water supply, heating and sewerage; 4.4.4. organization of formal and non-formal education, including English language and vocational training; 4.4.5. focus on human health care, construction of diagnostic centres, cultural facilities, sport facilities, improvement of veterinary services; and 4.4.6. support to capacity building for local governments and civil society. [SPT] [SPS]

4.5 In addition to the above, the Investor will support socio-economic development policies and activities undertaken by Southern Gobi local administration and will develop partnerships to ensure that sustainable benefits from the OT Project reach Mongolian people, including people in Umnugovi Aimag. [DDS] [SPS] [SPT]

4.6 The Investor shall conduct all of its local and regional socio-economic development programs and activities based on principles of transparency, accountability and public participation. [DDS]

4.7 The Investor shall continue to prepare, conduct, implement, update on an appropriate basis, and make public socio-economic baseline studies, socio-economic impact assessments, socio-economic risk analyses, as well as multi-year communities plans, community relations management systems, policies, procedures and guidelines, and mine closure plans, all of which shall be produced with community participation and input and be consistent with international best practice. [DDS]

---

14 See above for the understanding of these acronyms, added to the clauses by the researchers of the Task Force to attempt a categorization of standards.

4.8 The Investor shall give priority focus to those Umnugovi Aimag citizens and groups directly and indirectly impacted by the OT Project, as determined by socio-economic and environmental impact assessments and other relevant documents and, for this purpose, the Investor shall regularly engage with and support the public and local stakeholders in Umnugovi Aimag. [DDS] [SPT]

4.9 The Investor shall establish cooperation agreements with local administrative organisations in accordance with Article 42 of the Minerals Law and these agreements may include the establishment of local development and participation funds, local participation committees and local environmental monitoring committees. [DDS] [SPS] [SPT]

4.10 The Investor will consult with local administrative organisations to provide appropriate compensation upon resettlement of herder families located on the Contract Area who are directly impacted by the OT Project. [DDS] [SPS] [SPT]

4.11 The Investor shall make as a priority training, recruiting and employing citizens of local communities in the Southern Gobi region, with preference to Umnugovi Aimag. [DDS]

4.12 The Investor shall support special business development programs to assist in starting and growing local businesses so they can supply the OT Project, as well as the expansion and diversification of Mongolian business partners so that they are not fully dependent on the OT Project. [DDS]

4.13 The Investor shall continue to actively build and maintain productive working relationships, based on principles of transparency, accountability, accuracy, trust, respect and mutual interests, with non-governmental organizations, civic groups, civil councils and other stakeholders. [DDS].

Source: Contract No. 102 Mining Contract Mongolia 2009

To the same end, a different clause provides for the allocation of company equity (*"local share"*) in favour of residents in the project area, together with standards on the investor dividends policy:

ARTICLE 10.17 Local share

10.17.1 At the option of the Project Affected People, the Company agrees that the Project Affected People: [DDS] [SPT]

(A) required to be resettled and rehabilitated as a result of the Project; and

(B) who are natural persons and other natural persons residing permanently in the districts of the Project Area at the date on which the construction activities for the Project commence, shall, directly or indirectly, be sold or issued up to a maximum of ten per cent (10%) of all the Company Shares with the value of each share determined on the basis of the face value of such shares without applying any premium, which shall be exercised and the total value paid in full in the period from the date of Financial Close until the date which is three years after the Financial Close. GON shall work together with the Company to agree on a local share allocation plan and implement such effective mechanisms and processes that is not cumbersome in the ordinary course of business to the Company to give full effect to the transactions envisaged in this Section 10.17.1 (Local share). For the avoidance of doubt, the Company shall not be required to issue any Company Shares to the general public. [SPT] [DDS]

10.17.2 The Parties agree that it is their common intention that, subject to compliance with Company's dividend policy, Laws of Nepal and any obligations under the Financing Documents, at least two-third (2/3rd) of the Distributable Profits shall be paid as dividends to the Shareholders in respect of the shares in each financial year.

10.17.3 For the purposes of Section 10.17.2 (Local share), the term "Distributable Profits" means such profits of the Company available for distribution by the Company after it has identified (acting prudently) amounts which it considers should be retained in order:

(A) to meet commitments, contingencies capital and operating maintenance;
(B) to provide for unforeseen expenditure, reduction in revenue given the nature of the business and unplanned maintenance including setting aside reserves for such purpose pursuant to prudent utility practises, and
(C) to develop, implement and operate its business in accordance with the Transaction Documents; and
(D) to ensure that there is no breach of any covenant or undertaking given by the Company to any Lender under the Financing Documents at the time of the payment of any dividend;
(E) to maintain the sound financial standing of the Company;
(F) to ensure that the Company maintains such reasonable and proper reserves for working capital or otherwise as may be required by Applicable Law or as its board of directors may (acting reasonably) consider to be appropriate.

Source: Contract No. 110 Project Development Agreement Upper Trishull-1 Hydropower Project Nepal 2016

Finally, yet another clause provides standards of protection (customs and cultural traditions, welfare, community activities, hiring policy, and training) in favour of local or indigenous communities and/or citizens in the project area:

> SECTION 10: Rights and Obligations of the Parties.
> ln the development of the community: k.1: To recognize and respect the rights, customs and traditions of indigenous cultural communities over their ancestral lands and to allocate royalty payment of not less than one percent (1%) of the value of the gross output of minerals sold; k.2. To coordinate with proper authorities in the development of the host and neighboring communities in accordance with the SDMP and to promote the general welfare of the inhabitants living therein. Where traditional self-sustaining income and the community activities are identified to be present, the Contractor shall assist in the preservation and/or enhancement of such activities; and K.3. To give preference to Filipino citizens who have established domicile in the neighboring communities, in the hiring of personnel for its mining operations. If necessary skills and expertise are currently not available, the Contractor must immediately prepare and undertake a training and recruitment program at its expense. [DDS] [CSR].
> **Source:** Contract No. 111 Mineral Production Sharing Agreement Philippines 2011

4 Some Ways Forward

The UNIDROIT Working Group on Investment Contracts has the purpose of standardising, but also and above all modernising, the core provisions of IICs in the light of the new challenges to IIL and the widespread belief in a need for reconsideration of the main premises of such branch of international law. Within the debate on the logic and core principles of IIL, the need for a balance between protection of investments as established by the practice emerging from treaties and arbitral awards and new instances on environmental protection, sustainable development, and corporate social responsibility emerges. To find a reasonable balance, dynamics of IICs are considered in the light of the UPICC and other international standards and model clauses as reliable benchmarks of shared solutions. The requirement of privity of contract cannot be overcome, but the availability of recourse to arbitration in this context may help to achieve some openness to third-parties' interests and the contractualisation (and thus the shared responsibility between investor and State) of public goals. Within such context, possible ways forward would start from the current practice but need a wider gaze.

To that end, the UNIDROIT Working Group has not reached any final thoughts on any of the issues hereby discussed. The brief considerations that follow are thus exclusively those of the author, although being elaborated thanks in part to the discussions held by the Working Group.

A "procedural" duty on how to negotiate, as well as on how to govern business relationships. In the very first place, the inclusion of due diligence requirements seems to be the way forward, recommended also in commercial contracts by the OECD Guidelines, as well as domestic or regional legislation transforming this soft law instrument into hard law.[15] These are tools that mirror the logic of commercial due diligence, well known to the business world and routinely used in investment or merger-and-acquisition operations, but which have as their object the verification of conditions of environmental, social, and/or human rights protection.

Commercial due diligence normally operates in the initial phase of the investment, before it is actually realised, and usually determines the drafting of declarations and warranties in the agreement, reporting facts whose truthfulness the party guarantees. If these declarations and warranties prove to be false, the injured party will be entitled to compensation for the damage suffered (usually in the form of a penalty with a value pre-determined in the contract itself). A similar due diligence process is already frequently put in place for environmental or economic and social rights protection, where the party guarantees that it has complied with all relevant regulations and has not committed any illicit acts. This can be extended to all other due diligence mechanisms having as their object matters within the (widely defined) label of sustainable development (including human rights due diligence). The investor must therefore guarantee the counterparty that it has complied and will comply with all the standards imposed by the host country in the establishment of the investment.

As already mentioned (and as far as permitted by the legal system), the contract also allows the parties to take a further leap and commit to (and execute the due diligence based on) compliance with international standards rather than standards already embedded in national legislation. Any due diligence can thus address interests of third-parties and specific communities'

15 Maria Chiara Malaguti, 'From soft to hard law and interpretation: the case of the OECD Guidelines for Multinational Enterprises and the role of the National Contact Points' (2023) 10(2), Oslo Law Review, 1–17.

instances and make the investor responsible against the (contracting) State for violation of its own declarations to that end or possibly an unsatisfactory performance of the scope and means of such due diligence as agreed with the other party.

On the other hand, the logic of due diligence as traditionally known in investment law, whereby the investor must put itself in a position to know the regulations of the country where it invests and must adequately assess the latter's possible variations, also finds space in the context of sustainability, in the sense that the investor must evaluate what are the reasonable spaces of the host State to concretely implement its own right to regulate in matters of sustainability, climate change, human rights, and so on.

A second type of due diligence, however, exists and consists in the operator's duty to monitor its business partners so that they comply with those same sustainability standards. This tool has yet a different origin: the practice of codes of conduct which, in companies of the same group, can be implemented and respected throughout the group thanks to careful due diligence on the behaviour of the various controlled companies, is extended to a wider category of business partners, even if only linked by a contractual relationship. As known, this is embedded in the OECD Guidelines and the domestic and regional laws that have implemented such Guidelines. In this way, the entrepreneur/investor is obliged to implement an efficient system for monitoring compliance with the code.

Any monitoring mechanism, however, occurs against one or more specific standards. In this context, it is, therefore, essential that the parties clearly define the applicable standards to make the commitment concrete and stringent. Furthermore, the concrete consequences of failure to adequately monitor must be determined, since, in this context, the investor only violates a monitoring obligation, not necessarily the underlying standard itself.

Obligations not to do versus obligations to do. Aside from the obligation of due diligence, however intended, which certainly makes the investor responsible but is limited to sanctioning the lack of due care in establishing (and operating) an investment in full understanding of the context in which one operates and in full compliance with it, there is obviously the establishment of direct obligations on the part of the investor in the establishment and subsequent management of the investment. Failure to comply with them may determine the possibility for the counterparty to obtain compensation for damages or any other contractual remedy that the parties deemed appropriate to include.

The logic of insertion of new obligations does not seem to depart from the traditional setting of contractual protection of the rights of the counterparty and the attendant possible remedies. The real debate here would be on whether a violation of obligations to the benefit of local communities or affecting general interests could somehow permit a challenge by such local communities. Privity of contract would conflict in this case with the need to protect either individual third parties affected by the violation or indeed common goods. This of course unless the parties are ready to insert clauses permitting to recognise (some) third parties as beneficiaries of (certain) contractual parties' undertakings and thus possibly recognise protection to such third parties and even the possibility to protect these rights through adjudication. Some considerations on this point are made below when discussing the role of ADR in this context.

In a crescendo of investor responsibility, a positive duty of collaboration between the investor and the State for the achievement of certain objectives can also be established. In this case, it is not just a matter of sanctioning the violating behaviour of the investor, but of affirming a positive duty so that the two parties collaborate, each to the extent of its competence and role, to guarantee shared sustainability objectives. The violation of such a duty can determine, as a remedy, a *facere* obligation more easily than in the case of a "simple" violation of an obligation to respect the standard.

ADR and protection of third-parties' interests. Finally, for any obligation to be effective, it is necessary that the affected right be adequately protected. This brings one to the issue of dispute resolution.[16]

As already mentioned, the contract transforms a potential counterclaim into an ordinary unilateral claim. The real issue here concerns which remedies would be appropriate, and, indeed, the most adequate dispute mechanisms to choose.

However, the matters we are dealing with inevitably raise the question of the protection of the rights of third parties, including those who feel harmed by the investor not as individuals but as a community, and therefore of their possible intervention in a contractual dispute. As already mentioned, some consider arbitration (contractual but also investment arbitration), at least under some circumstances, unsuitable for resolving disputes of this kind.[17]

16 Vera Korzun, 'Enforcing Soft Law in International Investment Arbitration' (2023) 56(1), Vanderbilt Law Review.

17 Challenges arise from the fact that some issues call for application of tort or criminal law, and the collective nature of the damages would physiologically take to class actions. See Joana Setzer and Catherine Higham, 'Global trends in climate change litigation: 2024 Snapshot' (2024) LSE Policy Papers; see also Belén Olmos Giupponi and Raul Partido Figueroa, 'Navigating ESG arbitrability challenges in energy and climate: an in-depth analysis and future perspectives' (2024) 12(1), European Energy Journal.

However, it cannot be overlooked how, on the contrary, the instruments for alternative dispute resolution, mediation as well as arbitration,[18] have the kind of flexibility that could also allow for the consideration of third-party interests, as the institution of the *amicus curiae*[19] at least partially already does, or possibly for their participation as proper parties, by, for instance, availing a contractual clause that grants them *locus standi* as third-party beneficiaries of the contract. In fact, more and more often, scholars and practitioners point to arbitration and mediation as tools for solving ESG and climate change issues.[20]

From this point of view, the road is probably still long in the sense that many questions of both a substantive and procedural nature need to be resolved, including the very complex issue of the quantification of damages, especially when prospective and in the absence of canons that easily determine the causal link between the act and the damages.

In this context, however, the instrument of appointing an expert arbitrator or a technical committee (frequently used in commercial arbitration), which judges on a specific technical aspect (for example, precisely in terms of prospective damages), could open new perspectives and a composite system of dispute resolution that is, in some way, also open to the protection of third (non-contractual) parties. It is not the overcoming of privity, but a sort of "socialisation" of solutions of disputes within a larger context, or – said in the reverse – a sort of "contractualisation" of third-parties' interests and the protection of the general interest.

---

18 Maria Chiara Malaguti, 'ADR in International Investment Law: Recent Trends (A Specific Focus on Mediation)' (2024) ILA Italy Yearbook (to be published).

19 Maria Chiara Malaguti, 'Amicus curiae e tutela del public interest – Potenzialità dell'istituto alla luce della giurisprudenza in controversie in materia di investimenti tra Stato e privati' in Lucia Serena Rossi and Elisa Baroncini (eds), *Rapporti tra ordinamenti e diritti dei singoli* (Editoriale Scientifica 2023) 475–491.

20 Anja Ipp and Annette Magnusson (eds), *Investment Arbitration and Climate Change* (Wolters Kluwer 2023).

CHAPTER 5

Enforcing International Environmental and Climate Change Law on Investors: Reflections on the Investment Protocol to the African Continental Free Trade Area and Beyond

Jackson Shaw Kern and Mohit Khubchandani[1]

1 Introduction

Undeniable scientific indicators suggest that we have now entered firmly into an uncertain "Anthropocene era" in which human activity is irreversibly altering the natural systems of the Earth.

This reality is reflected in recent reports of the Intergovernmental Panel on Climate Change, against the backdrop of the 2015 Paris Agreement. Meanwhile, mass-scale investments in the renewable energy sector are on the rise, including State-led initiatives as well as those occurring under the aegis of the Green Climate Fund and veteran multilateral institutions such as the World Bank and International Monetary Fund. Sustainability provisions featuring within newer economic treaties equally give testament to the prominent place that environmental issues have come to occupy in the space of international law and policy.

Yet one may reasonably question whether the organs of international justice are reliably suited to the magnitude of the task at hand. Environmental obligations already acknowledged to be binding upon States in international law (whether by force of custom or convention) suffer from jurisdictional gaps that often deny effective fora for their policing and enforcement. Unlawful environmental harms inflicted by non-State actors pose an additional order of challenge. One observer has written, in respect of a different international scourge, that the respective international conventions "continue to arrogate

1 When he co-authored this piece, Mohit Khubchandani was a Visiting Foreign Lawyer at Wilmer Cutler Pickering Hale and Dorr LLP, London, where he got the support and encouragement of Prof. Steven Finizio to write it. The views expressed in this article are the authors' alone.

 | HTTPS://DOI.ORG/10.1163/9789004769854-006

the prerogatives of curbing and prosecuting" to national authorities, "thus depriving these instruments and the international legal order of any real control function".[2] Such language resonates in the environmental realm, where national judiciaries operate at the frontlines while often facing austere limitations in their quest to confer environmental justice.[3] Perhaps foremost amongst these is their limited jurisdictional reach, coupled with the limited scope for international enforceability of their judgments.

More than a decade ago, in its World Investment Report 2012, the United Nations Conference on Trade and Development (UNCTAD) noted that a "new generation" of investment policies aimed at systematically integrating sustainable development had begun to emerge.[4] By 2019, a group of diverse human rights experts, appointed and mandated by the United Nations Human Rights Council, dispatched an open letter to the United Nations Commission for International Trade Law (UNCITRAL) in the context of its Working Group III on Investor–State Dispute Settlement Reform, stating the need to bring "systemic structural changes to the architecture" of international investment arbitration.[5]

In the Protocol on Investment to the Agreement Establishing the African Continental Free Trade Area (AfCFTA Investment Protocol/Investment Protocol/

---

2 AP Llamzon, *Corruption in International Investment Arbitration* (Oxford University Press, 2018) para. 11.03. He has also written that "the primary shortcoming of current international anticorruption treaties has precisely been the abdication of the control function to domestic institutions". Ibid., para. 4.121. See, in this respect, JD Amado, JS Kern, and MD Rodriguez, 'Elevating Corruption to an International Tort' in *Investors' International Law* (J Ho and M Sattorova, eds.) (Bloomsbury, 2021).

3 Recent years have, however, seen some notable progress in matters of transnational environmental litigation, particularly in the courts of The Netherlands and the UK, including in respect of parent company liability. See, in this respect, Protocol on Investment to the Agreement Establishing the African Continental Free Trade Area, art 47 (AfCFTA Investment Protocol).

4 UNCTAD, *World Investment Report 2012: Towards a New Generation of Investment Policies* (New York, 2012) 102.

5 Letter dated 7 March 2019, Mandates of the Working Group on the issue of human rights and transnational corporations and other business enterprises; the Special Rapporteur on the right to development; the Special Rapporteur on the issue of human rights obligations relating to the enjoyment of a safe, clean, healthy, and sustainable environment; the Independent Expert on the effects of foreign debt and other related international financial obligations of States on the full enjoyment of all human rights, particularly economic, social, and cultural rights; the Special Rapporteur on the rights of indigenous peoples; the Independent Expert on the promotion of a democratic and equitable international order; and the Special Rapporteur on the human rights to safe drinking water and sanitation (OL ARM 1/2019).

Protocol), one glimpses a new offering in the struggle that is currently underway for the future of that very architecture. Amongst numerous other investor obligations, the Protocol heralds the advent of a regime under which international investors might be held directly liable before an international tribunal for environmental breach, with accompanying internationally enforceable arbitral remedies, and in which the international arbitral machinery may thus play a significant role in ensuring access to justice for the various victims of environmental harm.

In this chapter we seek to explore the methods and manners by which such mechanism might best be actualised, including via the forthcoming dispute settlement Annex of the Investment Protocol. In this way, treatymakers might establish an international environmental control function that is better matched to the realities of unhindered international capital flows, in better defence of the Global Commons that are dear to us all.

Section II thus proceeds with an examination of the Protocol's substantive environmental prescriptions when viewed in light of general international environmental law and emerging international climate change law. Section III then proposes to integrate these norms into the procedural edifice of investment arbitration. Section IV offers brief concluding thoughts for the future direction of international investment law in Africa and beyond.

2 Investors' Environmental Obligations under the Investment Protocol: Substantive Principles

International environmental law, historically reserved to imposing obligations (whether it be by convention or custom) upon the States, can no longer be viewed so narrowly. The natural systems of the Earth now coming under threat transcend national boundaries and reach far into the realm of the Global Commons. At the same time, we are witnessing the emergence of treaty instruments imposing environmental obligations upon non-State actors, and thereby directly regulating their conduct. The time is thus ripe to assess and apply the principles of international environmental law (including the duties of due diligence and environmental impact assessment as well as the precautionary principle and the principle of prevention of transboundary harm) in the context of investment protection. Investment tribunals have long recognised that the regime of international investment law cannot be interpreted in isolation from the broader body of public international law – including human rights law.[6]

2.1 Overview of Investor Obligations under Article 34 of the Protocol

In 2016, the States of the African Union concluded the draft Pan-African Investment Code (PAIC or the Code). Article 24 of the Code governs investor compliance with business ethics and "internationally recognized human rights".[7] The Code was ultimately agreed to be non-binding, thus serving largely as a guide in future rounds of treatymaking. The now-adopted Investment Protocol provides, in a binding manner, that intra-African investors and their investments shall, in carrying out their business activities, respect and protect the environment and, in particular, shall respect the right to a clean, healthy, and sustainable environment; shall comply with the principles of prevention and precaution; shall carry out environmental impact assessments in accordance with applicable laws and standards; shall apply the precautionary principle to their environmental impact assessments; shall, where their business activities cause environmental harm, take steps to mitigate and restore impacted sites; and shall not exploit or use natural resources to the detriment of the rights and interests of the host State and its local communities.

2.1.1 The Right to a Clean, Healthy, and Sustainable Environment

Article 34(1)(a) of the Investment Protocol compels investors to respect the "right to a clean, healthy and sustainable environment" by reference to the African Charter on Human and Peoples' Rights (ACHPR) and the resolution of the United Nations General Assembly bearing that title.[8] The right to health is codified in various international instruments.[9] The UN Committee on International Eco-

---

6 *Phoenix Action v. Czech Republic,* ICSID Case No. ARB/06/5, Award (15 Apr. 2009), para. 78. See also *AAPL v. Sri Lanka,* ICSID Case No. ARB/87/3, Award (27 June 1990), para. 21.

7 *Draft Pan-African Investment Code* (2016) <https://au.int/sites/default/files/documents/32844-doc-draft_pan-african_investment_code_december_2016_en.pdf> accessed 4 October 2023.

8 See UNGA, 'The human right to a clean, healthy and sustainable environment' (28 July 2022) UN Doc A/RES/76/300, art 24 (African Charter on Human and Peoples' Rights (1981)).

9 Universal Declaration of Human Rights (1948), art 25; International Covenant on Economic, Social and Cultural Rights (1966), art 12; Convention on the Rights of the Child, 1577 UNTS 3 (20 November 1989), art 24; African Charter on Human and Peoples' Rights (1981), art 16.

Article 34
Environmental Protection

1. Investors and their investments shall, in carrying out their business activities, respect and protect the environment, and, in particular shall:

   a. respect the right to a clean, healthy and sustainable environment, as reflected in Article 24 of the African Charter of Human and Peoples' Rights, and the Resolution of the United Nations General Assembly A/RES/76/300 ("The human right to a clean, healthy and sustainable environment");

   b. comply with the principles of prevention and precaution when conducting their business activities to anticipate and prevent any risk of significant harm to the environment;

   c. carry out an environmental impact assessment, in accordance with the best international standards and practices and as required by domestic law;

   d. apply the precautionary principle to their environmental impact assessment and to decisions taken in relation to a proposed investment, including any necessary mitigating or alternative approaches to the investment, or precluding the investment if necessary; and

   e. where their business activities cause harm to the environment, take steps to mitigate the harm, to restore impacted sites and ensure a clean, healthy and sustainable environment.

2. Investors shall not exploit or use natural resources to the detriment of the rights and interests of the Host State and local communities.

FIGURE 5.1 Protocol on investment to the agreement establishing the African continental free trade area, final draft adopted, January 2023, Article 34

nomic, Social and Cultural Rights has interpreted this right as including the right to a healthy environment,[10] which right is itself independently recognised.[11] Other

10 UN Committee on Economic, Social and Cultural Rights, 'General Comment No. 14: The right to the highest attainable standard of health (Article 12 of the International Covenant on Economic, Social and Cultural Rights)' (11 August 2000) UN Doc E/C.12/2000/4, para. 4.

11 African Charter on Human and Peoples' Rights (1981), art 24; Protocol of San Salvador to the American Convention on Human Rights (1969), art 11; IACtHR, 'State Obligations in Relation to the Environment in the Context of the Protection and Guarantee of the Rights to Life and Personal Integrity: Interpretation and Scope of Articles 4(1) and 5(1) in Relation to Articles 1(1) and 2 of the American Convention on Human Rights' (Advisory Opinion OC-23/17, 15 November 2017), para. 79; Regional Agreement on Access to Information, Public Participation and Justice in Environmental Matters in Latin America and the Caribbean, arts 1, 4, 4.

universal soft[12] and hard[13] law instruments also enshrine this right. These hard law instruments impose obligations heretofore cast upon States. The question that thus arises is: how may standards existing as between and amongst the States be operationalised vis-à-vis investors? The regime of international responsibility reflected in the Articles on the Responsibility of States for Internationally Wrongful Acts (ARSIWA)[14] – even as its title suggests – is not created with investors in mind. As the drafters of the Protocol have evidently and soundly concluded, international responsibility may nonetheless be cast upon investors precisely via the vehicle of obligations articulated in investment treaties, treaties which concurrently confer upon those investors' generous international protections.

It must be noted in passing that investment tribunals have already found various international obligations to be incumbent upon investors, even in the absence of express treaty language to this effect. By way of example, in the case of *Urbaser v. Argentina*, that tribunal rejected an investor's submission that the human right to water creates a duty borne uniquely by the State.[15] The tribunal further found as follows:

> 1195. [...] [I]nternational law accepts corporate social responsibility as a standard of crucial importance for companies operating in the field of international commerce. This standard includes commitments to comply with human rights in the framework of those entities' operations conducted in countries other than the country of their seat or incorporation. [...] ***[I]t can no longer be admitted that companies operating internationally are immune from becoming subjects of international law.*** [...]. The focus must be, therefore, on contextualizing a corporation's specific activities as they relate to the human right at issue in order to determine whether any international law obligations attach to the non-State individual.[16]

12 UN Conference on the Human Environment, 'Declaration of the United Nations Conference on the Human Environment' (5–16 June 1972), UN Doc A/CONF.48/14/Rev.1, pt I, ch I; UN Conference on Environment and Development, 'Rio Declaration on Environment and Development' (3–14 June 1992) UN Doc A/CONF.151/26 (Vol I), Annex I; UNHRC, 'The human right to a clean, healthy and sustainable environment' (8 October 2021) UN Doc A/HRC/RES/48/13.

13 UNGA, 'Universal Declaration of Human Rights' (10 December 1948) UN Doc A/RES/217 (III)A; International Covenant on Economic, Social and Cultural Rights, art 12.

14 ILC, 'Draft Articles on Responsibility of States for Internationally Wrongful Acts, with Commentaries' (2001) UN Doc A/56/10, Supp No 10 (ARSIWA).

15 *Urbaser v Argentina* ICSID Case No. ARB/07/26, Award (8 Dec 2016), para. 1193.

16 Ibid., para. 1195 (emphasis added).

The tribunal further discussed the Universal Declaration of Human Rights[17] and the International Covenant on Economic, Social, and Cultural Rights[18] in opining that "the human right for everyone's dignity and its right for adequate housing and living conditions are complemented by an obligation on all parts, public and private parties, not to engage in activity aimed at destroying such rights".[19] In the case of *David Aven and others v. Costa Rica,* the tribunal similarly found that "[i]t is true that the enforcement of environmental law is primarily to the States, but it cannot be admitted that a foreign investor could not be subject to international law obligations in this field".[20] The tribunal relied upon the findings of the International Court of Justice (ICJ) in *Barcelona Traction* to note that, if environmental obligations were not imposed upon the investor, such would run counter to the *erga omnes* nature of customary international law obligations where all States have a legal interest in ensuring preservation of the natural environment.[21]

2.1.2 Principles of Prevention and Precaution in Business

For perhaps the past fifty years since the Stockholm Declaration (and certainly the past thirty years since the 1992 Rio Declaration), the precautionary principle has been a tenet of international environmental law. According to the principle, "[w]here there are threats of serious or irreversible damage, lack of full scientific certainty shall not be used as a reason for postponing cost-effective measures to prevent environmental degradation".[22] Numerous multilateral conventions, such as the Convention on International Trade in Endangered Species,[23] the Convention on Biological

17 Ibid., para. 1196.

18 Ibid., para. 1197.

19 Ibid., para. 1199.

20 *Aven and others v. Costa Rica* ICSID Case No. UNCT/15/3, (Final Award 18 Sept 2018), para. 737.

21 *Barcelona Traction, Light and Power Company, Limited* (*Belgium v. Spain*) (Preliminary Objections, Judgment) [1970] ICJ Rep 3, para. 33.

22 UN Conference on Environment and Development, 'Rio Declaration on Environment and Development' (3–14 June 1992), Annex I, principle 15; United Nations Framework Convention on Climate Change, art 3(3); Vienna Convention for the Protection of the Ozone Layer (1985), 1513 UNTS 293.

23 The 1994 Conference of Member States of CITES set out a twofold mechanism to protect species at risk: first, in clear deference to the precautionary principle, species that may be at risk but where scientific uncertainty remains qualify for classification in Annex I and II; second, uncertainty may not be invoked to justify failure to take protective measures.

Diversity,[24] the Vienna Convention on the Protection of the Ozone Layer,[25] and the International Convention Relating to Intervention on the High Seas in Cases of Oil Pollution Casualties,[26] call for the implementation of the precautionary principle in a manner akin to the Rio Declaration. The collective purpose and subject matter of these conventions – i.e., guarding against environmental harm to species, biodiversity, air, and water – are all-encompassing, and these issues now frequently arise in investment arbitration.

International investment agreements increasingly contain clauses[27] that encourage foreign investors to adopt responsible business conduct in respect of human rights and environmental protection.[28] Many investment treaties have also endorsed these principles in some form within the broader context of corporate social responsibility generally.[29] As of 2026, at least 38 States[30]

---

24 Convention on Biological Diversity, pmbl. (5 June 1992), 1760 UNTS 79 (stating in its preamble that "where there is a threat of significant reduction or loss of biological diversity, lack of full scientific certainty should not be used as a reason for postponing measures to avoid or minimize such threat").

25 Vienna Convention on the Protection of the Ozone Layer, pmbl. (1985) 1513 UNTS 293. Since the adoption of this convention, States have called for a precautionary principle approach when regulating greenhouse gases. For example, the Montreal Protocol on Substances that Deplete the Ozone Layer (16 September 1987) 1522 UNTS 3 (as amended 29 June 1990) (specifying that Member States should take precautionary measures to control emissions of substances degrading the ozone layer).

26 International Convention Relating to Intervention on the High Seas in Cases of Oil Pollution Casualties (adopted 29 November 1969) 970 UNTS 211, art V(3)(a) (requiring that action be taken when the coasts are endangered, considering, inter alia, "the extent and probability of imminent damage if those measures are not taken").

27 See AfCFTA Investment Protocol, art 34(1)(b).

28 See Working Group on the Issue of Human Rights and Transnational Corporations and Other Business Enterprises (UNWG on Business and Human Rights), 'International Investment agreements (IIAs) and Human Rights: Report on Human Rights-Compatible International Investment Agreements' (27 July 2021) UN Doc A/76/238, para. 41.

29 Indian Model BIT (2015), art 12; Brazil–Angola Cooperation and Facilitation Investment Agreement, art 10, Annex 2.

30 In alphabetical order: Argentina – launched November 2023; Belgium – launched July 2017, updated April 2024; Chile – launched July 2017, updated March 2022; Colombia – launched December 2015, updated December 2020; Czech Republic – launched October 2017; Denmark – launched April 2014; Finland – launched October 2014; France – launched April 2017; Germany – launched December 2016; Indonesia – launched September 2023; Ireland – launched November 2017; Italy – launched December 2016; Japan – launched October 2020; Kenya – launched June 2019; Liberia – launched August 2024; Lithuania – launched February 2015; Luxembourg – launched June 2018; Mongolia – launched June 2023; Nepal – launched December 2023; Netherlands – launched December 2013, updated July 2022; Nigeria – launched April 2023; Norway – launched October 2015; Pakistan – launched October 2021; Peru – launched June 2021; Poland – launched

have implemented stand-alone national action plans on business and human rights (or chapters on business and human rights).[31] These include Denmark,[32] Italy,[33] Sweden,[34] Norway,[35] Japan,[36] France,[37] Thailand,[38]

May 2017, updated October 2021; Slovenia – launched November 2018; Spain – launched July 2017; Sweden – launched August 2015; Switzerland – launched December 2016; Thailand – launched October 2019; Uganda – launched August 2021; United Kingdom of Great Britain and Northern Ireland – launched September 2013, updated May 2016; United States of America – launched December 2016, updated March 2024; Vietnam – launched July 2023. Additionally, China has adopted the Business and Human Rights Chapter within China's Human Rights Action Plan of China (2021–2025); Georgia has adopted the Business and Human Rights Chapter within Georgia's Human Rights NAP; South Korea has adopted the Business and human rights VIII chapter within South Korea Human Rights NAPs; México has adopted the Business and human Rights Chapter within Mexico's Human Rights NAP (2020–2024).

31 See UN OHCHR, 'National Action Plans on Business and Human Rights' (UN Working Group on Business and Human Rights, updated 2025) <https://www.ohchr.org/en/special-procedures/wg-business/national-action-plans-business-and-human-rights> accessed 7 October 2024. See also Working Group on the Issue of Human Rights and Transnational Corporations and Other Business Enterprises, 'International Investment Agreements (IIAs) and Human Rights: Report on Human Rights-Compatible International Investment Agreements' (27 July 2021) UN Doc A/76/238, para. 36.

32 Denmark, 'Danish National Action Plan: Implementation of the UN Guiding Principles on Business and Human Rights' (March 2014) 31 <https://www.ohchr.org/Documents/Issues/Business/NationalPlans/Denmark_NationalPlanBHR.pdf> accessed 16 November 2024.

33 Italy, 'Italian National Action Plan on Business and Human Rights 2016–2021' (December 2016) 25 <https://faolex.fao.org/docs/pdf/ita214593.pdf> accessed 22 January 2024.

34 Sweden, 'Action Plan for Business and Human Rights' (August 2015), 29 <https://globalnaps.org/wp-content/uploads/2024/01/NAP-Sweden-2017-open-Swedish.pdf> accessed 16 November 2024.

35 Norway, 'Business and Human Rights: National Action Plan for the Implementation of the UN Guiding Principles' (October 2015) 26–27 <https://www.regjeringen.no/globalassets/departementene/ud/vedlegg/mr/business_hr_b.pdf> accessed 11 November 2024.

36 Japan, 'National Action Plan on Business and Human Rights: 2020–2025' (October 2020), 21. <https://www.ohchr.org/Documents/Issues/Business/NationalPlans/Japan-NAP.pdf> accessed 11 November 2024.

37 France, 'National Action Plan for the Implementation of the United Nations Guiding Principles on Business and Human Rights' (April 2017) 21 <https://www.ohchr.org/Documents/Issues/Business/NationalPlans/NAP_France_EN.pdf> accessed 11 November 2024.

38 Thailand, 'First National Action Plan on Business and Human Rights (2019–2022)' (October 2019) <https://www.ohchr.org/Documents/Issues/Business/NationalPlans/NAPThailandEN.pdf> accessed 11 November 2024.

Germany,[39] The Netherlands,[40] Belgium,[41] and Kenya[42] who have adopted national plans bringing them into conformity with international best practices based upon the OECD Guidelines for Multinational Enterprises and the UN Guiding Principles on Business and Human Rights.

Under Article 34 of the Protocol, investors shall now adhere mandatorily to the principles of prevention and precaution.

2.1.3 Environmental Impact Assessment (including Precautionary Principle)

An environmental impact assessment (EIA)[43], as a national instrument, shall be undertaken for proposed activities likely to yield a significant adverse impact on the environment.[44] The ILC Draft Articles on Prevention of Transboundary Harm establish requirements relating to the dispersal of information on environmental impacts of activities in good faith.[45] In the *Pulp Mills* case, even though the ICJ did not prescribe a particular form or threshold of EIA, it did note that the EIA "has gained so much acceptance among States that it may now be considered a requirement under general international law".[46] The

39 Germany, 'National Action Plan: Implementation of the UN Guiding Principles on Business and Human Rights 2016–2020" (December 2016) 13 <https://www.ohchr.org/Documents/Issues/Business/NationalPlans/NAP_Germany.pdf> accessed 20 May 2025.

40 The Netherlands, 'National Action Plan on Business and Human Rights' (December 2013), 20 <https://www.ohchr.org/Documents/Issues/Business/NationalPlans/Netherlands_NAP.pdf> accessed 11 November 2024.

41 Belgium, 'Plan d'action national: enterprises et droits de l'homme' (23 June 2017), action point 17 <https://globalnaps.org/wp-content/uploads/2026/04/Belgium-NAP-Business-and-Human-Rights-2.0-English-simplified.pdf> accessed 11 November 2024.

42 Kenya, 'National Action Plan on Business and Human Rights' (June 2019), 21 <https://www.ohchr.org/Documents/Issues/Business/NationalPlans/2019_FINAL_BHR_NAP.PDF> accessed 11 November 2024.

43 See AfCFTA Investment Protocol, art 34(1)(c)(d).

44 Convention on Environmental Impact Assessment in a Transboundary Context (adopted 25 February 1991) 1989 UNTS 309, arts 2(1), (4), (5); UN Conference on Environment and Development, 'Rio Declaration on Environment and Development' (3–14 June 1992) UN Doc A/CONF.151/26 (Vol. I), Annex I, principle 17.

45 ILC, 'Draft Articles on Prevention of Transboundary Harm from Hazardous Activities' (2001) UN Doc A/56/10, Supp No 10, arts 8(1), 9(1).

46 *Pulp Mills on the River Uruguay (Argentina v. Uruguay)* [2010] ICJ Rep 14 204.

International Tribunal for the Law of the Sea (ITLOS) endorsed this position the following year.[47]

Investment tribunals, for their part, have endorsed the EIA requirement for decades.[48] Most recently, the tribunal in the case of *Lopez-Goyne Family Trust v. Nicaragua* has interpreted provisions of the Dominican Republic–Central America–United States Free Trade Agreement (DR-CAFTA) as impliedly requiring an EIA from the investor.[49] The requirement of an EIA is expressly enshrined in numerous investment treaties and trade agreements,[50] including in the form prescribed by the Espoo Convention.[51]

As is equally explicit in the language of the Protocol's Article 34, investors shall comply with a general obligation to conduct an EIA "in accordance with the best international standards and practices and as required by domestic law" in the host State.[52]

2.1.4 Mitigation and Remediation of Harm

Article 31 of the ARSIWA relates to reparations. The accompanying commentary notes that an element "affecting the scope of reparation is the question of mitigation of damage" and that "[e]ven the wholly innocent victim of wrongful conduct is expected to act reasonably when confronted by the injury".[53] This principle is clearly established by the ICJ in the *Gabčíkovo–Nagymaros Project* case, where the Court found as follows:

> 80. [...] [Slovakia] stated that: 'It is a general principle of international law that a party injured by the non-performance of another contract party must seek to mitigate the damage he has sustained.' It would follow from such a principle that an injured State which has failed to take the necessary measures to limit

47 *Responsibilities and Obligations of States Sponsoring Persons and Entities with Respect to Activities in the Area* (ITLOS Advisory Opinion, 1 February 2011), para. 145.

48 *Maffezini v Spain* ICSID Case No. ARB/97/7, Award (13 Nov 2000), para. 67.

49 *The Lopez-Goyne Family Trust v. Nicaragua* ICSID Case No. ARB/17/44, Award (1 March 2023), para. 462.

50 See e.g., Chile–Malaysia Free Trade Agreement (2010), art 9.5; Colombia–Republic of Korea Free Trade Agreement (2013); EU–UK Trade and Cooperation Agreement (2020), art 393.

51 EC–Kazakhstan Cooperation Agreement (1995), art 54.

52 AfCFTA Investment Protocol, art 34(1)(c)-(d).

53 International Law Commission, 'Commentary on the Draft Articles on Responsibility of States for Internationally Wrongful Acts' (2001) UN Doc A/56/10, art 31, para. 11.

> the damage sustained would not be entitled to claim compensation for that damage which could have been avoided. While this principle might thus provide a basis for the calculation of damages, it could not, on the other hand, justify an otherwise wrongful act.[54]

Investment tribunals have equally recognised the duty to mitigate. In *Middle East Cement v. Egypt*, the tribunal noted in relevant part:

> 167. The duty to mitigate damages is not expressly mentioned in the [relevant treaty]. However, this duty can be considered to be part of the General Principles of Law which, in turn, are part of the rules of international law which are applicable in this dispute according to Art. 42 of the ICSID Convention.[55]

Investment agreements and model treaties involving the participation of African States have already featured provisions on the mitigation of harm in the environmental context.[56] For example, Article 13 of the Southern African Development Community (SADC) Model BIT[57] and Article 14 of the 2016 Morocco–Nigeria BIT[58] create specific mitigative obligations in the context

54 *Gabčíkovo–Nagymaros Project (Hungary/Slovakia)* [1997] ICJ Rep 7, para. 80.

55 *Middle East Cement v. Egypt*, ICSID Case No. ARB/99/6, Award (12 Apr 2002), para. 167. Further, in *AIG v. Kazakhstan* ICSID Case No. ARB/01/6, Award (7 Oct 2003), para. 10.6.4, the tribunal also noted that "[m]itigation of damages, as a principle, is applicable in a wide range of situations. It has been adopted in common law and in civil law countries, as well as in International Conventions and other international instruments [...]".

56 See AfCFTA Investment Protocol, art 34(1)(e).

57 SADC, 'Model Bilateral Investment Treaty Template with Commentary' (2012), art 13.4. <https://investmentpolicy.unctad.org/international-investment-agreements/treaty-files/2875/download> accessed 11 June 2023 notes: "Investors, their Investments and the Host State authorities shall apply the precautionary principle to their environmental impact assessment and to decisions taken in relation to a proposed investment, including any necessary mitigating or alternative approaches to the Investment, or precluding the Investment if necessary. The application of the precautionary principle by Investors and Investments shall be described in the environmental impact assessment."

58 Reciprocal Investment Promotion and Protection Agreement between Morocco and Nigeria (signed 3 December 2016), art 14(3) <https://investmentpolicy.unctad.org/international-investment-agreements/treaty-files/5409/download> accessed 12 April 2024, notes: "Investors, their investment and host state authorities shall apply the precautionary principle to their environmental impact assessment and to decisions taken in relation to a proposed investment, including any necessary mitigation or alternative approaches of the precautionary principle by investors and investments shall be described in the environmental impact assessment they undertake." The treaty further undertakes to specifically define both EIA ("the process used to predict the environmental consequences (positive or negative) of a plan, policy, program, or project prior to

of EIA, such that a duty of mitigation applies not only to the innocently injured but also expressly to the investor as well. Indeed, immediate mitigative measures by those actors present on the scene (often including the injuring wrongdoer) may be essential in minimising otherwise irreparable harms. Insofar as remediation is concerned, arbitral tribunals may be guided by Article 35 of the ARSIWA, according to which offending actors ought to "re-establish the situation which existed before the wrongful act was committed".[59] Compensation may be owed "for the damage caused [...] insofar as such damage is not made good by restitution".[60]

Under Article 34 of the Protocol, investors shall thus be bound to the mitigative and remediative responsibilities.

2.1.5 Obligation Not to Exploit Natural Resources to the Detriment of the Rights and Interests of the Host State and Local Communities

A right of public access to information, participation, and justice in environmental matters is firmly established in various conventions.[61] Although local communities often have much at stake in foreign investment initiatives and the disputes arising from them, these communities may seem "invisible under the current international investment agreement system".[62] This truth renders investment law sometimes indifferent to the great advances towards their protection under broader international law.

In one example, the ICCPR stipulates that no one shall be subjected to arbitrary or unlawful interference with privacy, family, or home.[63] Environmental degradation plainly may adversely affect the well-being of individuals and communities and constitute a serious and foreseeable violation of private

---

move forward with the proposed action") and Social Impact Assessment ("the process of assessing or estimating in advance the social consequences that are likely to follow from specific actions project development, particularly in the context of appropriate national, state or provincial environment policy legislation").

59 ARSIWA, art 35.

60 ARSIWA, art 36. See also Sec. III *infra*.

61 Convention on Access to Information, Public Participation in Decision-making, and Access to Justice in Environmental Matters (adopted 25 June 1998) 2161 UNTS 447, art 9; Regional Agreement on Access to Information, Public Participation, and Access to Justice in Environmental Matters in Latin America and the Caribbean (Escazú Agreement) (4 March 2018), art 8.

62 Nicolás Perrone, 'The "Invisible" Local Communities: Foreign Investor Obligations, Inclusiveness, and the International Investment Regime' (2019) 113 AJIL Unbound 16, 16–21.

63 International Covenant on Economic, Social and Cultural Rights (adopted 16 December 1966) 993 UNTS 3, art 17.

and family life.[64] Children – as part of local communities – hold special rights under international law. The UN Convention on the Rights of the Child (UNCRC) is the world's most extensively ratified treaty.[65] Article 24 of the UNCRC acknowledges that children have the right to the highest attainable standard of health and that States must consider environmental pollution risks when ensuring access to food and water.[66] Relatedly, Article 14(2)(h) of the African Charter on the Rights and Welfare of the Child also deals with Health and Health Services to be provided by member States to the Charter to children.[67] The UN Declaration on the Rights of Indigenous Peoples (UNDRIP) also expressly recognises indigenous peoples' right to the full enjoyment, collectively and as individuals, of all fundamental freedoms featuring in the Charter of the United Nations, the Universal Declaration of Human Rights, and international human rights law.[68] Further, the ILO Convention No. 169, titled the Indigenous and Tribal Peoples Convention, provides under its Article 7(4) that "[g]overnments shall take measures, in co-operation with the peoples concerned, to protect and preserve the environment of the territories they inhabit".[69]

By force of the Protocol's Article 34,[70] investors too are brought under the obligation not to impair the rights and interests of local communities or of the host State itself.[71]

---

64 Ibid., para. 8.12.

65 All countries have ratified the UNCRC, with the sole exception of the United States. See UN OHCHR, 'Ratification Status for CRC – Convention on the Rights of the Child' (UN OHCHR, updated) <https://tbinternet.ohchr.org/_layouts/15/TreatyBodyExternal/Treaty.aspx?Treaty=CRC> accessed 10 March 2023 (UNCRC).

66 UNCRC, art 24.

67 African Charter on the Rights and Welfare of the Child (adopted 11 July 1990), OAU Doc CAB/LEG/24.9/49, art 14(2)(h).

68 For the authoritative commentary on the Declaration, see M Weller and J Hohmann (eds), *The UN Declaration on the Rights of Indigenous Peoples: A Commentary* (OUP 2017).

69 Indigenous and Tribal Peoples Convention (adopted 27 June 1989) 1650 UNTS 383, art 7(4).

70 See AfCFTA Investment Protocol, art 34(2).

71 For lesser undertakings in earlier treaties, see Article 13.3 of the SADC ("Investors or their Investments shall make the environmental and social impact assessments: (a) public [including via the Internet] and (b) accessible to the local communities, or other areas with potentially affected interests, in an effective and sufficiently timely manner so as to allow comments to be made to the Investor, Investment and/or government prior to the completion of the Host State processes for establishing an Investment") and Brazil–Angola Agreement on Cooperation and Facilitation of Investment, Article 10, Annex 2 ("The investors and their investments shall strive to carry out the highest level possible of contributions to the sustainable development of the host State and the local community, by means of the adoption of a high degree of socially responsible practices, taking as a reference the voluntary principles and standards defined in Annex [X] – 'Corporate Social Responsibility'") (unofficial translation).

2.2 Other Standards in International Environmental Law

The obligations set out in Article 34 of the Protocol evoke other environmental standards existing in international law.

2.2.1 The Duty of Due Diligence

In the *Pulp Mills* case, the ICJ famously noted that "the principle of prevention, as a customary rule, has its origins in the due diligence that is required of a State in its territory" – the principle of prevention and the standard of due diligence are thus intrinsically wedded together.[72] By way of an emerging example in the investment law context, Article 7(3) of the 2019 Dutch Model BIT states the following:

> The Contracting Parties reaffirm the importance of investors conducting a due diligence process to identify, prevent, mitigate, and account for the environmental and social risks and impacts of its investment.[73]

Commentators have noted that "this provision appears to encourage investors to conduct due diligence to account for the wider impact of their protected investments" but that "[i]t is, however, unclear what consequences flow from the failure to exercise such due diligence".[74] Article 34 of the Protocol now stands in a position to dispel this uncertainty by attaching consequences for the investor's non-compliance.

2.2.2 The Duty to Cooperate

The duty to cooperate is one of the most significant norms of contemporary international environmental law.[75] Abiding by this duty is imperative to com-

72 *Pulp Mills on the River Uruguay* (*Argentina v. Uruguay*) [2010] ICJ Rep 14, para. 101.

73 Netherlands, 'Model Investment Agreement' (22 March 2019), art 7(3).

74 Kabir AN Duggal and Laurens H van de Ven, 'The 2019 Netherlands Model BIT: Riding the New Investment Treaty Waves' (2019) 35(3) Arbitration International 347.

75 United Nations Environment Programme, 'Cooperation in the Field of the Environment Concerning Natural Resources Shared by Two or More States' (Draft Decision, UNEP/GC/101, 1978). See also, e.g., *The South China Sea Arbitration* (*Philippines v. China*) PCA Case No 2013–19, Award (12 July 2016), para. 984 ("Article 197 of the [UN] Convention [on the Law of the Sea] requires States to cooperate on a regional basis to formulate standards and practices for the protection and preservation of the marine environment"); Rio Declaration on Environment and Development (adopted 14 June 1992) UN Doc A/CONF.151/26 (Vol I); Convention on Biological Diversity (5 June 1992) 1760 UNTS 79;

bating biodiversity loss and the impacts of excessive burning of fossil fuels. The ICJ noted in the *Pulp Mills* case that the obligation to consult included an obligation for Uruguay to provide Argentina with the results of an EIA prior to authorisation of the project.[76] The Court further found that Uruguay had violated certain procedural obligations, most notably the obligation to inform and consult Argentina on the very construction of the mills.[77] Such a duty is also recognised in investment treaties such as the EU–Japan Economic Partnership Agreement[78] and the UK–Japan Comprehensive Economic Partnership Agreement,[79] which underscore cooperation amongst the States party in order to promote a positive contribution of trade towards climate-resilient development.

2.2.3 The Principle of Preventing Significant Transboundary Harm

This principle mandates that States ensure activities carried out within their jurisdictions do not harm the environment or territory of other States.[80] The obligation concerns the prevention of harm exceeding a certain threshold of tolerability.[81] Several investment and free-trade agreements explicitly refer to the principle. Nearly three decades ago, the EC–Kazakhstan Cooperation Agreement called for "combating local, regional, and transboundary air and water pollution".[82] Many agreements have also affirmed the parties' commitment to the 1989 Basel Convention on the Control of Transboundary Movements of Hazardous Wastes and their Disposal[83] while the recent UK–Australia Free Trade Agreement recognises the importance of "imple-

United Nations Convention to Combat Desertification in Those Countries Experiencing Serious Drought and/or Desertification, Particularly in Africa (14 October 1994) 1954 UNTS 3; UNGA Res 3281 (XXIX) 'Charter of Economic Rights and Duties of States' (12 December 1974) UN Doc A/RES/29/3281, art 3.

76 *Pulp Mills on the River Uruguay (Argentina v. Uruguay)* [2010] ICJ Rep 14, para. 121.

77 Ibid., paras 111 and 122.

78 EU–Japan Economic Partnership Agreement (2018), art 16.4.

79 UK–Japan Comprehensive Economic Partnership Agreement (2020), art 16.4.

80 *For example, The South China Sea Arbitration (Philippines v. China)*, PCA Case No. 2013–19, Award (12 July 2016), para. 941; *Corfu Channel (UK v. Albania)* [1949] ICJ Rep 4.

81 See Arie Trouwborst, *Precautionary Rights and Duties of States* (Matrinus Nijhoff 2006) 44.

82 EC–Kazakhstan Cooperation Agreement (1995), art 54; see also EU–Turkmenistan Partnership and Cooperation Agreement (1998), art 53.

83 See, for example, Colombia–Ecuador–EU–Peru Trade Agreement (2012), art 270; Central America–EU Association Agreement (2012), art 287; ASEAN–Japan Comprehensive Economic Partnership Agreement (2008), art 16; EU–Korea Framework Agreement (signed 10 May 2010), art 23.

mentation of measures to reduce domestic and transboundary air pollution"[84] and the EU–Vietnam Framework Partnership and Cooperation Agreement specifically refers to "ozone depleting substances".[85]

2.2.4 The Polluter Pays Principle

The polluter pays principle establishes the requirement that the costs of pollution shall be borne by those responsible for causing it. As early as the *Trail Smelter* case of 1941, Canada was ordered to pay $78,000 as compensation to the U.S. where a smelter plant owned by a Canadian corporation emitted hazardous fumes (sulphur dioxide), causing damage to plant life, forest trees, soil, and crop yields across the border in Washington State over several years.[86] The polluter pays principle is enshrined in various binding[87] and non-binding[88] legal instruments. It is also echoed in Principles 22 and 16 of the Stockholm and Rio Declarations, respectively.[89] In the investment treaty context, the recently negotiated EU–UK Trade and Cooperation Agreement reaffirm the principle under its Article 393.[90]

2.3 The Scope for Climate Change Litigation

No discussion of contemporary international environmental law is complete without reference to climate change. In 2015, the Paris Agreement was reached, calling for the States to voluntarily adopt Nationally Determined Contributions for the reduction of carbon emissions, with the aim of holding

---

84 United Kingdom–Australia Free Trade Agreement (2021), art 22.9.

85 EU–Viet Nam Framework Partnership and Cooperation Agreement (2012), art 30(4)(b).

86 Russell Miller, 'Trail Smelter Arbitration' in Rudiger Wolfrum (ed), *Max Planck Encyclopedia of Public International Law* (OUP, 2007).

87 Rotterdam Convention on the Prior Informed Consent Procedure for Certain Hazardous Chemicals and Pesticides in International Trade (1998) 2244 UNTS 337; Stockholm Convention on Persistent Organic Pollutants (2001) 2256 UNTS 119; Convention on Cooperation for the Protection and Sustainable Use of the Danube River (1994) 1997 ATS 22.

88 See e.g., Protocol for the Protection of the Mediterranean Sea against Pollution from Land-Based Sources and Activities (adopted 17 May 1980) 1328 UNTS 105; Convention on Civil Liability for Damage Resulting from Activities Dangerous to the Environment (adopted 21 June 1993) 1993 ETS 150; International Convention on Oil Pollution Preparedness, Response and Co-operation (adopted 30 November 1990) 1891 UNTS 51.

89 UN Conference on the Human Environment, 'Stockholm Declaration' (16 June 1972) UN Doc A/CONF.48/14/Rev.1, principle 22; UN Conference on Environment and Development, 'Rio Declaration on Environment and Development' (3–14 June 1992) UN Doc A/CONF.151/26 (Vol I), annex I, principle 16.

90 See also EU–Georgia Association Agreement (signed 27 June 2014) [2014] OJ L261/4.

"the increase in the global average temperature to well below 2°C above pre-industrial levels" and pursuing efforts "to limit the temperature increase to 1.5°C" above pre-industrial levels.[91]

2.3.1 The Recent Advisory Opinions of International Courts and Tribunals regarding States' Obligations in Respect of Climate Change

In the past few years alone, three monumental climate change advisory opinions have been rendered by international courts and tribunals. These have shed further light on many of the obligations discussed above. These opinions will also inevitably have an impact on the conduct of investors. The import of these opinions in the context of corporate liability and investment arbitration is discussed below in reverse chronology of their occurrence.

2.3.1.1 The Opinion of the International Court of Justice (23 July 2025)

On 17 April 2023, following a resolution unanimously adopted by the UNGA, the ICJ undertook to clarify the climate obligations of States in consonance with seven international instruments.[92]

In 2025, the Court rendered a historic Advisory Opinion (endorsed by the UNGA in 2026).[93] It is one of the most significant developments in international law in recent times. It has been largely welcomed by scholars and academics.[94] However, when it comes to international investment arbitration

91 Paris Agreement (adopted 12 December 2015) 3156 UNTS 1, art 2. In their NDCs, countries communicate actions they will take to reduce their greenhouse gas emissions in order to reach the goals of the Paris Agreement. Countries also communicate in their NDCs actions they will take to build resilience to adapt to the impacts of climate change <https://unfccc.int/process-and-meetings/the-paris-agreement> accessed 18 March 2025. In the context of the United States, one of the world's largest polluters, see Mohit Khubchandani, 'The United States and the Paris Agreement on Climate Change' (2019) 22(1) Max Planck Yearbook of United Nations Law Online 70, 70–82.

92 These instruments are the UN Charter, Universal Declaration of Human Rights (UDHR), International Covenant on Civil and Political Rights (ICCPR), the International Covenant on Economic, Social and Cultural Rights (ICESCR), United Nations Framework Convention on Climate Change (UNFCCC), the Paris Agreement, and the United Nations Convention on the Law of the Sea (UNCLOS).

93 Obligations of States in Respect of Climate Change, Advisory Opinion, ICJ (23 July 2025); see also, UNGA Res. A/RES/80/263, adopted on 20 May 2026 <https://docs.un.org/en/A/80/L.65> accessed 3 July 2026.

94 Mohit Khubchandani and Jason Rudall, Counting the Cost of Climate Change: Hits, Misses and the Future of Environmental Compensation After the ICJ's Advisory Opinion, Opinio Juris, 13.02.2026 <https://opiniojuris.org/2026/02/13/counting-the-cost-of-climate-change-hits-misses-and-the-future-of-environmental-compensation-after-the-icjs-

and corporate liability, one might need to explore further than what appears to the naked eye to fully appreciate its considerable impact on the topics being discussed in this article.

On the one hand – especially in stark contrast to the high hopes that were set by the Inter-American Court of Human Rights (IACtHR) Advisory Opinion in the context of corporate liability, which was rendered just weeks before the ICJ Opinion[95] – the Court's Opinion may seem "underwhelming"[96] but upon inspection, it is not.

To critically discuss the impact of the Opinion, it may usefully be divided into what the Court did not say (and what may be inferred therefrom) and what it did say.

What the Court did not say:

If one only searched for the phrase investment arbitration or investment law in the 140-page Opinion, there appears to be just one singular mention. In that context too, the Court simply notes that "the most directly relevant applicable law consists of the Charter of the United Nations, the UNFCCC, the Kyoto Protocol, the Paris Agreement, UNCLOS, the ozone layer treaties, the Biodiversity Convention, the Desertification Convention" and additional customary and other rules.[97] It notes that such an analysis was "most directly relevant" while being without prejudice to "other rules of international law" including "international investment law".[98] Judge Cleveland, in her Separate Declaration – in a brief section dedicated to international investment law – seems not to entirely endorse this assessment by the Court of what is the most directly relevant law. She notes – as was also stressed by many participants at the hearing – "the potentially negative influence of international investment law on efforts taken by States to combat climate change".[99] A further observation she makes is of particular relevance for the regulation of investors' obligations in international law:

---

advisory-opinion/>; see also Maria Antonia Tigre, Maxim Bönnemann, and Antoine De Spiegeleir (eds.), The ICJ's Advisory Opinion on Climate Change, Verfassungsbooks, doi: 10.17176/20251210-183825-0 <https://verfassungsblog.de/wp-content/uploads/2025/12/Tigre-Bonnemann-DeSpiegeleir_TheICJsAdvisoryOpinionOnClimateChange_2025.pdf>.

95 See further in relation to the IACtHR Advisory Opinion.

96 Harro van Asselt, The Private Life of the ICJ Advisory Opinion on Climate Change, Völkerrechtsblog, 15.08.2025, doi: 10.17176/20250815–122331-0.

97 ICJ Climate Change Advisory Opinion (n 93), at para. 172.

98 Ibid, para. 173.

99 Separate Opinion, J. Cleveland, para. 21.

> 22. It is therefore important to underscore that [...] the climate system impose(s) significant responsibilities on States to adopt and implement appropriate environmental regulations to mitigate and adapt to climate change, including in co-operation with other States, while allowing States some discretion with respect to the particular regulatory paths that may be chosen. Accordingly, the **interpretation of investment instruments must be informed by States' obligations in respect of climate change under international law**, including the stringent due diligence standard to which States are bound in implementing such obligations.[100]

What the Court did say:

States' Duties of Due Diligence to Monitor the Acts of Private Actors in Their Jurisdiction

At the same time, it is important to clarify that even the Court's silence regarding investment arbitration does not mean – at least through an implied reference – that conduct of private actors is spared without regulation. The Court crucially notes that domestic mitigation obligations under Article 4(2) of the Paris Agreement includes States parties' obligations in carrying out due diligence by monitoring "activities carried out by private actors".[101] The Court also makes clear – in line with its settled jurisprudence in this regard[102] – that while the conduct of private actors is not directly attributable to States, "[...] a State may be responsible where [...] it has failed to exercise due diligence by not taking the necessary regulatory and legislative measures to limit the quantity of emissions caused by private actors under its jurisdiction".[103] From the perspective of investment arbitration, this lends support to States' rights in adopting their preferred domestic policies and rendering decisions in a manner compliant with the Opinion, thereby standing to impact upon the investor's suite of international claims.

States' Duties to Monitor Production, Licensing, and Subsidisation of Fossil Fuels

The above understanding may also be buttressed by the Court's recognition of burning of fossil fuels being a major contributor of climate change.[104] While

100 Ibid, para. 22.

101 ICJ Climate Change Advisory Opinion (n 93), para. 252. Also see paras 276, 403.

102 *Pulp Mills on the River Uruguay (Argentina v. Uruguay), Judgment* I.C.J. Reports 2010 (I) 79–80, para. 197.

103 ICJ Climate Change Advisory Opinion (n 93), para. 428.

104 Ibid., para. 72.

relying on IPCC reports, the Court adds that States ought to be mindful of activities of these industries in relation to "production, licensing and subsidizing of fossil fuels".[105] Any such failure would amount to an internationally wrongful act.[106] Notably, Judges Bhandari and Cleveland in their joint declaration – in a dedicated section – go further to elaborate on how there is a need for a stricter regulation of what States might authorise as acceptable fossil fuel production, licensing and subsidies through EIAs and such considerations being reflected in the NDCs.[107] This includes an assessment of downstream consequences of such activities in other jurisdictions.[108]

The Renewed 1.5°C Temperature Goal

Perhaps one of the most crucial and impactful observations by the Court in the Opinion is that the 1.5°C to 2°C (a huge margin in practical reality) of the Paris Agreement's regime – including, also, through the IPCC and other reports – has been firmly set and revised as "*1.5°C* [which now] *has become the scientifically based consensus target under the Paris Agreement*".[109] This would require corporate actors and investors to realign their policies. In particular, standards for private actors, such as the Science-Based Targets Initiative[110] would need to be amended for investors to pitch their climate credentials as supporting the 1.5°C target through their investments into prospective host States.

Causation

Finally, with respect to establishing causation, the Court has dismissed suggestions of practical impossibility owing to "the diffuse nature of climate change" by opining (in the context of State responsibility) that the prevailing standard requiring "a sufficiently direct and certain causal nexus" between an alleged wrongful action or omission and the alleged damage "is flexible

---

105 Ibid., para. 94.

106 Ibid., para. 427.

107 Joint Declaration of Judge Bhandari and Cleveland, para. 10.

108 Ibid., paras 11 & 12.

109 In para. 224 of the Opinion, the Court relies upon subsequent COP decisions through the 3rd and 5th CMA and notes that these are subsequent agreements under arts. 31(3)(a) of the VCLT to arts. 2 and 4 of the Paris Agreement. Accordingly, it decided that the "well below 2°C above pre-industrial levels as a goal" of 2015 is no more a practical reality or solution to combat climate change.

110 SBTi Corporate Net-Zero Standard (Version 1.2) (October 2024).

enough to address the challenges arising in respect of the phenomenon of climate change".[111]

∴

In sum, while the full Court may not have directly spoken to investment law, viewed in this light, the Opinion does tend to acknowledge that investment protection guarantees cannot override States' climate obligations – and it arguably lends support to States negotiating or re-negotiating investment treaties, including to expressly incorporate investor obligations on these subject-matters.

2.3.1.2 The Opinion of the Inter-American Court of Human Rights (3 July 2025)

On 9 January 2023, Chile and Colombia jointly requested an advisory opinion from the IACtHR to clarify the scope of State obligations in responding to the climate crisis under international human rights law, particularly with respect to the human right to a healthy environment as protected under the American Convention on Human Rights. Two and a half years later, and just 20-days before the ICJ Opinion, the IACtHR delivered an Opinion which is by far the most robust in relation to corporate liability and carries "significant implications for international investment law and arbitration".[112]

The Court follows the same line of reasoning as the ICJ in relation to due diligence obligations, while clarifying further that this includes States' "mitigation strategy, in particular with regard to foreign investment, finance and international trade".[113] It emphasises, in a dedicated section on "regulating behaviour of companies"[114] that companies must prevent their activities from causing or contributing to human rights violations.[115] Most significantly,

111 ICJ Climate Change Advisory Opinion (n 93), paras 434, 436 (citing *Certain Activities Carried Out by Nicaragua in the Border Area (Costa Rica v. Nicaragua), Compensation, Judgment* [2018] ICJ Rep 1, 26, para. 32*; Armed Activities on the Territory of the Congo (Democratic Republic of the Congo v. Uganda)*, (Reparations, Judgment) [2022] ICJ Rep 1, 48, para. 93).

112 Nicolò Andreotti, Climate Change and Investment Arbitration: The IACtHR's 2025 Advisory Opinion as a Regulatory Defense Tool, (Kluwer Arbitration Blog, 9 August 2025), <https://legalblogs.wolterskluwer.com/arbitration-blog/climate-change-and-investment-arbitration-the-iacthrs-2025-advisory-opinion-as-a-regulatory-defense-tool/> accessed 17 November 2025.

113 Inter-American Court of Human Rights Advisory Opinion (3 July 2025), para. 344.

114 Ibid., para. 345.

115 Ibid.

while relying on the United Nations Working Group on Business and Human Rights, the Court notes that "not only States, but also companies 'have obligations and responsibilities with regard to climate change and [its] impacts [...] on human rights.'"[116] This language is evocative of observations by the *Urbaser* arbitral tribunal that investors are not immune from becoming subjects of international law.[117]

Unlike the ICJ, the Inter-American Court enters the domain of what States must specifically do in this regard to fulfil their due diligence obligations. According to the Court, States should:[118]

> Call upon all ***companies domiciled or operating in their territory and jurisdiction*** to take effective measures to combat climate change and related human rights impacts;
>
> Enact legislation obliging companies to conduct human rights and climate change due diligence along the entire value chain;
>
> Require companies, state-owned and private, to disclose in an accessible manner the greenhouse gas emissions of their value chain;
>
> Require companies to take measures to reduce such emissions, and to address their contribution to climate and climate mitigation goals, throughout their operations;
>
> *Adopt a set of standards to discourage greenwashing and undue influence by companies in the political and regulatory sphere in this area, and support the actions of human rights defenders.*

The Court also notes that different private actors should have differing responsibilities in relation to "the risk to human rights that they pose".[119] "The Court also stresses the importance of the [...] role played by the different components of economic conglomerates and transnational corporations, so

116 Ibid., para. 346, *relying upon* Working Group on the issue of human rights and transnational corporations and other business enterprises, "Information Note on Climate Change and the Guiding Principles on Business and Human Rights, 2023" 5 <https://media.business-humanrights.org/media/documents/Information-Note-Climate-Change-and-UNGPs.pdf> accessed 17 November 2025.

117 *Urbaser* (n 15).

118 IACtHR Opinion (n 113), para. 347.

119 Ibid., para. 350.

that States can attribute legal responsibilities to parent companies, or companies that exercise control over others, according to the greenhouse gas emissions generated by their subsidiaries or by the companies they control."[120]

Most unequivocally – in relation to investment arbitration – the Court also found that:

> 351. ***States should also review their existing trade and investment agreements, as well as investor-state dispute settlement mechanisms***, to ensure that they do not limit or restrict efforts on climate change and human rights.[121] (Emphasis added)

In a manner perhaps more overt than the ICJ, the Inter-American Court has here offered direct support to the notion of investment treaty recalibration by the States.

2.3.1.3 The Opinion of the International Tribunal for the Law of the Sea (21 May 2024)

The ITLOS, on 12 December 2022, received a request for an advisory opinion from the Commission of Small Island States on Climate Change and International Law. The Commission requested clarification of obligations of States party to the United Nations Convention on the Law of the Sea (UNCLOS) (including under its Part XII) to prevent, reduce, and control pollution of the marine environment related to climate change impacts such as ocean warming, sea level rise, and ocean acidification caused by anthropogenic greenhouse gas emissions. The ITLOS rendered its advisory opinion on 21 May 2024, in which it concluded that "States Parties to the Convention have specific obligations under Article 194 of UNCLOS to take all necessary measures to prevent, reduce, and control marine pollution from anthropogenic GHG emissions and to endeavour to harmonize their policies in this connection."[122] The tribunal

---

120 Ibid., para. 350, *relying upon* the Report of the Special Representative of the Secretary-General on the issue of human rights and transnational and other business enterprises, John Ruggie, 'Guiding Principles on Business and Human Rights: Implementing the United Nations "Protect, Respect and Remedy" Framework' (21 March 2011) UN Doc A/HRC/17/31, Principle 13(b).

121 Ibid., para. 351.

122 *Request for an Advisory Opinion submitted by the Commission of Small Island States on Climate Change and International Law (Advisory Opinion)* ITLOS Case No 31 (21 May 2024), para. 243 <https://www.itlos.org/fileadmin/itlos/documents/cases/31/Advisory_Opinion/C31_Adv_Op_21.05.2024_orig.pdf> accessed 16 September 2024.

further found that Article 194, paragraph 1 of UNCLOS[123] imposes a due diligence standard on the States that is "stringent".[124]

In the context of corporate liability, the ITLOS Opinion reaches to a similar extent as that of the ICJ when it comes to due diligence obligations. On a simple search of this 153-page Opinion, the word "investment" finds no mention. However, the Tribunal does note – in the context of corporate liability – that the *Pulp Mills* test[125] propounded by the ICJ, ought to be respected.[126] Thus, Article 194(1) includes regulation of activities of private entities.[127] Then, the Tribunal further notes that the obligation under Article 194(2)[128] in relation to the phrase "activities under their jurisdiction or control" "refers to activities carried out by both public and private actors".[129] Further, the Tribunal makes clear that the obligation to conduct EIAs that concern "planned activity" includes those activities by "private entities".[130]

These observations are very crucial, especially in relation to the developing investment arbitration and law of the sea jurisprudence,[131] and stand to impact both off-shore and on-shore investments around the sea.

2.3.1.4 The African Court on Human and Peoples' Rights Is Next

On 9 May 2025, the Pan African Lawyers Union (PALU) also filed a similar request to the African Court of Human and Peoples' Rights, Arusha.[132]

123 Art. 194 (1) reads: States shall take, individually or jointly as appropriate, all measures consistent with this Convention that are necessary to prevent, reduce, and control pollution of the marine environment from any source, using for this purpose the best practicable means at their disposal and in accordance with their capabilities, and they shall endeavour to harmonize their policies in this connection.

124 Ibid., para. 258.

125 *Pulp Mills on the River Uruguay (Argentina v. Uruguay)*, Judgment, I.C.J. Reports 2010 (I), 79–80, para. 197.

126 ITLOS Climate Change Advisory Opinion (n 122) para. 235.

127 Ibid., para. 236.

128 Art. 194 (2) reads: States shall take all measures necessary to ensure that activities under their jurisdiction or control are so conducted as not to cause damage by pollution to other States and their environment, and that pollution arising from incidents or activities under their jurisdiction or control does not spread beyond the areas where they exercise sovereign rights in accordance with this Convention.

129 ITLOS Climate Change Advisory Opinion (n 122) para. 247.

130 Ibid., para. 358. See also para. 367 in this regard, in relation to the EIA obligation under art. 206.

131 *Pildegovics and North Star v. Norway: Peteris Pildegovics and SIA North Star v. Kingdom of Norway* (ICSID Case No. ARB/20/11) (2020).

132 Pan African Lawyers Union, Request for an Advisory Opinion (2 May 2025) <https://climatecasechart.com/wp-content/uploads/non-us-case-documents/2025/20250502_99025_petition.pdf> accessed 18 May 2025.

Observers had earlier noted that:

> [A]n advisory opinion … would be desirable insofar as the material scope of the Court's advisory jurisdiction extends both to the African Charter itself and to 'any other relevant human rights instrument'. Such an opinion would give the Court the opportunity to build on jurisprudence recently established by UN treaty bodies with respect to the International Covenant on Civil and Political Rights (Torres Strait Islanders Petition) in matters of climate change or the […] IACtHR 2017 advisory opinion on States' extraterritorial obligations to refrain from committing environmental harm (Advisory Opinion OC-23/17). It could even comment on the recent Human Rights Council (UN Human Rights Council 2021) and General Assembly (UN General Assembly 2022) resolutions affirming the human right to a clean, healthy and sustainable environment in light of climate change. Such resolutions reinforce Article 24 of the African Charter and may therefore enhance the prospects of successful climate litigation on the continent.[133]

∵

The African Court has now been invited to add its voice to the chorus – what is evident is that we have already seen a considerable expansion of public international law regimes tending to pave the way for better-understood obligations in relation to climate change. Investment tribunals have already held that investors should anticipate regulatory changes in volatile sectors such as the environment, especially when they emanate from constitutional or treaty-based rights.[134] Tribunals are also less likely to make a finding of arbitrariness if the regulatory measures relate to climate change obligations.[135] A degree of at least transitory uncertainty may be unavoidable,[136] and climate

---

133 Suedi & Fall, 'Climate Change Litigation before the African Human Rights System: Prospects and Pitfalls' (2023) XX J Journal of Human Rights Practice 1, 8.

134 *Tecmed v Mexico* ICSID Case No. ARB(AF)/00/2, Award (29 May 2003), para. 154; *Plama v. Bulgaria* ICSID Case No. ARB/03/24, Award (27 Aug 2008), para. 333; *Urbaser* (n 15) para. 248.

135 See, e.g., *Pildegovics* (n 131), para. 543.

136 *Lone Pine v. Canada* (ICSID Case No. UNCT/15/2), Award (25 Feb 2020), paras 623–24; *Red Eagle v. Colombia* (ICSID Case No. ARB/18/12), Award (12 Mar 2024), para. 309; *Montauk Metals v. Colombia* (ICSID Case No. ARB/18/6), Award (21 Aug 2023), para. 937; *Gabriel Resources v. Romania* (ICSID Case No. ARB/15/31), Award (15 Dec 2023), para. 1320; *Discovery Global v. Slovak Republic* (ICSID Case No. ARB/21/30), Award (18 Mar 2024), para. 629.

change is one such dynamic area of the law. Further, all applicable laws may now be analysed in light of these forward-looking advisory opinions.

Thus, these opinions of international courts and tribunals may assist in further delineating the bounds of State obligations in respect of harms caused by climate change, presenting a useful aid in guiding also the course of investor liability under Article 34 of the AfCfTA Protocol and other emerging international investment instruments.

2.3.2 Moving beyond Advisory Opinions: Judgments of Regional Human Rights Courts concerning Environment and Climate Change

While there is some jurisprudence from municipal systems that deals with the subject-matter of climate change, the present analysis is limited to State responsibility emanating out of climate-induced harms, and what the reciprocal obligations on investors could look like. For this purpose, recent jurisprudence from regional human rights courts is instructive. By way of example, on 9 April 2024, while the European Court of Human Rights (ECHR) did not, in *Verein Klima Seniorinnen Schweiz and Others v. Switzerland* [*GC*][137] rule in favour of the claimants for procedural reasons, it nonetheless crucially found in favour of reimagining how causality thresholds could be lowered and noted the following in the context of climate change:

> [T]he causal link between the acts or omissions on the part of State authorities in one country, and the harm, or risk of harm, arising there, was necessarily more tenuous and indirect compared to that in the context of local sources of harmful pollution. Furthermore, from the perspective of human rights, the essence of the relevant State duties in the context of climate change related to the reduction of the risks of harm for individuals. Conversely, failures in the performance of those duties entailed an aggravation of the risks involved, although the individual exposures to such risks would vary in terms of type, severity and imminence, depending on a range of circumstances. Accordingly, in this context, issues of individual victim status or the specific content of State obligations could not be determined on the basis of a *strict conditio sine qua non requirement.*[138]

---

137 *Verein KlimaSeniorinnen Schweiz and Others v. Switzerland* App No 53600/20 (ECtHR, 9 April 2024).

138 Ibid.

Likewise, the recently decided *Duarte Agostinho v. Portugal* case concerned several climate change-related claims by six Portuguese nationals relating to "a breach of Articles 2, 3, 8, and 14 of the Convention owing to the existing and serious future, impacts of climate change imputable to the respondent States, and specifically those in relation to heatwaves, wildfires, and smoke from wildfires, which affected their lives, well-being, mental health, and the amenities of their homes".[139] However, the case was ultimately dismissed on admissibility grounds relating to the non-exhaustion of domestic remedies.[140]

While these cases were thus not decided on the merits in favour of the claimants, they nonetheless indicate a positive trend in favour of climate litigation and arbitration instituted against States at the regional level.

A landmark decision in this context was rendered by the IACtHR in the case of *La Oroya v. Peru*,[141] where the Court has perhaps set a path towards the process of evolving *jurisprudence constante* for climate reparations from toxic industrial pollution.[142] La Oroya is a small town in the heart of the Peruvian Andes; for more than 100 years, an industrial smelter exposed La Oroya to "extreme levels of toxic pollution".[143] Since 1922, the metallurgical facility Complejo Metalúrgico de La Oroya has been operating in the city.[144] In this timeline, its metallurgical activities affected 30,200 hectares of vegetation, as well as the air, soil, and water in La Oroya, causing it to be one of the 10 most contaminated cities in the world.[145] The town is so polluted that one study by Peru's Ministry of Health in 2005 found that 99.9 percent of children under six years old had high lead levels in their blood.[146]

The following are important takeaways from the judgment:

- ***Collective Climate Reparations***: The judgment gives momentum for collective reparations (such as to the inhabitants of the La Oroya town). This includes, *inter alia*, environmental remediation of the surrounding

139 *Duarte Agostinho and Others v. Portugal and 32 Others* App No 39371/20 (ECtHR, 9 April 2024), para. 3.

140 Ibid., para. 231.

141 *Case of the Inhabitants of La Oroya v. Peru* (Preliminary Objections, Merits, Reparations, and Costs) IACtHR (27 November 2023).

142 EarthJustice, 'La Oroya v. Peru: Historic Precedent on Human Rights and the Environment' (2024) <https://earthjustice.org/experts/jacob-kopas/la-oroya-v-peru-historic-precedent-on-human-rights-and-the-environment> accessed 16 February 2025.

143 Ibid.

144 La Oroya (n 141), para. 67.

145 Ibid., para. 76.

146 Human Rights Watch, 'Landmark Court Ruling Upholds Right to Healthy Environment' (2024) <https://www.hrw.org/news/2024/04/18/landmark-court-ruling-upholds-right-healthy-environment> accessed 16 February 2025.

ecosystem,[147] comprehensive and specialised health care for any inhabitant who presents symptoms,[148] and support for relocating inhabitants who wish to do so.[149]

- ***Guidelines for Mining Industries***: The mining industry is a considerable contributor to climate change. The judgment also gives guidelines for the mining industry, including aligning air quality standards with international standards,[150] guaranteeing that mining companies adhere to the UN Guiding Principles on Business and Human Rights,[151] and creating an information system that proactively provides updated air and water quality data in mining areas.[152]
- ***Causality Emanating from Air Pollution***: Air pollution is the biggest contributor to climate change. However, given that it happens over a prolonged period of time, it is difficult to establish direct causal links. When it comes to reparations for human health, it becomes cumbersome, since many communities lack access to proper health care and diagnostic tests, as some conditions, such as cancer, can be latent and undetected for years.[153] Taking stock of all these considerations and balancing them, the Court held that it was sufficient to show that an exposure to pollution created a significant health risk, without having to prove that the exposure caused a concrete condition or disease.[154] This approach – according to the Court – is in line with the precautionary principle, such that a lack of scientific certainty regarding risks cannot be an excuse for failing to adopt measures to protect public health.[155]
- ***Business and Human Rights Obligations***: While establishing the right to a clean and healthy environment as a *jus cogens* norm,[156] the Court noted that the effects of environmental contamination fall disproportionately on individuals.[157] Thus, States have attendant responsibilities, including to legislate that businesses must respect human rights and act with due dili-

147 La Oroya (n 141), para. 351.
148 Ibid., para. 348.
149 Ibid., para. 355.
150 Ibid., para. 346.
151 Ibid., para. 352.
152 Ibid., para. 354.
153 EarthJustice, (n 142).
154 La Oroya (n 141), para. 204.
155 Ibid., para. 207.
156 Ibid., para. 129.
157 Ibid., paras 134–141.

> gence, regardless of their size, sector, operational context, ownership, or structure.[158]

One author notes that the eco-centric approach taken by the Court in this case, as well as its discussion on the *jus cogens* status of the right to a clean and healthy environment, opens possibilities for future developments both within the Inter-American system and beyond it.[159] The impact of this judgment – as a corollary – stands to be felt in the realm of international investment law as well.[160]

In respect to the La Oroya saga, it must be noted that its proliferation of numerous parallel proceedings spanning over many years serves to showcase the potential utility of resolving such disputes in a unitary forum – perhaps an international arbitral forum empowered to order damages to victims.

2.3.3 The Impact of International Climate Change Law on International Investment Arbitration and Ensuing Investor Obligations

We have concluded the previous section with some food for thought as to how climate change obligations – traditionally incumbent upon States in the inter-State litigation and regional human rights courts contexts – may be transposed to investment law and, in particular, investor obligations. This section evinces how that might occur. To achieve the goals of the Paris Agreement, the United Nations Intergovernmental Panel on Climate Change (IPCC) urged States to take significant and rapid measures to prompt changes in virtually all fields of economic activity.[161] As a corollary, this translated into such States'

---

158 Ibid., paras. 109–111.

159 Patricio Trincado Vera, 'The Right to a Healthy Environment in *La Oroya v. Peru*: A Landmark Judgement of the IACtHR' (Opinio Juris, 25 May 2024) <https://opiniojuris.org/2024/05/25/the-right-to-a-healthy-environment-in-la-oroya-v-peru-a-landmark-judgement-of-the-iacthr/> accessed 16 February 2025.

160 K.K. Adnan, '*La Oroya v Peru* and *Renco v. Peru* (*II*): Prospects and Challenges of Regime Interaction and Cross-Fertilisation' Transnational Dispute Management (2024). See also José Saldaña, 'People from *La Oroya v Peru*, Inter-American Court of Human Rights: How Effective Is International Law to Protect the Environment in Extractive Contexts?' (EJIL: Talk!, 22024) <https://www.ejiltalk.org/people-from-la-oroya-vs-peru-inter-american-court-of-human-rights-how-effective-is-international-law-to-protect-the-environment-in-extractive-contexts/> accessed 17 February 2025.

161 Joeri Rogelj et al., 'Mitigation Pathways Compatible with 1.5°C in the Context of Sustainable Development' in IPCC (eds), *Global Warming of 1.5°C* (Cambridge University Press, 2018); Keywan Riahi et al., 'Mitigation Pathways Compatible with Long-Term Goals' in IPCC (eds), *Climate Change 2022: Mitigation of Climate Change: Contribution of Working Group III to the Sixth Assessment Report of the Intergovernmental Panel on Climate Change* (Cambridge University Press, 2022).

obligations under economic treaties regulating activities that contribute significantly to climate change.

As a result, since Paris, the world has begun to see a new age of bilateral and multilateral investment treaties having reference to the Agreement.[162] Many investment agreements recognise and reaffirm the parties' commitment to the UNFCCC and the Paris Agreement specifically.[163] Within the UNFCCC framework, parties also engage in information-sharing regarding carbon pricing, emissions trading, and the promotion of energy efficiency[164] as well as addressing deforestation and forest degradation.[165] The recent EU–UK Trade and Cooperation Agreement specifically refers to the targeted threshold of temperature increases not exceeding 1.5°C above pre-industrial levels.[166]

Suzanne Spears has noted that "[i]mplementing the IPCC's recommendations will necessarily involve a wide array of governmental regulations, some of which will significantly redefine the scope of previously authorised permissible activities and property rights in industries that involve high greenhouse gas (GHG) emissions or the destruction of carbon sinks" and that "[s]ome of these regulations will eliminate the economic viability of proprietary interests and acquired rights of private sector investors".[167] It is not difficult to foresee a possible collision course, as new regulations may impact upon investor rights while also giving rise to investor obligations.

Several possible scenarios may be mentioned in this context. States may defend against investment treaty claims on the basis that they acted *bona fide* in pursuit of the goals of the Paris Agreement.[168] Some will also argue that the legitimacy of their climate mitigation measures has been affirmed not only by the 194 States Parties to the Paris Agreement and the IPCC but also by the courts and tribunals that have interpreted and applied States' human rights and other obligations in line with new scientific evidence and a growing understanding of the threats that climate change poses to the rights of present and future generations.[169] They may assert that international

162 See, for example, EU–Singapore Free Trade Agreement (2018), art 12.6.

163 See e.g., EU–Japan Economic Partnership Agreement (2018), art 16.4.

164 See e.g., EU–Viet Nam Free Trade Agreement (2019), art 13.6.

165 See e.g., United Kingdom–Australia Free Trade Agreement (2021), art 22.5.

166 EU–UK Trade and Cooperation Agreement (2020), art 401.

167 Suzanne Spears, 'Chapter 9: Reconciling Human Rights and Investor Rights: The Case of Climate Change', in Annette Magnusson and Anja Ipp (eds), *Investment Arbitration and Climate Change* (Kluwer Law International 2023) 208.

168 Ibid.

169 Ibid.

investment treaties must be interpreted and applied, and any compensation be calculated, to reflect this ongoing evolution in human rights law.[170]

Thus, the issue may also impact upon quantum of any compensation awarded. The applicable test is whether a claimant "materially contributed" to its alleged injury by some "wilful or negligent" act or omission, which must be considered in "the determination of reparation".[171] Tribunals have taken account of an investor's misconduct or poor business judgment that contributed to its injury, reducing the compensation amount by 25% or more.[172] An author notes that in *RWE v. Netherlands*, a suspended fossil fuel phase-out (FFPO) dispute, the respondent highlighted how the claimants had wilfully abandoned their 2006 commitment to develop carbon capture and sequestration (CCS), thereby assuming the risk of injury from an eventual decision to reduce emissions by phasing out coal power.[173]

As for harms that are caused by investor conduct: as the current ISDS system stands, an actionable path for affirmative host State claims might be in the form of environmental counterclaims.[174] In this context, Prof. Maxi Scherer and Clara Reichenbach have recently noted that "[f]oreseeable climate-related counterclaims are likely to fall into two main categories – mitigation and adaptation":

> First, a host State may raise a counterclaim that the investor has failed to mitigate climate change in carrying out its investment. For instance, an investor may have exceeded emissions limits, failed to offset greenhouse gas emissions, or neglected to measure and report its emissions to regulatory authorities. Mitigation counterclaims depend on pre-existing obligations to take such measures

170 Ibid.

171 ARSIWA, art 39.

172 *Copper Mesa Mining Corporation v. Republic of Ecuador* PCA Case No. 2012–02, Award, paras. 6.91–6.102 (15 March 2016).

173 Oliver Hailes, 'Chapter 6: Valuation of Compensation in Fossil Fuel Phase-Out Disputes', in Annette Magnusson and Anja Ipp (eds), *Investment Arbitration and Climate Change* (Kluwer Law International 2023) 158–159, placing reliance upon *RWE AG and RWE Eemshaven Holding II BV v Kingdom of the Netherlands*, ICSID Case No. ARB/21/4, Respondent's Counter-Memorial, paras. 1169–1178 (5 September 2022) [RWE, Counter-Memorial].

174 In the context of the AfCFTA Investment Protocol, it may also be noted that the treaty includes a provision on denial of benefits, stating as follows: "A State Party may at any time deny an investor of another State Party and the investment of such investor the benefits of this Protocol if [...] an investor or investment has committed a breach of a specific binding obligation under Chapter 5 of this Protocol." AfCFTA Investment Protocol, art. 5(1)(g).

> [...]. Second, an investor, through its activities, may damage the environment in a manner that undermines the capacity of the host State to adapt to climate change.[175]

The challenges faced in the context of climate change are considerable. The States may wish to draw inspiration from other tools of public international law – treaties, customary law, general principles, and subsidiary sources – as well as scientific information from recognised bodies such as the IPCC to incorporate certain presumptions, particularly to ease the evidentiary burdens of establishing causation in the context of arbitrations invoking responsibility for climate change harms.

3 Enforcing Investors' Environmental and Climate Change Obligations via the Forthcoming Dispute Settlement Annex to the AfCFTA Investment Protocol: A Proposal

To be successful, host State claims and counterclaims for environmental harms need the requisite tools. Turning to procedural implementation of substantive norms and prescriptions, the example of the AfCFTA Investment Protocol is once again useful. Its text, as adopted in 2023, provides as follows:

> Rules and Procedures governing Dispute Prevention, management and resolution of disputes covered by the Protocol on Investment Settlement shall be set out in an Annex to this Protocol which shall be negotiated after the adoption of this Protocol by the Assembly of Heads of State and Governments and finalized within 12 months at the latest from the date of adoption of this Protocol.[176]

As early as 2019, in a joint report of the African Union, the African Development Bank, the UN Economic Commission for Africa, and the United Nations Conference on Trade and Development (UNCTAD) (titled *Assessing Regional Integration in Africa* or ARIA IX), this quartet of institutions endorsed the adoption of investor obligations (including environmental obligations), accompanied by arbitral remedies for the host State and its nationals, as one of four pillars of the anticipated Protocol:

175 Maxi Scherer and Clara Reichenbach, 'Chapter 5: Climate-Related Counterclaims in International Investment Arbitration', in Annette Magnusson and Anja Ipp (eds), *Investment Arbitration and Climate Change* (Kluwer Law International 2023) 106.

176 AfCFTA Investment Protocol, art 46(2).

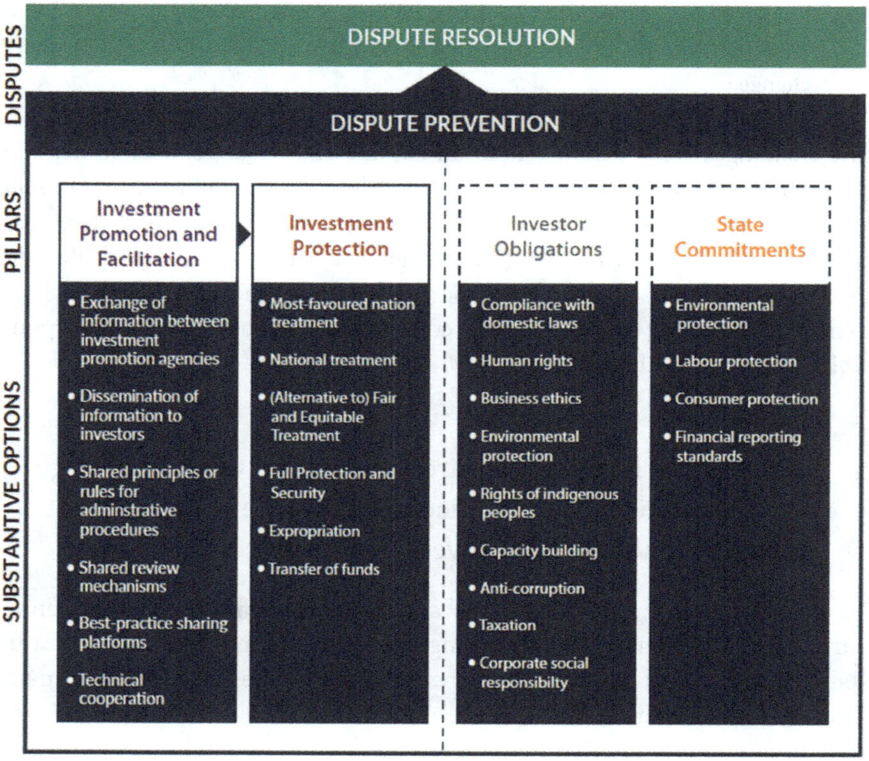

FIGURE 5.2 United Nations Economic Commission for Africa, African Union, and UNCTAD,"Next Steps for the African Continental Free Trade Area: Assessing Regional Integration in Africa IX" (July 2019), 187

The authors chose the following words:

> The international investment regime historically imposed obligations only on host States, not on private investors (Paulsson, 1995). However, as underscored by the [Pan-African Investment Code], [international investment agreements] may serve as vehicles for investor rights and also for their obligations, which could rebalance the regime. Investor obligations can be a source for claims against transgressing investors and for counterclaims by defending States. The

right to initiate proceeding may be bestowed upon the [host] State, its nationals or both (Amado, Kern and Rodriguez, 2017).[177]

This proposition encompasses both the substantive and procedural dimensions. The textual enfranchisement of investor obligations within the body of the Protocol itself has now been achieved.[178] In that sense, the promulgation of ***substantive rules*** is a *fait accompli* in the already-existing treaty instrument.[179] The States now seek ***procedural implementation*** via the vehicle of

177 United Nations Economic Commission for Africa, African Union & UNCTAD, 'Next Steps for the African Continental Free Trade Area: Assessing Regional Integration in Africa IX' (July 2019) 198 (emphasis added). The referenced works are Jan Paulsson, 'Arbitration without Privity', ICSID Review: Foreign Investment Law Journal 10(2) (1995) 232–257, and Jose Daniel Amado, Jackson Shaw Kern & Martin Doe Rodriguez, *Arbitrating the Conduct of International Investors* (Cambridge University Press, 2018). See also, for example, UNGA, 'Possible reform of investor–State dispute settlement (ISDS): multiple proceedings and counterclaims' (22 January 2020) UN Doc A/CN.9/WG.III/WP.193, para. 41 (stating that the Working Group III on Investor–State Dispute Settlement Reform "may wish to consider formulating provisions on investor obligations which would form the basis for a State's counterclaims" and that such obligations "may relate to the protection of human rights and the environment, compliance with domestic law, measures against corruption and the promotion of sustainable development") and note 26 (stating that the Working Group "may wish to consider whether the framework for counterclaims by respondent States could be expanded to allow for claims by third parties against investors") and UNGA, 'Report of Working Group III (Investor–State Dispute Settlement Reform) on the work of its thirty-seventh session (New York, 1–5 April 2019) UN Doc A/CN.9/970, paras. 31, 34–35.

178 As foreshadowed by the ARIA IX report and attested throughout this volume, the Protocol sets out in its Chapter 5 a slew of investor obligations which are not confined to the environmental realm alone. The foundation for their enforcement is thus now well in place. For example, the Protocol's Article 37 embodies an anti-corruption rule upon investors, in language that tracks the substantive proscription of the United Nations Convention against Corruption (UNCAC). See Protocol, art. 37 ("*Anti-Corruption*"). Thus, "[b]y calibrated engineering of international investment instruments; the UNCAC's proscription of corruption may be rendered directly applicable in international arbitration, and thereby requisitioned into the service of corruption's many victims". JD Amado, JS Kern, and MD Rodriguez, "Elevating Corruption to an International Tort" in J Ho and M Sattorova (eds), *Investors' International Law* (Bloomsbury, 2021). See also Chapter 6 in this volume.

179 It must be noted that, even in the absence of express treaty enfranchisement, a considerable body of jurisprudence regarding investor obligations has already emerged in the context of host State counterclaims. As seen above, in the case of *Urbaser* (n 15), that tribunal opined that "international law accepts corporate social responsibility as a standard of crucial importance for companies operating in the field of international commerce" and that "[t]his standard includes commitments to comply with human rights in the framework of those entities' operations conducted in countries other than the country of their seat or incorporation" and that "it can no longer be admitted that

the envisaged dispute settlement Annex. Section III of this Chapter now offers the theoretical basis and textual tool for achieving that end, in the manner earlier envisaged by ARIA IX, where such might be desired by the treaty-makers. In short, such may be realised by joining the substantive principles of international environmental law to the procedural mechanisms for arbitrating the conduct of international investors.

With regard to access, the evident candidates for *locus standi* are those nationals of the host State who suffer injury flowing from the investor's unlawful acts, as well as the host State itself. One must examine the Protocol's enumerated *investor obligations* in order to properly ascertain the identity of the corresponding *right-holder* (or right-holders). The first would seem, by its nature, to attach uniquely to natural persons, i.e., host State nationals. As seen, Article 34(1)(a) of the Protocol stipulates that "[i]nvestors and their investments" shall "respect the right to a clean, healthy and sustainable environment, as reflected in Article 24 of the African Charter [on] Human and Peoples' Rights, and the Resolution of the United Nations General Assembly A/RES/76/300 ('The human right to a clean, healthy and sustainable environment')".[180] Because this substantive obligation upon investors is explicitly framed in terms of a human right, it would seem to demand that a corresponding right of action be created in host State nationals as the relevant right-holders.

As for the remaining obligations set out under Article 34 of the Protocol, while they are equally woven from the thread of international norms traditionally binding upon States at international law, their reach too is extended by effect of the treaty instrument such that they be expressly applied to private parties, namely foreign investors and their investments.[181] Unlike the first one, these obligations are not definitionally linked or otherwise reserved to the protection of any single category of injured party; their breach may cause injury to either individuals (e.g., agricultural impacts causing loss of profits) or the host State itself (e.g., pollution to public waterways requiring remedi-

---

companies operating internationally are immune from becoming subjects of international law". *Urbaser* (n 15), para. 1195. In the case of *Aven and others v Costa Rica* (n 20), the tribunal found that "[i]t is true that the enforcement of environmental law is primarily to the States, but it cannot be admitted that a foreign investor could not be subject to international law obligations in this field". *Aven* (n 20), paras. 737. The *Aven* tribunal went further still, notably leaving open the question of whether host States might claim unilaterally against investors before an international tribunal under Article 10, Section B of DR-CAFTA. *Aven* (n 20), paras. 735–736.

180 AfCFTA Investment Protocol, art 34(1)(a). See also Sec. II *supra*.

181 See Sec. II *supra*.

ation). Indeed, the last one expressly extends its protection to both.[182] Thus, the obligations match to both public and private corresponding claimants.

The fitting resolution lies in access to justice for the victims of environmental harm. It might be said that the following three elements form the common core of extra-contractual liability across diverse legal traditions:

i. the respondent has committed or authorised the act of breach (or perhaps failed to take reasonable steps to prevent it);
ii. the claimant has suffered damage; and
iii. there is a causal link between the act (or omission) and the damage.

It is, of course, essential to first establish the wrongfulness of the act and also that the putative claimant or claimants have incurred injury. With respect to establishing causation, it may be argued that arbitral tribunals should apply a lower standard of proof concerning environmental harms.[183] By way of example, in 2022, the ICJ, in its reparations judgment (including environmental compensation) in *Armed Activities on the Territory of the Congo*, emphasised flexibility in the standard of proof required when a long time had lapsed since the injurious activity (war in that case) had occurred (over a period of five years from 1998 to 2003).[184] The ICJ has expressly found in the *Certain Activities Carried Out by Nicaragua in the Border Area* case that "damage to the environment, and the consequent impairment or loss of the ability of the environment to provide goods and services, is compensable under international law".[185] In the context of climate change, the Committee on the Rights of the Child has found in *Sacchi et al v. Argentina* that the collective nature of climate change causation does not absolve a State from responsibility for harms caused by emissions originating within its territory.[186] These principles regarding causation have now been recognized by the ICJ in

182 See Protocol, art 34(2) (requiring that "[i]nvestors shall not exploit or use natural resources to the detriment of the rights and interests of the Host State and local communities"); see also Sec. II *supra*.

183 As noted by Judge Christopher Greenwood in his Separate Opinion in the *Pulp Mills Case* (when comparing environmental harms to genocide), *Pulp Mills Case* (n 46), Sep Op (Greenwood), para. 26.

184 *Armed Activities on the Territory of the Congo (Democratic Republic of the Congo v. Uganda) (Reparations, Judgment) [2022] ICJ Rep, paras 120–26.*

185 *Certain Activities Carried Out by Nicaragua in the Border Area (Costa Rica v. Nicaragua) (Compensation, Judgment) [2018] ICJ Rep, para. 42.*

186 UN Committee on the Rights of the Child, *Sacchi et al v. Argentina* (Decision) (22 September 2021) UN Doc CRC/C/88/D/104/2019, para. 10.10.

its July 2025 Advisory Opinion, and these precepts may be applied by analogy to the investor; indeed, that is what Article 34 requires.

A question might be raised as to what precisely is the applicable law of reparations in the instance of claims for an investor's environmental breach. The standard generally recognised in international law (full reparation per the *Chorzów Factory* judgment of the inter-war Permanent Court of International Justice and as reflected in the ARSIWA) is traditionally reserved for representing that measure of compensation owed for wrongful State conduct. If needed, the standard may readily and permissibly be adapted to other permutations of claimants and respondents by *lex specialis*, namely the Protocol itself, in the form of the dispute settlement Annex.[187] Victims of environmental harm may seek judgment (in the form of an arbitral award that declares a finding of wrongful acts) and accompanying compensation for damage, with the precise measure to be determined under application of the full reparation rule by a learned arbitral tribunal.

Thus, where jurisdiction *ratione personae* is properly conferred, an arbitral tribunal established under the Protocol might serve to order monetary compensation or other relief for injury against offending foreign investors. Acts of environmental breach lay a basis for liability to those who would bring claims for harm flowing from the injurious acts. By firmly establishing an international forum to adjudicate such liability, the Annex might better elevate environmental breach toward the status of an internationally justiciable delict.

The liable party (or parties) may include an "investment" enterprise or, alternatively, an intermediary or ultimate beneficial owner of the "investment" (i.e., an "investor").[188] Jurisdiction may be attained by the crafting of

187 If the drafters should prefer a slightly higher degree of specificity in setting out the bounds of qualifying injury, a useful guide might consider that categories of compensable harm shall include "material damage, loss of profits, and non-pecuniary loss". See Civil Law Convention, art 3(2).

188 The Protocol contains an enterprise-based definition of "investment" which is stated to mean "an enterprise or company […] which is established, acquired, or expanded in conformity with the laws and regulations of a Host State by an investor which maintains substantial business in the territory of that Host State" and which enterprise "may possess assets". Protocol, art. 1. In its scope of application, the Protocol provides that it "sets out the rights and obligations for State Parties, investors, and investments" while applying to "all investments of investors of State Parties". Ibid., art 3(1),(2). "Investor" is meanwhile defined to mean "a natural person, who is a national of a State Party in accordance with its laws and regulations, who has made an investment in the territory of another State Party" or "a legal or juridical person, in accordance with the definition of the legal or juridical person of the Home State in this article, that has made an investment in the territory of the Host State". Ibid., art 1.

calibrated treaty text such that investor consent is obtained as a pre-condition to admission or establishment of an investment or as a pre-condition to the bringing of any claim for breach of the standards of investment protection (**Option I**).[189] However, allowing the investor a unique privilege of arbitral initiation gives rise to a residual asymmetry; the better approach is to obtain treaty jurisdiction over the investor by the simple fact of admission or establishment of the investment *ab initio* (**Option II**).[190] The investor's offer of arbitration may concurrently be extended to host State nationals as non-party beneficiaries of the instrument, in a manner similar to the position of investors under the "standing offer" of thousands of contemporary investment agreements.[191]

189 In this model, the investor must give his express consent to arbitration of the environmental obligations as a condition to issuance of a requisite investment authorisation or as a necessary procedural step in constituting an arbitral tribunal to hear his own claims. See JD Amado, JS Kern, and MD Rodriguez, *Arbitrating the Conduct of International Investors* (Cambridge University Press 2018) 87–90 and Annex, Model 6 ("Contingent Consent Clause").

190 See Ibid., 90–93 and Model 7 ("Jurisdiction without Privity"); see also the Netherlands–Indonesia Agreement on Economic Cooperation (with Protocol and Exchanges of Letters dated 17 June 1968) (signed 7 July 1968, entered into force on 17 July 1971), 799 UNTS 13, art 11 ("[t]he Contracting Party in the territory of which a national of the other Contracting Party makes or intends to make an investment, shall assent to any demand on the part of such national, and any such national shall comply with any request of the former Contracting Party to submit, for conciliation or arbitration, to [ICSID] any dispute that may arise in connection with the investment") and the Declaration of the Government of the Democratic and Popular Republic of Algeria concerning the settlement of claims by the Government of the United States of America and the Government of the Islamic Republic of Iran (19 January 1981), art II. By according to such a treaty, the investor's home State exercises a sovereign power to compel its nationals to the jurisdiction of an international tribunal.

191 The Hague Rules on Business and Human Rights Arbitration, substantially derived from the UNCITRAL Arbitration Rules, offer a thoroughly modern and progressive body of procedural rules well-suited to this purpose. City of The Hague and Center for International Legal Cooperation, *The Hague Rules on Business and Human Rights Arbitration*, (launched 12 December 2019). It is noted that "[t]he characterization of the dispute as relating to business and human rights is not necessary for jurisdiction where all the parties to the arbitration have agreed to settle a dispute under [the Hague] Rules". Ibid., art 1. The PCA's 2001 Optional Rules for Arbitration of Disputes Relating to Natural Resources and/or the Environment also offer a viable option and are equally available even in disputes between private parties. In similar manner, under art. 1(1) of those Rules, "[t]he characterization of the dispute as relating to natural resources and/or the environment is not necessary for jurisdiction where all the parties have agreed to settle a specific dispute" under said Rules.

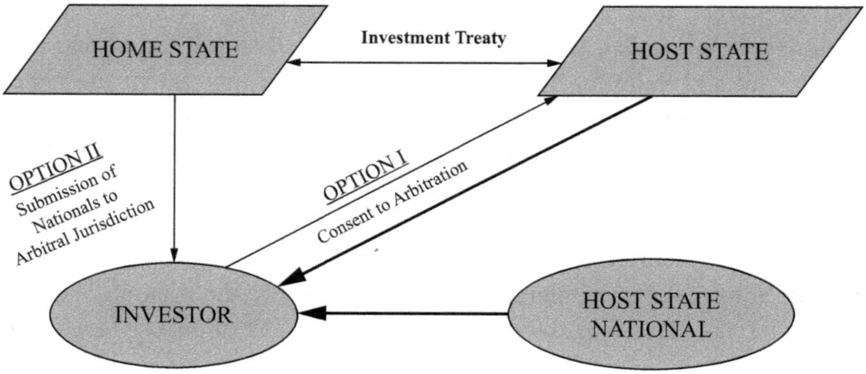

FIGURE 5.3 Obtaining Jurisdiction over the Investor.

A text for inclusion into the dispute settlement Annex of the Protocol might read as follows:

> The State Parties hereby agree that the Host State and its nationals shall be entitled to submit claims [for full reparation] for breach of those obligations enumerated in [Chapter 5] [Article 34] of the Protocol against an Investor having the nationality of another State Party to international arbitration in accordance with the provisions of this Annex.[192]

In the case of mass-scale environmental events, claims might be advanced by a designated representative acting to prosecute mass or collective claims on behalf of all victims.[193] Avenues may also exist (or may be drafted into the municipal laws of host States) for nationals to assign their claims to the State itself, in order that the State may "espouse" those claims against the investor, in a sort of reverse diplomatic protection.[194] Conversely, the State might designate or "deputise" one or more of its nationals to prosecute the State's own claims in a *qui tam* model formulation.[195]

The Investment Protocol is notable in that its provisions have been formulated into a single mega-multilateral convention whose accession spans across the African continent, thereby striving towards a uniform position establishing environmental breach as a widely justiciable international wrong. Further,

192 The proposed text is adapted from Amado, Kern & Doe Rodriguez, Annex, Model 7 "Jurisdiction Without Privity".

193 See Amado (n 177), ch 4.

194 Ibid., 25–55.

195 Ibid., 55–66.

the Protocol serves to extinguish the effect of many prior investment treaties of its contracting States. The drafters have wisely foreseen this necessity: within Article 49 (*"Relationship with Other International Investment Agreements"*) it is provided that "[e]xisting bilateral investment treaties concluded between the State Parties are terminated within five (5) years from the entry into force" and further that "[u]pon termination [...] their survival clauses shall also be terminated".[196]

The interplay of the Protocol with existing extra-African investment agreements is not dealt with so easily. In this respect Article 49 states that, "State Parties *may take into account* the requirements of this Protocol when negotiating international investment agreements and when reviewing existing international investment agreements concluded with Third Parties".[197] This language reflects the legalistic limitations of privity where the Protocol naturally cannot require a particular result in renegotiating instruments involving non-parties (though it could theoretically require their unilateral termination). Nonetheless, one might wish that the provision had adopted a slightly stronger posture. Otherwise, the Protocol may open the way to perverse incentives for intra-African investors to structure their investments via extra-African entities in order to avail the investment protections of earlier-generation treaties while escaping the Protocol's investor obligations.[198]

4 Conclusion

It is now evident that general principles of international environmental law and international human rights law have percolated into the regime of investor–State dispute settlement. It is also evident – from existing counterclaims indicators – that certain tools are already at the disposal of the States. Given the urgent calls from the UN and other international bodies to safeguard the environment and intertwined human rights, Article 34 of the Investment Protocol may serve as a template for others to follow suit.

The advantages of the arbitral forum for the bringing of claims by victims of environmental harm are evident. In the absence of such a forum, victims are left to navigate the world of transnational remedies, seeking to establish juris-

196 Protocol, art 49(1).

197 Protocol, art 49(4) (emphasis added).

198 Such a loophole might be closed by availing **Option II** for obtaining jurisdiction over offending investors, where considered in conjunction with the established definitions of "Investor" and "Investment" under the Protocol.

diction in either the courts of the host State, the courts of the investor's home State, or, more remote still, some third State. Even where jurisdiction lies, a court might dismiss the claim on grounds of *forum non conveniens* or other similar doctrine existing in the civil law traditions. There may be numerous barriers in compelling the offending investor to be a defendant in these various courts, and in winning an enforceable judgment.

In arbitration, victims might find a unitary forum serving to overcome many of the obstacles, and one that is better suited to the pursuit of effective remedies.[199] These realities call for the establishment of an international jurisdiction in which claims for compensation for environmental breach may be finally resolved, with accompanying international remedies for victims. This international jurisdiction is on the cusp of gaining life by virtue of the Investment Protocol. It is left only for the dispute settlement Annex to confer robust *locus standi* to enforce via the vehicles of claiming States party and/or their many aspiring nationals,[200] thus putting arbitration to use in defence of the Global Commons.[201]

In conclusion, the optimal point of equilibrium in investment law reform might be found precisely in allowing robust (but defined and delimited) investor protections while equally imposing countervailing investor obligations, with the traditionally accompanying suite of arbitral avenues. The Protocol has been made for this moment. If accompanied by a suitably tailored dispute settlement Annex, it is uniquely situated to deliver a return to the reciprocity that is arbitration's essence and to propel the progressive innovation of the mixed-claims model forward into a next generation.

---

199 See, in this regard, Amado (n 177), ch 6.

200 It has been written that "[a]scriptions of nationality allow states to allocate control over a scarce and valuable resource: people." M Casas, 'Nationalities of Convenience, Personal Jurisdiction, and Access to Investor-State Dispute Settlement' (2016) 49 NYU J Int L & Pol 1.

201 For a proposal that privileges the creation of a permanently standing dispute settlement body with in-built appellate mechanism, see W Kidane, *The Case for an African Investment Court (AIC)*, available at <http://dx.doi.org/10.2139/ssrn.6233798> accessed 3 July 2026.

CHAPTER 6

Investors' Treaty Imposed Anti-Corruption Obligations

Won Kidane and Jackson Shaw Kern

1 Introduction

Imposing anti-corruption obligations on investors via international treaties has become fashionable.[1] International tribunals' treatment of corruption allegations has also attracted considerable scholarly commentary,[2] mainly because of the many investor–State arbitrations to date involving questions of corruption.[3]

---

1 For example, contemporary Regional Economic Communities in Africa, including ECOWAS, COMESA, and SADC, all provide for investors' anti-corruption obligations in various instruments. Similarly, the Pan-African Investment Code also provides for anti-corruption investor obligations. These instruments have collectively inspired the anti-corruption provisions of the Protocol on Investment to the Agreement Establishing the African Continental Free Trade Area (AfCFTA Investment Protocol).

2 Charles N Brower and Jawad Ahmad, "The State's Corruption Defence, Prosecutorial Efforts, and Anti-Corruption Norms in Investment Treaty Arbitration" in Katia Yannaca-Small (ed), *Arbitration Under International Investment Agreements: A Guide to the Key Issues* (2nd edn, OUP 2018) 455; John R Crook, "Remedies for Corruption" (2015) 9(3) World Arbitration and Mediation Review 303–316; Despina Christofi, "The Relationship between Allegations of Economic Crimes in Foreign Investments and the Adjudicative Power of Investor–State Tribunals" (2021) 36(1) ICSID Review 129, 147; Domitille Baizeau and Tessa Hayes, "The Arbitral Tribunal's Duty and Power to Address Corruption Sua Sponte" in Andrea Menaker (ed), International Arbitration and the Rule of Law: Contribution and Conformity (ICCA Congress Series No 19, Kluwer Law International 2017) 225, 234–237, 258; L Yves Fortier, "Arbitrators, Corruption, and the Poetic Experience: 'When Power Corrupts, Poetry Cleanses'" (2015) 31(3) Arbitration International 367–380; Emmanuel Obiora Igbokwe, *Dealing with Bribery and Corruption in International Commercial Arbitration: To Probe or Not to Probe* (International Arbitration Law Library, Kluwer Law International 2023); Yueming Yan, "The Inclusion of Anti-corruption Clauses in International Investment Agreements and Its Possible Systemic Implications" (Singapore Management University) <https://ink.library.smu.edu.sg/cgi/viewcontent.cgi?article=5890&context=sol_research> accessed 17 April 2025.

3 Most notably, *World Duty Free Company Limited v. Republic of Kenya,* ICSID Case No ARB/00/7, Award (25 September 2006, dispatched 4 October 2006) IIC 277 (2006) (ICSID); see also *Niko Resources (Bangladesh) Ltd v. Bangladesh Petroleum Exploration & Production Company Ltd,* ICSID Case Nos ARB/10/11 and ARB/10/18, Decision on the Corruption Claim (25 February 2019); *Spentex Netherlands BV v. Republic of Uzbekistan,* ICSID Case

 | HTTPS://DOI.ORG/10.1163/9789004769854-007

This essay will weigh the means and mechanisms by which international anti-corruption norms might operate upon investors, with a particular focus on the investor-specific obligations within the Protocol on Investment to the Agreement Establishing the African Continental Free Trade Area (AfCFTA Investment Protocol). Its Article 37 reads as follows:

> Investors and their investments shall not offer, promise or give any unlawful or undue pecuniary or other advantage or present, whether directly or through intermediaries, to a public official of a State Party, or to a member of an official's family or business associate or other person in order to obtain a favour or that the official or other person act or refrain from acting in relation to the performance of official duties.
>
> Investors shall cooperate with State Parties in preventing and eliminating corruption in public governance and shall not encourage, incite, aid, abet or conspire with any official or another person or any entity to commit or authorise the commission of an act of corruption, taking into account applicable and relevant domestic laws and regulations, the African Union Convention on Preventing and Combatting Corruption, the United Nations Convention against Corruption and other applicable international legal instruments.
>
> Notwithstanding relevant international obligations of State Parties regarding anti-corruption, a breach of this Article by an investor is deemed to constitute a breach of the domestic laws and regulations of the Host State concerning the establishment and operation of an investment.[4]

In light of this provision, this essay will seek to conduct a stress test of the instrument by considering possible manners of its actual operation once the Protocol enters into force,[5] while also examining the extent of various chal-

---

No ARB/13/26, Award (27 December 2016); *Glencore International AG v. Republic of Colombia*, ICSID Case No ARB/16/6, Award (27 August 2019); *Metal-Tech Ltd v. Republic of Uzbekistan*, ICSID Case No ARB/10/3, Award (4 October 2013).

4 African Continental Free Trade Area (AfCFTA) Investment Protocol, art 37 ("Anti-corruption") (January 2023) <https://edit.wti.org/document/show/e5d51824-c467-4e24-922b-3fb376d89550> accessed 17 April 2025.

5 These notions are derived and adapted in part from a 2021 essay which explored the space prior to the existence of the AfCFTA Investment Protocol. See Jose Daniel Amado, Jackson Shaw Kern, and Martin Doe Rodriguez, "Elevating Corruption to an International Tort" in Jean Ho and Mavluda Sattorova (eds), *Investors' International Law* (Hart Publishing 2021) 352.

lenges faced. In the end, the essay will illustrate that while theoretically possible, there are numerous obstacles (both doctrinal and practical) to establishing and ensuring investor liability for corruption at the international level.

Ultimately, it might be argued that the inclusion of these provisions in the Protocol appears to be a risky prescriptive experimentation conducted by Africans in Africa, for at least two fundamental reasons: (i) it invites international arbitral or judicial tribunals into complex domestic criminal and civil disputes that they are unlikely to be able to determine with accuracy;[6] and (ii) it injects a new set of untested substantive rules which may add unnecessary inconsistency and incoherence into the already complex international investment jurisprudence.

2 The Status Quo of International Anti-corruption Law

2.1 The Anti-corruption Conventions

For a fuller appreciation of context, it is helpful to overview two of the key instruments regulating State obligations in the sphere of anti-corruption measures. Core provisions of the 2003 African Union Convention on Preventing and Combating Corruption (the AU Convention) and the United Nations Convention Against Corruption (the UNCAC), which are expressly mentioned within the AfCFTA Investment Protocol, will be briefly set out.

The AU Convention states as its first fundamental principle a "respect for democratic principles and institutions, popular participation, the rule of law

6 As of this writing, the mechanism of dispute settlement that the Protocol will adopt remains unknown. The Protocol provides as follows:

1. "In the event of a dispute between an investor of a State Party and a Host State relating to an alleged breach of this Protocol, the investor and the Host State shall initially seek to resolve amicably the dispute through consultations, negotiations, conciliation, mediation or other amicable dispute resolution mechanisms available in the Host State.

2. Notwithstanding the outcome of the dispute prevention and grievances management process under Article 45, in the event that an investor of a State Party and the Host State are unable to amicably resolve the dispute in accordance with Paragraph 1, they may seek to resolve such dispute in accordance with the dispute resolution mechanisms to be provided in the Annex referred to in Paragraph 3.

3. Rules and Procedures governing Dispute Prevention, Management and Resolution of disputes covered by this Protocol, shall be set out in an Annex to this Protocol. The Annex shall be negotiated after the adoption of this Protocol by the Assembly of Heads of State and Government of the Africa Union, and finalised within 12 months at the latest from the date of adoption of this Protocol. The Annex, upon adoption by the Assembly of Heads of State and Government of the African Union, shall form an integral part of this Protocol."

AfCFTA Investment Protocol art 46.

and good governance".[7] It then seeks to criminalise both demand- and supply-side bribery (i.e., both the seeking and the offering) but states, in aspirational language only, that its States party "undertake" to "[a]dopt legislative and other measures that are required to establish as offences" the acts of corruption defined therein.[8] The AU Convention does not prescribe any particular exercise of jurisdiction but rather states only that each State party "has jurisdiction" over acts of corruption in accordance with principles of territoriality and nationality.[9] As these two bases of jurisdiction are long recognised by international law, the statement may be little more than a truism.[10]

The UNCAC, for its part, provides that it "shall apply [...] to the prevention, investigation, and prosecution of corruption and to the freezing, seizure, confiscation and return of the proceeds of offences established in accordance" therewith.[11] The UNCAC seeks to criminalise both supply and demand-side bribery of national public officials in the following mandatory terms:

> Each State Party shall adopt such legislative and other measures as may be necessary to establish as criminal offences, when committed intentionally:
>
> (a) The promise, offering or giving, to a public official, directly or indirectly, of an undue advantage, for the official himself or herself or another person or entity, in order that the official act or refrain from acting in the exercise of his or her official duties;
> (b) The solicitation or acceptance by a public official, directly or indirectly, of an undue advantage, for the official himself or herself or another person or entity, in order that the official act or refrain from acting in the exercise of his or her official duties.[12]

The UNCAC separately sets forth an offence upon the supply side of transnational bribery, imposing upon States party the obligation to:

---

7 African Union Convention on Preventing and Combating Corruption (AU Convention), art 3(1).
8 Ibid., art 5(1).
9 Ibid., art 13(1)(a)-(b).
10 The AU Convention also states that each State party "has" jurisdiction "when the offence, although committed outside its jurisdiction, affects, in the view of the State concerned, its vital interests or the deleterious or harmful consequences or effects of such offences impact on the State Party". AU Convention, art 13(1)(d).
11 United Nations Convention against Corruption (UNCAC), art 3(1).
12 Ibid., art 15.

> [A]dopt such legislative and other measures as may be necessary to establish as a criminal offence, when committed intentionally, the promise, offering or giving to a foreign public official or an official of a public international organization, directly or indirectly, of an undue advantage, for the official himself or herself or another person or entity, in order that the official act or refrain from acting in the exercise of his or her official duties, in order to obtain or retain business or other undue advantage in relation to the conduct of international business.[13]

Lastly, in setting out its general jurisdictional principles, the UNCAC mandatorily prescribes each State party to legislate the corruption offences where committed in its territory,[14] and permissively where committed by its nationals.[15] As of 2025 the UNCAC has attained no fewer than 192 States parties;[16] indeed, only a handful have not joined, amongst them North Korea, Syria, and Eritrea.[17]

In sum, the anti-corruption conventions do not impose direct obligations upon non-State actors such as investors nor do they create any direct right of action in an international jurisdiction but rather rely upon their States party to be implemented.

2.2 Arbitral Practice to Date

As a general matter, the presently prevailing view is that any use of corrupt practices will operate to foreclose access to arbitral remedies. As Judge Gunnar Lagergren famously held in a 1963 arbitral award, "[p]arties who ally themselves in [such] an enterprise [...] must realise that they have forfeited any right to ask for assistance of the machinery of justice (national courts or arbi-

---

13 Ibid., art 16(1).

14 UNCAC, art 42(1)(a). The UNCAC also contains a mandatory prescription with regard to offences "committed on board a vessel that is flying the flag of that State Party or an aircraft that is registered under the laws of that State Party" at the time of commission: Ibid., art 42(1)(b). This too is a basis of jurisdiction that is well established in international law, often known as the flag principle.

15 Ibid., art 42(2)(b). In an acknowledgement of corruption's victims, the UNCAC also includes a permissive basis of jurisdiction where the offence is committed not by, but against, a national of the relevant State party, sometimes known as the passive personality principle: Ibid., art 42(2)(a).

16 United Nations Office on Drugs and Crime, "UNCAC Signature and Ratification Status", <http://www.unodc.org/unodc/en/corruption/ratification-status.html> accessed 1 July 2026.

17 Ibid.

tral tribunals) in settling their disputes".[18] As seen in that award, the status of international public policy *contra* corruption was achieved long prior to the emergence of the anti-corruption conventions.[19] In 2007, two years after the UNCAC entered into force, an arbitral tribunal reaffirmed the international public policy in a contractual dispute governed by municipal laws in the case of *World Duty Free v. Kenya*, which it described as "an international consensus as to universal standards and accepted norms of conduct"[20] while similarly dismissing the claimant's claim.

The result of dismissal has subsequently been reached in treaty-based arbitrations. For example, in the case of *Metal-Tech Ltd v. Uzbekistan*, while acknowledging a seeming "unfair advantage" to the shielded respondent State, the tribunal nonetheless found that "the idea [...] is not to punish one party at the cost of the other, but rather to ensure the promotion of the rule of law, which entails that a court or tribunal cannot grant assistance to a party that has engaged in a corrupt act".[21] Certain nuances amongst these cases must be identified. In *World Duty Free*, the tribunal applied principles of separability to "examine the relative evidence of corruption in the underlying contract in order to determine its enforceability",[22] ultimately concluding in the negative.[23] This marks a distinction from Judge Lagergren's case, which concerned not corruption in the *making* of the contract but rather corruption as the *object* of the contract. Meanwhile, in a treaty case, corruption in the making of the investment may vitiate a tribunal's jurisdiction by operation of a legality clause requiring investments to be established in accordance with law, a defect which no separability presumption may cure.[24]

18 *Award in ICC Case No 1110 of* 1963 (1996) 21 Yearbook Commercial Arbitration 47, 56.

19 See Ibid., where Judge Lagergren recorded as follows:
"[T]here exists a general principle of law recognized by civilized nations that contracts which seriously violate *bonos mores* or international public policy are invalid or at least unenforceable and that they cannot be sanctioned by the courts or arbitrators [...] such corruption is an international evil; it is contrary to the good morals and to an international public policy common to the community of nations."

20 *World Duty Free Co Ltd v. Republic of Kenya*, ICSID Case No. ARB/00/7, Award (4 October 2006), 46 ILM 339 (2006), para 139.

21 *Metal-Tech Ltd v. Uzbekistan*, ICSID Case No. ARB/10/3, Award (4 October 2013), para 389.

22 RZ Torres-Fowler, "Undermining ICSID: How the Global Antibribery Regime Impairs Investor–State Arbitration" (2012) 52(4) Virginia Journal of International Law 995, 1011 fn 71, 1012.

23 For a perspective on the case, see W Kidane, "The Culture of Investment Arbitration: An African Perspective" (2019) 34(2) ICSID Review – Foreign Investment Law Journal 411.

24 Tribunals have also ruled that an illegal acquisition of an investment renders the investor's claim inadmissible, even in the absence of an express legality clause. See, for example, *Plama Consortium Ltd v. Bulgaria*, ICSID Case No. ARB/03/24, Award

Judge Lagergren's reasoning, applied as it was in a case of commercial bribery (it was a dispute over a contract as between two private parties the object of which, Judge Lagergren came to be convinced, included the paying of bribes to Argentine officials),[25] may not serve very well in investor–State arbitration.[26] It is difficult to escape the notion that behind the treaty case dismissals may lie a fear that any other result would be seen to punish innocent peoples following corrupt acts of their ruling elites, in a time when investor–State arbitration has fallen under great scrutiny. This dilemma has produced a perverse position in the law. As observed by Aloysius Llamzon, "[c]urrent case law suggests that host States can only be held responsible for bribe solicitations or attempts at extortion" committed by their officials,[27] but "when corruption is 'successfully' consummated such that the public action or inaction purchased by the bribe has occurred, host States are *not* internationally responsible for such corruption".[28] Further than this, not only is the State not internationally responsible for the corruption, but the corrupt act may give rise to the unpalatable spectre of a penalty shield to be raised against any State responsibility for *other* conduct that is alleged to be internationally wrongful, thus raising a considerable moral hazard. Equally, the extent of the asymmetry in consequences between an investor and a host State has been

(27 August 2008), para 135, and *Phoenix Action Ltd v. Czech Republic,* ICSID Case No ARB/06/5, Award (15 April 2009), para 101.

25 The respondent conceded that its sole reason for retaining the claimant was "the quite remarkable degree of influence which he had with the political appointees of the Peronista Government". Torres-Fowler, 1011, fn 71.

26 For an elaboration of the argument, see AB Spalding, "Deconstructing *Duty-Free*: Investor–State Arbitration as Private Anti-Bribery Enforcement" (2016) 49(2) University of California Davis Law Review 443, 488–493.

27 Aloysius Llamzon and Anthony Sinclair, "Investor Wrongdoing in Investment Arbitration: Standards Governing Issues of Corruption, Fraud, Misrepresentation and Other Investor Misconduct" in AJ van den Berg (ed), *Legitimacy: Myths, Realities, Challenges* (Kluwer Law International 2015) 468, 496, para 11.07. Such might constitute a breach of, for example, a treaty guarantee of fair and equitable treatment of investments. See, for example, *EDF (Services) Ltd v. Romania*, ICSID Case No ARB/05/13, Award (8 October 2009).

28 Ibid., (emphasis in original). One observer has, however, opined that any fairness objection may be misguided where "[t]he 'state' derives no benefit from corruption. Bribes are not paid into the public revenue. Rather, the 'state' suffers a significant loss when assets or other valuable legal entitlements are transferred into private hands for less than their real value through corrupt transactions. The actors that benefit from corruption are the particular individuals or groups exercising state authority corruptly and the individuals or groups with which they corruptly transact."
See J Bonnitcha, "Investment Treaties and Transition from Authoritarian Rule" (2014) 15 (5–6) Journal of World Investment and Trade 965, 1000.

deemed a factor in tribunals' general reluctance to make findings of corruption, as well as their application (transparently or not) of a much more rigid standard of proof to such allegations.[29]

3 The *Pro* Position: Actioning Investors' Anti-corruption Obligations

It is as yet unknown whether the substantive investor obligations set out in the AfCFTA Investment Protocol will be joined by an international arbitral (or other) forum for their direct enforcement. The Protocol provides at Article 46 that "Rules and Procedures governing Dispute Prevention, Management and Resolution of disputes covered by this Protocol" shall be "set out in an Annex [which] shall be negotiated […] and finalised within 12 months at the latest from the date of adoption of this Protocol".[30] The Annex presently remains pending.

On the one hand, it is evident that there are certain factors commending the possible use of arbitration for this purpose. Arbitration is firmly established as the predominant mechanism for the resolution of disputes in international commerce and investment. As Llamzon observes in his seminal work on corruption in international investment law, the anti-corruption conventions (such as the AU Convention and the UNCAC) "continue to arrogate the prerogatives of curbing and prosecuting corruption to national authorities, thus depriving these instruments and the international legal order of any real control function for combating transnational corruption".[31] He concludes that "the only potentially effective mechanism under the international legal order for the control of transnational corruption currently available is international investment arbitration".[32] Meanwhile, diverse constituencies have

---

29 Aloysius Llamzon and Anthony Sinclair, "Investor Wrongdoing in Investment Arbitration: Standards Governing Issues of Corruption, Fraud, Misrepresentation and Other Investor Misconduct" in AJ van den Berg (ed), *Legitimacy: Myths, Realities, Challenges* (Kluwer Law International 2015) 468, 496.

30 AfCFTA Investment Protocol, art 46(3) <https://www.bilaterals.org/IMG/pdf/en_-_draft_protocol_of_the_afcfta_on_investment.pdf>.

31 Llamzon (n 27), para. 11.03. He further notes that "[p]lans for effective anti-corruption monitoring and dedicated dispute settlement mechanisms to decide cases of transnational corruption (including a U.N. proposal for an arbitral framework) have not borne fruit" (Ibid.). For more on the unavailing U.N. initiative, see Ibid., paras 4.77–4.79.

32 Ibid., He has also written that "[g]iven the lack of any concerted international mechanism to enforce anti-corruption norms, investor-State arbitration has, almost by default, emerged as one of the few areas in the international legal order where the infrastructure

urged that, in addition to the historical role of treaty-born arbitration as a forum for the foreign investor to enforce obligations of investment protection upon the host State, the regime might impose a reciprocal responsibility to the investor.[33]

In any case, it seemed that the barring of an investor's affirmative claims marked the extent of any mechanism to directly confront corruption in international investment law – until now. In further developing the space by reference to the AfCFTA Investment Protocol, one might see an emerging role for arbitration which moves beyond the simple barring of claims. If jurisdiction is properly conferred, an international tribunal might serve to order monetary compensation or other relief – acts of corruption by a foreign investor and/or by a public official of the host State may lay a basis for liability to those who suffer injury flowing from the corrupt acts. The liable party (or parties) may include (i) the briber, who may come in the form of a natural person (or persons) found to have committed a corrupt act (and/or a business entity or other principal on whose behalf this person purported to act); or (ii) the bri-

---

is already in place to regulate foreign investment, including those tainted with corruption, in an authoritative and controlling manner" (Ibid., para 1.05), and that "this key public issue will for the foreseeable future have to be addressed through existing international systems; and investment arbitration is currently the closest thing the international legal order has to a standing system able to extract direct accountability from those who engage in corruption" (Ibid., para 11.47).

33 See, for example, United Nations Economic Commission for Africa, African Union & UNCTAD, "Next Steps for the African Continental Free Trade Area: Assessing Regional Integration in Africa IX" (July 2019) 198 ("The international investment regime historically imposed obligations only on host States, not on private investors (Paulsson, 1995). However, as underscored by the [Pan-African Investment Code], [international investment agreements] may serve as vehicles for investor rights and also for their obligations, which could rebalance the regime. Investor obligations can be a source for claims against transgressing investors and for counterclaims by defending States. The right to initiate proceedings may be bestowed upon the [host] State, its nationals, or both (Amado, Kern & Rodriguez, 2017)") (citations omitted); see also UNGA, "Possible reform of investor-State dispute settlement (ISDS): Multiple proceedings and counterclaims" (22 January 2020) UN Doc A/CN.9/WG.III/WP.193, para 41 (stating that Working Group III on Investor–State Dispute Settlement Reform "may wish to consider formulating provisions on investor obligations which would form the basis for a State's counterclaims" and that such obligations "may relate to the protection of human rights and the environment, compliance with domestic law, measures against corruption, and the promotion of sustainable development") and note 26 (stating that the Working Group "may wish to consider whether the framework for counterclaims by respondent States could be expanded to allow for claims by third parties against investors") and UNGA, "Report of Working Group III (Investor–State Dispute Settlement Reform) on the work of its thirty-seventh session" (New York, 1–5 April 2019) UN Doc A/CN.9/970, paras 31, 34–35. See also Chapter 1 in this volume.

bee, who may come in the form of a public official (i.e., a natural person) and/or his State. In setting out the bounds of qualifying injury in instances of corruption, a useful guide is found in the Council of Europe's Civil Law Convention on Corruption, which provides that categories of compensable harm shall include "material damage, loss of profits and non-pecuniary loss".[34] With regard to remedy, victims may seek judgment (in the form of an arbitral award that declares a finding of corrupt acts) and accompanying compensation for damage.

Finally, with regard to access, the evident candidates for standing are those nationals of the host State who suffer injury flowing from the corrupt acts, or indeed the host State itself, which might seek to recover from either the corrupted investor(s) or official(s) (or both). Jurisdiction may be attained by the crafting of calibrated treaty text within the dispute settlement Annex to the AfCFTA Investment Protocol, such that investor consent is conferred as a condition to admission or establishment of an investment,[35] or by the simple fact of such admission or establishment *ab initio*,[36] and an offer of arbitration may equally thereby be extended to defined host State nationals as beneficiaries of the instrument.[37] It must be noted that the burden will be upon the claiming

34 Council of Europe, Civil Law Convention on Corruption (4 November 1999), ETS 174, art 3(2).

35 In this model, the investor must give his express consent to arbitration of the anti-corruption norms as a condition to issuance of a requisite investment licence or authorization. See JD Amado, JS Kern, and MD Rodriguez, *Arbitrating the Conduct of International Investors* (Cambridge University Press 2018) 87–90 and Annex, Model 6 ("Contingent Consent Clause").

36 See Ibid., 90–93 and Model 7 ("Jurisdiction without Privity"); see also The Netherlands–Indonesia Agreement on Economic Cooperation (with Protocol and Exchanges of Letters dated 17 June 1968) (signed 7 July 1968, entered into force 17 July 1971) 799 UNTS 13, art 11 ("[t]he Contracting Party in the territory of which a national of the other Contracting Party makes or intends to make an investment, shall assent to any demand on the part of such national and any such national shall comply with any request of the former Contracting Party, to submit, for conciliation or arbitration, to [ICSID] any dispute that may arise in connection with the investment") and the Declaration of the Government of the Democratic and Popular Republic of Algeria concerning the settlement of claims by the Government of the United States of America and the Government of the Islamic Republic of Iran (19 January 1981) art II. By according to such a treaty, the investor's home State exercises a sovereign power to compel its nationals to the jurisdiction of an international tribunal.

37 The Hague Rules on Business and Human Rights Arbitration, substantially derived from the UNCITRAL Arbitration Rules, offer a thoroughly modern and progressive body of procedural rules well-suited to this purpose. City of The Hague and Center for International Legal Cooperation, *The Hague Rules on Business and Human Rights Arbitration* (launched 12 December 2019). It is noted that "[t]he characterization of the dispute as relating to business and human rights is not necessary for jurisdiction where all the parties to the arbitration have agreed to settle a dispute under [the Hague] Rules"

party (or parties) to prove causation of injury, which is often a difficult task in the case of ills such as corruption, whose effects are highly diffuse. Perhaps the best-situated claimant is the State itself, which may seek damages corresponding to its "assets or other valuable legal entitlements" which have been "transferred into private hands for less than their real value"[38] or may perhaps pursue corrupted investors for their ill-gotten gains.

Possible advantages of the arbitral forum for the bringing of claims by victims of corruption are evident. In the absence of such a forum, and as presumed under the UNCAC and the Council of Europe's Civil Law Convention on Corruption, victims are left to navigate the world of transnational remedies, seeking to establish jurisdiction in either the courts of the host State, the courts of the investor's home State, or, more remote still, some third State. Even where jurisdiction lies, a court might dismiss the claim on grounds of *forum non conveniens* or other similar doctrine existing in the civil law traditions.[39] There are numerous barriers in constraining both the allegedly corrupted investor and official (or his State) to be defendants in the same court, and in winning an enforceable judgment. Some of these difficulties are captured in an explanatory note to the Civil Law Convention:

> [D]ifficulties may relate, for instance, to the transmission of judicial and extra-judicial acts, to the choice of jurisdiction to seek redress, the uncertainties of the applicable law in a situation where several different alternatives may be possible, the obligation for the company to advance security for legal costs if the law suit is filed with the courts of another country and difficulties in having the judgement recognised and executed in a foreign country.[40]

(Ibid., art 1). Claims might be advanced by a designated representative acting to prosecute mass or collective claims on behalf of all victims. See Amado, Kern & Rodriguez (n 5) Ch 4.

38 See J Bonnitcha, "Investment Treaties and Transition from Authoritarian Rule" (2014) 15 (5–6) Journal of World Investment and Trade 965, 1000.

39 See generally R Brand and S Jablonski, *Forum Non Conveniens: History, Global Practice, and Future Under the Hague Convention on Choice of Court Agreements* (Oxford University Press 2007). See also Z Douglas, *The International Law of Investment Claims* (Cambridge University Press 2009) 395–396 (noting that "[a]lthough the doctrine of *forum non conveniens* is a creature of the common law, some commentators have observed that the flexibility built into jurisdictional rules in civilian systems is such that the gulf between the two legal traditions in the respect is more apparent than real"), citing AS Bell, *Forum Shopping and Venue in Transnational Litigation* (Oxford University Press 2003) 72.

40 Council of Europe, Civil Law Convention on Corruption (4 November 1999), ETS 174, Explanatory Report, para 87.

In arbitration, victims might find a unitary forum serving to overcome many of the obstacles of international judicial cooperation upon which the anti-corruption conventions rely,[41] and one that is better suited to the pursuit of effective remedies. The "uncertainties of the applicable law" are dispelled where the governing law emerges directly from the treaty instrument itself (e.g., Article 37 of the AfCFTA Investment Protocol), and "difficulties in having the judgement recognised and executed in a foreign country" are relieved where arbitral awards enjoy broader international enforceability than national court judgments.[42]

4 The *Contra* Position: Insurmountable Obstacles

On the other hand, the implementation of investors' treaty-imposed anti-corruption obligations faces grave challenges.

4.1 Structure and Content of the Anti-corruption Rules

As noted, the anti-corruption investor obligation lies in Article 37 of the January 2023 AfCFTA Investment Protocol, which reads as follows in full:

> Investors and their investments shall not offer, promise or give any unlawful or undue pecuniary or other advantage or present, whether directly or through intermediaries, to a public official of a State Party, or to a member of an official's family or business associate or other person in order to obtain a favour or that the official or other person act or refrain from acting in relation to the performance of official duties.
>
> ***Investors shall cooperate with State Parties in preventing and eliminating corruption in public governance and shall not encourage, incite, aid, abet or conspire with any official*** or another person or any entity to commit or authorise the commission of an act of corruption, ***taking into account applicable and relevant domestic laws and regulations***, the African Union Convention on Preventing and Combatting Corruption, the United Nations Convention against Corruption and other applicable international legal instruments.

41 See, for example, UNCAC, Chapter IV. Furthermore, these extensive provisions regarding international cooperation are all but exclusively targeted toward purposes of criminal penalties. For a treaty provision regarding international cooperation toward civil remedies, see CLC, art 13.

42 See, in this regard, Amado, Kern & Rodriguez (n 5) Ch 6.

> ***Notwithstanding relevant international obligations of State Parties regarding anti-corruption, a breach of this Article by an investor is deemed to constitute a breach of the domestic laws and regulations of the Host State concerning the establishment and operation of an investment.***[43]

Because investors and their investments are the obligated subjects of this provision, its focus is upon the supply side of bribery only, i.e., the offering (as opposed to the seeking) of any bribe, in notable contrast to the anti-corruption conventions comprising both.

4.2 Commentary

Article 37 of the Protocol sets out a substantive rule. It defines and prohibits acts of corruption. The first issue that may be raised is the immense challenge that will be faced by distant and delocalised international tribunals in obtaining and accurately assessing evidence, and thus in "getting it right" on the facts.

Indeed, it is fair to question whether arbitration is ever well-suited to the adjudication of corruption in view of the inherent evidentiary challenges that arbitral tribunals face. Tribunals do not enjoy investigative powers and are generally unable to compel the production of evidence in the absence of judicial assistance. Llamzon has put forth a proposal for an evidentiary regime that he describes as "equal to the task of unearthing inherently clandestine corruption" by addressing "the various evidentiary matters that have led to difficulties in proving corruption, including the burdens of proof, standards of proof, and the use of inferences, presumptions, and 'red flag' indicia".[44] Another observer has similarly examined in extensive detail five possible solutions to ease the evidentiary challenges, namely: (i) drawing adverse inferences; (ii) placing greater reliance on circumstantial evidence; (iii) lowering the standard of proof; (iv) shifting the burden of proof; and (v) drawing on factual findings in domestic proceedings.[45] One is left to consider whether these proposals are ultimately insufficient and unsatisfactory.

---

43 AfCFTA Investment Protocol, art 37 ("Anti-corruption") (emphasis added).

44 Llamzon (n 27) para 1.41.

45 C Rose, *"Questioning the Role of International Arbitration in the Fight against Corruption"* (2014) 31(2) *Journal of International Arbitration* 183.

Furthermore, the Protocol provides that a breach of its anti-corruption provision is deemed a breach of the domestic laws of the host State. In that sense, it essentially replaces the domestic anti-corruption rules of both the host and home States, to the extent they overlap. This is even more interesting because, as far as investors are concerned, it seemingly seeks to supplant the substantive anti-corruption rules that flow from corruption-specific international treaties, including the AU and UN conventions.

This is particularly problematic because the Protocol goes beyond and upsets the careful balance that these international instruments strike in terms of criminalising corrupt practices. For example, the investor assumes the obligation (it is not clear in what way) of cooperating with the host State in preventing corruption: "Investors shall cooperate with State Parties in preventing and eliminating corruption in public governance and shall not encourage, incite, aid, abet or conspire with any official."[46] This provision imposes an affirmative obligation that goes beyond simply refraining from corrupt practices. The point is critical because it relates, in turn, to the provisions concerning admission requirements, denial of benefits, and dispute settlement. Each is addressed in turn.

First, the admission requirement relates to the definition of the term "investment" which reads:

> 'Investment' means an enterprise or company […] which is established, acquired, or expanded ***in conformity with the laws and regulations of a Host State*** by an investor which maintains substantial business in the territory of that Host State.[47]

To qualify for protection, the commitment of capital or resources must fall under this definition of investment, which requires it to be "established, acquired or expanded in conformity with" domestic law. The Protocol presumably requires such domestic law to be substantively consistent with the Protocol's definition of corruption, including the affirmative duty to cooperate in preventing corruption; thus, the investor may be excluded from protection under the Protocol not only for acts that it may have committed but also for any omission in its affirmative duties of cooperation. It is not difficult to imagine how this could raise a serious and complex jurisdictional controversy.

These interlocking provisions of the Protocol pose a significant challenge not only because they invite more complexity but also because the Protocol

46 AfCFTA Investment Protocol, art 37.

47 Ibid., definition of terms (emphasis added).

applies only to African investors in Africa. It is hard to imagine that advanced capital-exporting countries would voluntarily accept such a kind of uncertainty. To be sure, the problem is not the elevated anti-corruption standard for Africans but rather the jurisdictional and other uncertainties that accompany uncertain investor obligations, such as a failure to cooperate in prevention measures.

Secondly, this obligation links directly to the treaty's denial-of-benefits provision, which states, in relevant part:

> A State Party may at any time deny an investor of another State Party and the investment of such investor the benefits of this Protocol if: [...] (g) an investor or investment has committed a breach of a specific binding obligation under Chapter 5 of this Protocol.[48]

One of these binding obligations is the anti-corruption provision set out above.

Thus, the way this plays out in reality is that the host State pleads both grounds as jurisdictional or admissibility defences. It would claim that the investor failed in its duty to cooperate in prevention – therefore, the "investment", no matter its size, may be definitionally disqualified or may freely be denied the protections of the treaty. The tribunal seized of the matter would then have to determine, on the basis of evidentiary submissions, whether the investor indeed failed to cooperate. This is more difficult than simply determining whether the investor engaged in corrupt activity, which in itself is not an easy task for international tribunals or international courts to perform.

In the realm of corruption matters, one must thus reconsider whether the better approach is to leave these matters to national law and national court jurisdiction while strengthening local institutions of governance. The introduction of new and possibly inconsistent substantive anti-corruption provisions through investment treaties may unnecessarily complicate matters while assigning to international tribunals a fact-finding task that they cannot meaningfully perform.

Finally, this difficulty must also be considered in light of further investor liability rules under the Protocol. Its Article 47 states as follows:

> 1. Investors and their investments shall, where applicable and in accordance with domestic laws and regulations, ***be subject to civil actions for liability in the judicial process of their Home State for the acts, decisions***

48 Ibid., art 5(1)(g).

> ***or omissions made in the Host State in relation to the investment where such acts, decisions or omissions lead to damage, personal injuries or loss of life in the Host State.***
>
> 2. State Parties shall develop rules and procedures that allow for, or do not prevent or unduly restrict, the bringing of court actions relating to the civil liability of investors in the territory of their Home States, taking into account rules governing conflict of laws and the recognition and enforcement of foreign judgments.
> 3. For greater certainty, this Article does not exclude the possibility of bringing civil actions against investors and their investments before the domestic courts of the Host State.[49]

The Protocol thus purports to confer *locus standi* to foreign claimants to bring lawsuits against the investor in its home State for actions that it undertook or failed to do in the host State. It also seeks to grant extraterritorial jurisdiction to the home State's courts. There is nothing mechanically impermissible for a treaty to require the domestic laws to create this jurisdictional space, but it fails to select any substantive rules for the determination of liability. Presumably, the Protocol's substantive rules would apply. This would include the anti-corruption rules.

A competitor, for example, could sue the foreign investor in its home jurisdiction after losing a bid because of the investor's offer of a bribe. This lawsuit could be brought in both the host State and home State courts. These courts would then have to struggle with parallel litigation, conflicts of laws, differing procedural allocation of burden and standard of proof, and, of course, factual and evidentiary uncertainties.

5 Conclusion

The various anti-corruption conventions that culminated in the nearly universal UNCAC embody swift and impressive achievements in international law. Nonetheless, their success is sometimes constrained at the will or whim of diverse States party in enacting and enforcing the anti-corruption norms. A vigorous anti-corruption campaign is undoubtedly established as a matter of international or transnational public policy. However, the fact that the conventions' norms are, by design, applied only indirectly, via the lenses of disparate municipal laws, weighed against any identifiable status of corruption as

49 Ibid., art 47 (emphasis added).

an internationally justiciable wrong – until the emergence of direct investors' anti-corruption obligations, as in the AfCFTA Investment Protocol. The prior austere limitations might be overcome by establishing an international jurisdiction for the direct application of substantive anti-corruption norms, with accompanying international remedies to victims. Such an experiment seems to have now been undertaken, though the precise form of the Protocol's dispute settlement Annex remains yet to be seen.

At the same time, it is possible that the Protocol, in its practical effect, does not simplify matters but rather makes them more complicated. The Protocol (i) introduces new and uncertain substantive anti-corruption principles; (ii) makes disputes more likely both because of the definition of investment and denial of benefits provisions; (iii) seemingly involves international decision-makers into complex domestic law disputes that they are unlikely to correctly assess on the facts; (iv) duplicates domestic court litigation by giving extraterritorial jurisdiction to the home State courts (without necessarily defining the substantive rule of decision); and (v) risks parallel litigation, anti-suit injunctions, and differing or even conflicting outcomes.

At the policy level, it disfavours African investors and encourages them to incorporate in jurisdictions that give greater treaty protections while incurring no investor obligations. If the purpose of the Protocol is to encourage intra-African investment, it may not succeed in that endeavour until such time as the rest of the world levels the playing field by following the Protocol's example.

All of these factors must be weighed carefully in further pursuing the experiment of investors' anti-corruption obligations in international law, both on the African continent and beyond.

CHAPTER 7

Socio-Political Obligations in Investment Treaties

Makane Moïse Mbengue

1 Introduction

Foreign investments and investors have often been at the heart of delicate socio-political situations in their host countries.[1] Within living memory, conflicts have erupted between governments and investors, for instance during a wave of oil industry nationalisations under President Hugo Chávez, which led to dozens of investor–State arbitrations; or when Bolivian President Evo Morales likewise nationalised hydrocarbons and other industries. While investors called these expropriations unlawful, the government defended them as an exercise of sovereignty to improve national welfare.

African countries have faced similar clashes: Tanzania's government in 2017 passed laws asserting "permanent sovereignty" over natural resources – mandating between 16% and 50% State ownership of mining projects, raising royalty rates, and eliminating access to international arbitration – moves that alarmed foreign mining companies. South Africa provides another example: after foreign investors brought an arbitration claim challenging South Africa's Black Economic Empowerment policies, the government concluded that bilateral investment treaties (BITs) focused too narrowly on investors' economic rights while "matters of national interest" – like correcting historic racial inequalities – were left exposed to unpredictable arbitration. South Africa responded by terminating its BITs and enacting a domestic investment law to preserve policy space for such socio-economic objectives.

These cases illustrate the recurring tension between investors' private rights and host States' public policy goals, explaining why calls have grown for investors to bear socio-political obligations in addition to enjoying investment protections.

Defining socio-political obligations with precision, however, is challenging. The term is not exactly a term of art in traditional investment treaties, as it

1 As put by T. Frank, Fairness in the International Legal and Institutional System (1993) *Receuil des cours*, p. 442: "One need not be an economist to be able to predict that investment by rich, developed economies in poor, underdeveloped ones is likely to give rise to social and political tensions capable of vitiating any potential economic benefits."

HTTPS://DOI.ORG/10.1163/9789004769854-008

encapsulates a range of duties that foreign investors might have in respect of the host State's society and political order. Generally, it refers to obligations on investors to respect the host country's sovereignty, laws, socio-cultural values, and to refrain from unwarranted political interference or harmful social impacts. Different treaties and authors use varying formulations – such as, investor "responsibilities", "corporate social responsibility", or obligations regarding human rights, environment, and anti-corruption – which overlap with the concept. Even drafters of modern instruments have noted "a certain lack of clarity"[2] in the scope of so-called socio-political obligations.

In broad terms, these obligations mean that investors should not act as unruly imperial agents within the host State but rather align their conduct with the host's development needs, public order, and governance prerogatives.

As detailed further in this chapter, this is far from being a new idea in international economics law: to the contrary, it has roots in general international law (Section 2), and early expressions in African practice (Section 3). These precursors finally led to this notion's crystallisation in the new African Continental Free Trade Area (AfCFTA) Investment Protocol (Section 4).

2 Roots of Socio-political Obligations under General International Law

The notion that foreign investors should respect certain socio-political duties of conduct is rooted in principles that emerged during the era of decolonisation and the push for a New International Economic Order (NIEO). In the 1960s and 1970s, developing countries frequently accused foreign investors (and the multinational corporations behind them) of undermining the sovereignty and social objectives of host nations. Underlying this call for a NIEO was, in particular, a concern for making sure that the key principle of non-intervention applies as well to economic relations as to the use of force.[3]

This led to a series of United Nations resolutions asserting the primacy of host State control over foreign investment. Notably, UN General Assembly Resolution 1803 (XVII) of 1962, entitled "Permanent Sovereignty over Natural Resources", declared that the right of peoples and nations to use and dispose

2 IISD, "Harnessing Investment for Sustainable Development – Inclusion of investor obligations and corporate accountability provisions in trade and investment agreements" (January 2018), available online, p. 18.

3 M. Jamnejad, & Michael Wood, "The Principle of Non-intervention" (2009) 22 *Leiden Journal of International Law* 2, pp. 345–381.

of natural wealth "must be exercised in the interest of [the nation's] development and of the well-being of the people".[4] The Resolution also stressed that exploration and exploitation of resources by foreign capital must conform to the host State's laws and regulations and align with its national interests, while warning that the violation of a people's sovereignty over its natural resources is contrary to the UN Charter and impedes global peace and cooperation. In essence, as early as 1962 the international community acknowledged that foreign investors could not be allowed to operate as a law unto themselves – their activities were subject to the host State's socio-political prerogatives, including economic independence and public welfare.

This theme was expanded in the 1974 Charter of Economic Rights and Duties of States.[5] The Charter, a key document of the NIEO movement, provides in its Article 2 that States have the inalienable right to regulate foreign investment within their jurisdiction, and to exercise authority over transnational corporations. While the Charter is phrased primarily as a declaration of States' rights (e.g. the right to nationalise with appropriate compensation, and to require investors to obey local laws), it carries the corollary that investors have a duty to respect the host State's sovereignty and laws. Developing countries at the time emphasised that foreign investors must not interfere in internal affairs or dictate national policies; for example, the Charter's preamble condemns political or economic conditions imposed on developing States "which conflict with the interests of the recipient State". The clear message was that investment agreements or conduct that undermines a host State's political independence or chosen development path are unacceptable. These principles reflect the general international law norm of non-intervention in internal affairs: just as States must not intervene in each other's domestic politics, a foreign investor (as a non-State actor) likewise should not subvert the host State's political sovereignty.

Arbitral practice in the 1970s grappled with these emerging norms. A famous example is *Texaco/Calasiatic v. Libya* (1977), an arbitration arising from Libya's nationalisation of oil concessions.[6] The sole arbitrator, Professor René-Jean Dupuy, acknowledged Libya's argument that it had a sovereign right to nationalise, citing and reviewing materials such as Resolution 1803, and noting that the latter's emphasis on permanent sovereignty reflected principles of

4 Resolution 1803 (XVII) of 14 December 1962, "Permanent sovereignty over natural resources", UN Doc A/RES/3171(XXVIII).

5 Resolution 3281 (XXIX) of 12 December 1974, Charter of Economic Rights and Duties of States, UN Doc A/RES/3281(XXIX).

6 *Texaco Overseas Petroleum Co. and California Asiatic Oil Company v. Libya*, Award, 19 January 1977.

customary international law.[7] However, Dupuy also balanced that sovereign right with other international law obligations – ultimately ruling that Libya must pay compensation pursuant to the contracts it had repudiated. The *Texaco* award thus recognised both sides of the coin: host States have a right to assert control (a key socio-political prerogative), and investors in turn cannot ignore the State's sovereignty, but the State's actions must also respect certain legal obligations (e.g. compensation).

Yet, the *Texaco* case and others in that era reveal that concerns about foreign investor conduct were central to NIEO debates. Libya and its supporters argued that foreign oil companies had long dictated Libya's policies and drained its resources – a form of political and economic interference that needed rectification. The arbitral tribunal's partial validation of Resolution 1803 underscored that investors are not above a State's sovereign decisions. Likewise, other NIEO-era instruments (such as the 1974 UN Declaration on the Establishment of a New International Economic Order[8] and related resolutions) called for transnational corporations to respect the sovereignty, laws, and development priorities of host States, implicitly outlining socio-political obligations even if not in legally binding language.

As such, the roots of investors' socio-political obligations can be traced to general international law principles asserting host State sovereignty, permanent resource sovereignty, and non-interference. By the late 20th century, it was widely accepted that a foreign investor ought not to engage in activities that undermine the host State's political independence or social welfare. This foundational understanding set the stage for a reform of the investment regime that would entail more concrete formulations of investor obligations and duties, especially as many developing countries grew disillusioned with the traditional investor-centric BIT regime.[9]

---

7 *Ibid.*, paras. 81 *et seq.*

8 Declaration on the Establishment of a New International Economic Order, 1 May 1974, UN Doc A/RES/3201(S-VI).

9 As put by A.-G. Sipowo, "Accountability of multinational corporations for human rights violations in investment regimes in Africa" in Yenkong Ngangjoh Hodu & Makane Moïse Mbengue (eds), *African Perspectives in International Investment Law* (2020), p. 88, the question was whether "the investment regime is capable of introspection to respond to one of its major critiques, this is that it only confers rights and does not impose obligations or responsibilities upon corporations".

3 Early Practice from African States regarding Investors' Socio-political Obligations

African States were among the pioneers in translating the above principles into actual investment treaty provisions. Beginning in the 2000s, several African regional organisations adopted instruments that impose explicit obligations on investors – effectively codifying socio-political duties at the regional level.

This trend emerged as part of a broader re-balancing of investment law in favour of sustainable development and host State policy space. International investment law in the early 2000s and 2010s experienced a well-known "backlash",[10] as it was widely perceived that, under the existing international instruments in force, "only the investor is protected, and not the host state itself".[11] At the same time, and concurrently, the reform of international investment law met the growing trend towards the adoption of norms whereby States were deemed responsible for the regulation of the multinational enterprises they had jurisdiction over, and notably with a view to ensuring these private actors' compliance with sustainability standards.[12]

Concretely, these trends took shape in the adoption of new language that expected more – both of States and investors, and did so by touching on their socio-political obligations. One early example is the Southern African Development Community (SADC) Protocol on Finance and Investment of 2006, which is notable for its early endeavour to pursue socio-economic policy goals as an investor duty, and thus explicitly integrating investors into the host State's development strategy and legal framework. For instance, Article 11 on "Sourcing of Requisite Skills" approached the question of hiring with a view towards developing local capacity:

> ARTICLE 11
> SOURCING OF REQUISITE SKILLS
> State Parties shall, subject to their national laws and regulations, permit investors to engage key personnel and other necessary human resources of their choice, regardless of nationality under the following circumstances:

---

10 Michael Waibel *et al.* (eds), *The Backlash Against Investment Arbitration* (Kluwer Law International, 2010).

11 Makane Moïse Mbengue, "Les obligations des investisseurs" *in* Dubin Laurence *et al.*, *L'entreprise multinationale et le droit international* (Pedone 2017). p. 296.

12 Makane Moïse Mbengue & Damien Charlotin, "Role and Responsibilities of States to Ensure MNEs Compliance With Environment and Human Rights Obligations" (2023) ICC Institute Dossier XXI, p. 215.

> (a) where the skills do not exist in the Host State and the Region;
> (b) where State Parties are satisfied that the sourcing of such skills will be in compliance with regional policies;
>
> and where such sourcing would enhance the development of local capacity through skills transfer.

The emphasis was still, however, on *States* being proactive in this respect. Compare, however, with the Agreement issued the next year by the Common Market for Eastern and Southern Africa (COMESA), whose Article 16 explicitly obliged foreign investors to prioritise local and regional labour in their hiring practices. In other words, investors had the right to hire expatriate technical experts, but must give priority to comparably qualified citizens of the host State or other COMESA States if available.

More importantly, the COMESA Agreement also included a provision explicitly entitled "Investor Obligation", in Article 13, which simply stipulated that:

> COMESA investors and their investments shall comply with all applicable domestic measures of the Member State in which their investment is made.

While rather straightforward, this made the respect for domestic law a binding obligation under the treaty, rather than a mere exhortation, or – at most – a condition for jurisdiction over investment disputes.

Perhaps the most forward-looking of the early regional instruments was the ECOWAS Supplementary Act on Investments (adopted by West African States in 2008). The ECOWAS Supplementary Act devotes an entire chapter (Chapter III) to "Obligations and Duties of Investors and Investments", enumerating a comprehensive set of responsibilities. Article 11 sets the tone:

> ARTICLE 11: GENERAL OBLIGATIONS
> (1) Investors and Investments are subject to the laws and regulations of the host State
> (2) Investors and investments must comply with the host State measures prescribing the formalities of establishing an investment, and accept host State jurisdiction with respect to the investment.
> (3) Investors shall strive through their management policies and practices, to contribute to the development objectives of the host States and the local levels of government where the investment is located.
>
> [...].

In the same vein, investors were required to conduct environmental and social impact assessments for projects,[13] and to refrain from corrupt practices.[14] Investors must also maintain "liaison processes" with local communities to ensure their concerns are heard.[15] Crucially, the ECOWAS Act imposes human rights and labour obligations: Article 14(2) mandates that:

> Investors shall uphold human rights in the workplace and the community in which they are located. Investors shall not undertake or cause to be undertaken, acts that breach such human rights. Investors shall not manage or operate the investments in a manner that circumvents human rights obligations, labour standards as well as regional environmental and social obligations, to which the host State and/or home State are Parties.

In other words, an investor in an ECOWAS country has a direct duty to respect human rights and not to use the corporate form to evade the State's own international obligations. This is further reinforced by Article 14(3), which forbids investors from participating in or abetting human rights abuses "in times of peace or during socio-political upheavals" – a clear reference to not supporting violence or conflict. The Act also requires adherence to fundamental ILO labour standards by investors. Critically, the Act included a provision on Investor Liability:

> Investors shall be subject to civil actions for liability in the judicial process of their host State for acts or decisions made in relation to the investment where such acts or decisions lead to significant damage, personal injuries or loss of life in the host State.[16]

13 ECOWAS Supplementary Act on Investments, Article 12. This would later inspire an even more ambitious provision in the Reciprocal Investment Promotion and Protection Agreement between the Government of the Kingdom of Morocco and the Government of the Federal Republic of Nigeria of 3 December 2016.

14 Ibid., art 13.

15 Ibid., art 15.

16 Ibid., art 18(3). See also A.-G. Sipowo, "Accountability of multinational corporations for human rights violations in investment regimes in Africa" in Yenkong Ngangjoh Hodu & Makane Moïse Mbengue (eds), *African Perspectives in International Investment Law* (2020), p. 99: "The ECOWAS Supplementary Act appears to be the most advanced model BIT with regard to corporate liability in investment dispute arbitrations, allowing host or home States to initiate proceedings if investors breach obligations, including human rights."

Taken together, the ECOWAS rules in 2008 were a landmark: they explicitly turned many "soft" expectations (like doing social impact assessments or respecting human rights) into hard law obligations for investors operating in West Africa. This served as a model for later instruments, such as the SADC Model Bilateral Investment Treaty Template, which provided a model for member States to use in renegotiating BITs.[17]

All this paved the way, at the pan-African level, for the Pan-African Investment Code (PAIC), a non-binding draft model code finalised under the auspices of the African Union in 2016. The PAIC was the first continent-wide attempt to articulate a balanced approach to investment, and it explicitly consecrates investors' socio-political obligations. Steeped in the language of non-intervention that makes its origins explicit,[18] Article 20 of the PAIC is titled "Socio-political Obligations of Investors", and provides that:

1. Investors shall adhere to socio-political obligations including, but not exclusively, the following:
   a. respect for national sovereignty and observance of domestic laws, regulations and administrative practices;
   b. respect for socio-cultural values;
   c. non-interference in internal political affairs;
   d. non-interference in intergovernmental relations; and
   e. respect for labor rights.
2. Investors shall not influence the appointment of persons to public office or finance political parties.
3. Investors shall refrain from exercising restrictive practices and from trying to achieve gains through unlawful means.[19]

Per the following article, investors must also refrain from corrupt or fraudulent practices. Notably, the PAIC goes beyond the purely "political" sphere and incorporates corporate social responsibility (CSR) as a binding obligation – it requires investors to contribute to the social and economic development of

17 SADC Model Bilateral Investment Treaty Template – with Commentary (July 2012), available online.

18 Another likely influence, since many African States are also members of the Organization of the Islamic Community (OIC), was the OIC Investment Agreement of 1981, whose Article 9 had long included a provision requiring investors to comply with domestic laws and regulations, and to abstain from any behaviour/action that might disrupt public morals, order, or the public interest.

19 In turn, this language notably inspired Article 24 of the 2017 version of the SADC Model BIT.

the host State and local community. For example, PAIC Article 22 obliges investors to ensure their economic activities do not conflict with the host State's development policies and to "contribute to the economic, social and environmental progress" of the host.

Although the PAIC is a model code (it has not been enacted as a treaty), its significance lies in consolidating Africa's approach to investor obligations in one document. It represents the clearest statement that Africa sees investors as having enforceable duties: not to meddle in politics, not to harm society, and to act as partners in sustainable development. It proved highly influential, not only in shaping later treaties – such as the ECOWAS Common Investment Code of 2018, whose Article 32 mirrors Article 22 of the PAIC – but also national laws on investment: Ethiopia's 2020 Law on investment includes the following duty for investors:

> All investors shall give due regard to social and environmental sustainability values including environmental protection standards and social inclusion objectives in carrying out their investment projects.[20]

In summary, by the 2010s African States – through SADC, COMESA, ECOWAS, and the African Union's PAIC – had developed a body of "home-grown" practice on socio-political obligations for investors. This regional practice moved the concept from the realm of UN General Assembly declarations into actual treaty texts and models. Investors in many African jurisdictions could now be held to legal standards of behaviour: obey domestic law, respect sovereignty, avoid corrupting politics, uphold human rights, and so forth. These innovations set the stage for the next step: making such obligations truly enforceable, which is precisely what the latest African investment agreement aims to do.

4 Crystallisation in the AfCFTA Investment Protocol and Its Implications

The culmination of the African approach to socio-political obligations is found in the new Investment Protocol to the AfCFTA. Concluded in 2023, the AfCFTA Investment Protocol consolidates many of the earlier regional innovations and "crystallizes" these investor obligations into a binding multilateral treaty.

This development is potentially groundbreaking: it means that across the entire African continent, foreign investors will be subjected to a common set

20 Ethiopia, Investment Proclamation No. 1180/2020 (available online), art 54(2).

of socio-political obligations, enforced through a unified dispute settlement mechanism.

The AfCFTA Investment Protocol contains a dedicated section (Part IV of the Protocol) on Obligations of Investors and Investments, mirroring the structure of the PAIC. In particular, Article 36 of the AfCFTA Investment Protocol is titled "Socio-political Obligations", and once again lays out the clear influence of the duty of non-intervention, since it provides that:

> Investors shall refrain from any interference in the internal affairs of State Parties and in their intergovernmental relations, in particular to influence the appointment of persons to public office, finance political parties or undermine the political stability or security of the Host State or to influence public opinion in a manner contrary to this Article.[21]

In other words, this language directly targets the core political aspects of investor conduct: regime change meddling, political financing, or other subversive activities by investors are clearly prohibited treaty violations. Beyond Article 36, the AfCFTA Protocol imposes an array of related obligations: Article 37 on Anti-Corruption prohibits investors from offering bribes or undue advantages to public officials and requires investors to cooperate with States in fighting corruption. Article 38 on Corporate Social Responsibility calls on investors to "achieve the highest possible level of contribution to the sustainable development of the Host State and local community" by adopting socially responsible practices. This includes commitments to environmental protection, human capital development (e.g. training local employees), gender equality, and fair labour practices. Article 39 on Corporate Governance obliges investors to meet transparency and accountability standards in line with international best practices (e.g. proper disclosure of financial information). In short, the AfCFTA Investment Protocol translates the previously modelled investor duties (from SADC, PAIC, etc.) into binding obligations at a continental scale.

All this in particular sets the stage for the potential operationalisation of these obligations through dispute settlement. In this respect, the Protocol contains a sophisticated provision on investor liability that recognises the potential role of domestic courts in this respect:

---

21 As well, Article 34(2), which provides that '[i]nvestors shall not exploit or use natural resources to the detriment of the rights and interests of the Host State and local communities', also harks back to 20th century debates regarding sovereignty over natural resources reviewed *supra*.

Article 47
Investor Liability

1. Investors and their investments shall, where applicable and in accordance with domestic laws and regulations, be subject to civil actions for liability in the judicial process of their Home State for the acts, decisions or omissions made in the Host State in relation to the investment where such acts, decisions or omissions lead to damage, personal injuries or loss of life in the Host State.
2. State Parties shall develop rules and procedures that allow for, or do not prevent or unduly restrict, the bringing of court actions relating to the civil liability of investors in the territory of their Home States, taking into account rules governing conflict of laws and the recognition and enforcement of foreign judgments.
3. For greater certainty, this Article does not exclude the possibility to bring civil actions against investors and their investments before the domestic courts of the Host State.[22]

While the first two paragraphs echo earlier language found in previous African instruments, the third one is particularly interesting in what it signals: regulation of investors' misdeeds is not only the responsibility of the home State, but can also become that of the host State.[23]

The real test, however, will be if these obligations can also be operationalised in investor–State dispute settlement proceedings (ISDS). Traditional BITs did not allow host States to bring claims against investors – only investors could sue States,[24] although all depended on the wording of the treaty at

22 As contemplated in Makane Moïse Mbengue and Stefanie Schacherer, "The 'Africanization' of international investment law: The Pan-African Investment Code and the reform of the international investment regime" (2017) *Journal of World Investment and Trade* 18, p. 445, fn. 193: "There are other ways of enforcement of investors' obligations, such as by creating a monetary liability in domestic courts of the host State for a breach of the treaty obligations by an investor."

23 While, as mentioned above, the ECOWAS Supplementary Act also contemplated such actions by the host State, they were limited to particularly egregious conduct, such as "acts or decisions leading to significant damage, personal injuries or loss of life in the host State".

24 *Spyridon Roussalis v. Romania*, ICSID Case No. ARB/06/1, Award, 7 December 2011, paras. 859–877; *Antoine Goetz & Others and S.A. Affinage des Métaux v. Republic of Burundi*, ICSID Case No. ARB/01/2, Award, 21 June 2012. See also Jean Kalicki, "Counterclaims by States in Investment Arbitration" (*Investment Treaty News*, 14 January 2013, available online).

stake.[25] This was both a procedural and substantial issue: the underlying instrument might lack a pathway to make such counterclaims admissible in arbitral proceedings, and, even if a State was not barred from bringing counterclaims, the treaty might also be missing relevant obligations incumbent on the investor.[26] This meant that even if a treaty technically required investors to, say, obey local law, there was often no international forum for the State to hold the investor accountable.

While the final version of the Investment Protocol relegated ISDS provisions to an Annex (which still needs to be negotiated), an earlier "Zero Draft" version might show which way the wind is blowing.[27] Notably, Article 9(b) of the Zero Draft provided that:

> Article 9
> Consent to Arbitration
> Consent to arbitration shall be provided as follows:
> a. each State Party consents to the submission of a claim to arbitration under this Article in accordance with this Annex; and
> b. by submitting a claim to arbitration, the investor also consents to counterclaims by the Host State for an alleged breach of the Protocol.

In other words, if an investor initiates an arbitration, the State can counter-sue that investor within the same proceeding for any breaches.[28] If adopted, this approach would be a game-changer in operationalising socio-political obligations: a mining company suing an African government, for example, might find itself on the defensive if the government counterclaims that the company violated environmental standards, engaged in corruption, or interfered in local politics in breach of the Protocol's provisions. This would ensure that investor misconduct can be adjudicated in tandem with the investor's claims.[29]

---

25 UNCITRAL Working Group III, UN Doc A/CN.9/WG.III/WP.193, para. 36.

26 See, e.g., *United Agencies Limited SA v. Algeria*, ICSID Case No. ARB/20/01, Award, 25 July 2022, paras. 453–458, finding that the BIT's investor–State arbitration clause did not cover obligations under Algerian domestic law.

27 Protocol on Investment to the Agreement Establishing the African Continental Free Trade Area, ZERO DRAFT (Accra, November 2021), available online.

28 Similar language has found its way into more recent treaties: see, e.g. the Agreement between the Government of the Republic of Kazakhstan and the Government of Turkmenistan on the Mutual Promotion and Protection of Investments, executed in Ashgabat on 10 October 2024, art 13(7).

29 Here as well, the roots are deeper than seems at first glance: the ECOWAS Supplementary Act had already included similar provisions in its Article 18, "Relation of investor's liability to dispute settlement". The innovation of the Zero Draft's approach would be to

As commentators have observed, imposing such obligations can enhance investor accountability and restore credibility to the ISDS system.[30] This could result in tribunals reducing or offsetting the investor's damages, or even awarding damages to the State on a counterclaim. There are precedents for this approach: most recently, in *Qatar Pharma v. Saudi Arabia*,[31] an ISDS tribunal under the OIC Agreement took into account the investor's (minor) breaches of domestic laws in its assessment of the *quantum* of compensation. What's notable is that the tribunal did so in light of Article 9 of the OIC Investment Agreement, an early expression of States' concern for socio-political obligations.

As such, in practical terms, the AfCFTA investor obligations could significantly influence how investment disputes in Africa are argued and decided. Investors bringing claims would need to demonstrate their own compliance with the treaty's duties, not just the host State's breaches. We may see African arbitral tribunals considering issues such as: Did the investor conduct proper social and environmental impact assessments? Did it consult with local communities? Was it complicit in any corrupt dealings or political interference? These factors could become relevant in determining liability and remedies. For instance, a tribunal might find that a State's regulatory measure was justified (and thus not a treaty breach) because it was implemented to sanction the investor's non-compliance with environmental laws. Or, even if a State is found liable for breaching an obligation (say, expropriation), the damages awarded to the investor might be reduced if the investor also broke its own obligations, perhaps amounting to contributory fault.

The broader implication is a redefined investor–State relationship in Africa: one based not only on the investor's rights but also on mutual obligations aimed at sustainable development. Socio-political obligations in the AfCFTA regime anchor foreign investment in a framework of respect – respect for the host State's sovereignty, its people, and its laws. This does not mean investors will stop pursuing profits or that States will never be held to account for unfair treatment. Rather, it means that investment adjudicators will have a fuller toolkit to ensure that investment activities advance, rather than undermine,

straightforwardly ensure the investor's consent to such counterclaims, putting them starkly on notice.

30 Samuel Kahura, "ICCA Kigali 2025: Saving ISDS through Modernization - The AfCFTA Protocol on Investment as a Blueprint for Drafting of Investment Treaties" (*Kluwer Arbitration Blog*, 27 May 2025), available online.

31 *Qatar Pharma for Pharmaceutical Industries and Dr Ahmed Bin Mohammad Al Haie Al Sulaiti v. Kingdom of Saudi Arabia*, ICC Case No. 25830/AYZ/ELU, Final Award, 23 October 2024.

host countries' social and political objectives. This balance could help address the legitimacy concerns that have long dogged ISDS by showing that egregious investor behaviour will not be immunised.

5 Conclusion

In conclusion, the concept of socio-political obligations in investment treaties has evolved from vague ideological underpinnings to concrete legal commitments – especially within African investment instruments. From the NIEO resolutions condemning foreign corporate interference, to the regional African treaties embedding investor duties, and now to the AfCFTA Investment Protocol making those duties enforceable, there is a clear trajectory towards accountability and balance.

Investors in Africa are now expected not only to refrain from injurious political or social conduct but also to affirmatively contribute to the host State's sustainable development. This represents a paradigm shift in international investment law. While the full impact will depend on how ISDS might evolve, and how tribunals will apply these provisions in practice, Africa's leadership in this area could inspire similar reforms globally. Socio-political obligations in investment treaties ensure that the privilege of investing abroad comes with responsibilities – a development that many believe is essential for a fair and equitable international investment regime going forward.

CHAPTER 8

Soft Law or Hard Law? Selected International Labour and Indigenous Peoples' Rights Standards Transposable to Investor Obligations in New-Age Investment Treaties

Mohit Khubchandani

1 Introduction

Not many discuss that one century ago, during 1922–26, the Permanent Court of International Justice (PCIJ) endorsed, in three Advisory Opinions, the competence of the International Labour Organization (ILO) to deal with questions concerning the *international regulation of the conditions of labour of persons employed in agriculture*[1] and those concerning the regulation of the "personal work of the employer."[2] These judgments were rendered starting three years after the first-ever Hours of Work (Industry) Convention of 1919. Looking forward 100 years, the ILO recently approached the ICJ to deliver an Advisory Opinion and the ICJ confirmed that the right to strike exists in international law.[3]

In this context, at the public hearings in October 2025, the ILO's Legal Adviser, Ms. Tomi Kohiyama, emphasised that:

---

1 Competence of the ILO in regard to International Regulation of the Conditions of the Labour of Persons Employed in Agriculture, Advisory Opinion, 1922 P.C.I.J. (ser. B) No. 2 (Aug. 12); Competence of the ILO to Examine Proposal for the Organization and Development of the Methods of Agricultural Production, Advisory Opinion, 1922 P.C.I.J. (ser. B) No. 3 (Aug. 12).

2 *Competence of the ILO to Regulate Incidentally the Personal Work of the Employer* (Advisory Opinion) [1926] PCIJ Rep Ser B No 13.

3 The ILO formulated the following Request for Advisory Opinion: "[i]s the right to strike of workers and their organizations protected under the Freedom of Association and Protection of the Right to Organise Convention, 1948 (No. 87)?" < https://www.icj-cij.org/sites/default/files/case-related/191/191-20231110-req-01-00-en.pdf> accessed 16 November 2024 ("ILO Request for Advisory Opinion 2023"). See also Right to Strike Under ILO Convention No. 87 (ICJ, Advisory Opinion, 21 May 2026).

 | HTTPS://DOI.ORG/10.1163/9789004769854-009

> 32. The Permanent Court of International Justice laid the foundation for the future of our Organization. Three years following its establishment, the ILO sought the opinion of the Court on a matter intrinsic to its functioning and normative action: the designation of employers and workers as members of the national tripartite delegations to the International Labour Conference. That first advisory opinion remains to this day key to understanding tripartism and is still regularly cited by the Credentials Committee of the International Labour Conference.
>
> 33. Today, the Organization turns to the Court [International Court of Justice] on a matter of equal significance [the right to strike]: the interpretation of one of the ILO's fundamental conventions that gives effect to the constitutional principle of freedom of association, which is quintessential to the ILO in its role in bringing together governments, employers and workers, on an equal footing, I quote the Constitution, 'in free discussion and democratic decision with a view to the promotion of the common welfare'.[4]

Thus, labour activities (such as in agriculture) are not only regulated in terms of State conduct for the purposes of discerning State Responsibility. Where a subject-matter such as agriculture may be the ground of investments by "investors"[5] in the host States, and if the ILO has competence to regulate State conduct in this regard, it is arguable – as a corollary – that the ILO regime should influence conduct by investors as well.

More than thirty-five years ago the historic ILO Indigenous and Tribal Peoples Convention, 1989 (No. 169) (ILO 169)[6] was adopted to "[e]nsur[e] that members of these peoples benefit on an equal footing from the rights and opportunities which national laws and regulations grant to other members of the population"[7] and to ensure that "[t]he rights of the peoples concerned to the natural resources pertaining to their lands shall be specially safeguarded. These rights include the right of these peoples to participate in

4 *Right to Strike under ILO Convention No. 87* (Request for Advisory Opinion) (Verbatim Record of 6 October 2025) CR 2025/16, 32 <https://www.icj-cij.org/sites/default/files/case-related/191/191-20251006-ora-01-00-bic.pdf> accessed 16 November 2024.

5 An investor is defined differently in different investment agreements. However, by and large, they implicate similar meanings.

6 Indigenous and Tribal Peoples Convention (adopted 27 June 1989) 1650 UNTS 383 (ILO Convention No 169).

7 ILO Convention No 169, art 2(a).

the use, management and conservation of these resources."[8] The special needs and status of these communities should not only be preserved by States but also be respected by the investors.

Indigenous Peoples do not have an official definition in the UN system (or even in the UNDRIP); however, in some contexts, other terms such as Tribes, First Peoples/Nations, Aboriginals, Ethnic groups, Adivasi, or Janajati are utilised.[9]

According to the Chairperson of the Working Group on Indigenous Populations, relevant factors to categorise the concept of "Indigenous" include: (a) Priority in time with respect to the occupation and use of a specific territory. (b) The voluntary perpetuation of cultural distinctiveness, which may include the aspects of language, social organisation, religion and spiritual values, modes of production, laws, and institutions. (c) Self-identification, as well as recognition by other groups or by State authorities as a distinct collectivity. (d) An experience of subjugation, marginalisation, dispossession, exclusion, or discrimination, regardless of whether these conditions persist.[10]

Investors thus ought to be cognisant that the world history of indigenous peoples has been scarred by attempts to discriminate or erase their identities.[11]

Malignant investors can seriously impact the rights deserved by these distinct peoples. As an illustration, according to Statista, Apple's total net sales amounted to 383.29 billion U.S. dollars in the 2023 financial year alone.[12] In stark comparison, the entire Gross Domestic Product (GDP) of more than 100 countries is less than that figure.[13] In this context, it is safe to posit that not only

---

8 Ibid., art 15(1).

9 United Nations Permanent Forum on Indigenous Issues, 'Factsheet: Who Are Indigenous Peoples?' <https://www.un.org/esa/socdev/unpfii/documents/5session_factsheet1.pdf> accessed 29 June 2025.

10 UN OHCHR, 'The United Nations Declaration on the Rights of Indigenous Peoples: A Manual for National Human Rights Institutions' (August 2013) <https://www.ohchr.org/sites/default/files/Documents/Issues/IPeoples/UNDRIPManualForNHRIs.pdf> accessed 29 June 2025.

11 Amazon Watch, 'Respecting Indigenous Rights: An Actionable Due Diligence Toolkit for Institutional Investors' (April 2023) 14 < https://respectingindigenousrights.org/respecting-indigenous-rights.pdf> accessed 29 June 2025.

12 F Laricchia, 'Apple Revenue Worldwide 2024' (Statista, 5 November 2024) <https://www.statista.com/statistics/265125/total-net-sales-of-apple-since-2004/> accessed 27 November 2024.

13 Worldometer, 'GDP by Country' <https://www.worldometers.info/gdp/gdp-by-country/> accessed 27 September 2024.

do States, but in fact, more so, foreign investors many a time overstep the rights of labourers or indigenous peoples during the operation of their investment in a host State. It is thus no surprise that the asymmetry between investor rights and investor obligations in bilateral investment treaties and investment chapters of comprehensive economic agreements has also been criticised.[14]

To validate the progress towards the regulation of investor conduct, the ICSID tribunal – nearly a decade ago – in *Urbaser v. Argentina* made it clear that:

> 1195. [...] [I]nternational law accepts corporate social responsibility as a standard of crucial importance for companies operating in the field of international commerce. This standard includes commitments to comply with human rights in the framework of those entities' operations conducted in countries other than the country of their seat or incorporation. [...] **[I]t can no longer be admitted that companies operating internationally are immune from becoming subjects of international law.** [...]. The focus must be, therefore, on contextualizing a corporation's specific activities as they relate to the human right at issue in order to determine whether any international law obligations attach to the non-State individual.[15]

Thus, while some developments have been made in Investor–State Dispute Settlement (ISDS), whereby the ILO and other human rights treaty regimes have been referenced in investment treaties, this paper argues that much more needs to be done by a systematic selection of inter-related human rights regimes and tools applicable to investment law, rather than a hotch potch application.

Section 2 begins with the author's select overview of relevant soft and hard law tools and instruments at the disposal of States when negotiating investment treaties.

Section 3 discusses the relevant (albeit scant) case law that expands on investor obligations in the context of labour standards and rights of indigenous peoples.

---

14 N Bueno, A Yilmaz Vastardis, and I Ngueuleu-Djeuga, 'Investor Human Rights and Environmental Obligations: The Need to Redesign Corporate Social Responsibility Clauses' (2023) 24 J World Inv & Trade 179; N Monebhurrun, 'The (Mis)Use of Development in International Investment Law: Understanding the Jurist's Limits to Work with Development Issues' (2017) 10 Law & Dev Rev 451.

15 *Urbaser v. Argentina*, ICSID Case No. ARB/07/26, Award (8 Dec 2016), para 1193.

Section 4 discusses, in passing, the current investment agreements referencing labour standards, with particular emphasis on the recent African Continental Free Trade Area (AfCFTA) Draft Investment Protocol (AfCFTA Investment Protocol), which is a welcome development.[16]

Section 5 offers some concluding thoughts and proposes certain forward-looking solutions, such as: (a) pithier investor-centric obligations rather than generic mentions to labour standards and the ILO regime, which are thus more suitable to regulating State conduct; (b) careful drafting of treaties capturing the essence of practical implications of labour standards and rights of indigenous peoples; and (c) taking inspiration from the language of soft law instruments to include their essence as treaty obligations binding upon States and investors alike (notwithstanding the differences emanating out of State Responsibility).

2 The Relevant International Legal Regime at a Glance

The modern international investment law regime was conceived in the late 1950s, with the first BIT signed between West Germany and Pakistan.[17] However, on the other hand, the core principles of international labour law began to emerge much earlier, in 1919 (as discussed before). Authors such as Kaufmann have claimed that labour rights contained in the Universal Declaration of Human Rights (UDHR) constitute customary international law.[18] She has also noted that, given the large number of ILO member States, these obligations can also be considered *erga omnes* in nature.[19] Therefore, it is likely (or at least arguable) that investment treaties can greatly benefit from the languages

16 Edit, 'AfCFTA Protocol on Investment (2023)' (Electronic Database of Investment Treaties (EDIT) <https://edit.wti.org/document/show/e5d51824-c467-4e24-922b-3fb376d89550> accessed 24 October 2024.

17 Treaty for the Promotion and Protection of Investments (with Protocol and exchange of notes) (Germany–Pakistan) (signed 25 November 1959) <https://investmentpolicy.unctad.org/international-investment-agreements/treaty-files/1387/download> accessed 30 September 2024.

18 L-L Fontaine, "Christine Kaufmann, Globalisation and Labour Rights: The Conflicts between Core Labour Rights and International Economic Law, Oxford, Hart, 2007" (2007) 20 RQDI 471, 475; see UNGA, "Universal Declaration of Human Rights" (10 December 1948) UN Doc A/RES/217(III)A (UDHR).

19 Ibid., 76.

of instruments that have either (a) crystallised into customary international law or are (b) inspired from ILO or other instruments that have many States as parties or signatories (this is particularly helpful when negotiating multilateral investment treaties). States are, of course, also free to take inspiration from progressive domestic labour legislations.[20]

Investors' labour standards obligations and indigenous peoples' rights-related obligations appearing in investment treaties are only a recent phenomenon, and there is still a long way to go. Thus, at first, it is imperative to systematically select the core focal regime of international labour law relevant for investors – so it can be reflected well in progressive investment treaties. This is because: (a) there are scores of international labour law and indigenous peoples' rights' related instruments (having varying levels of binding or persuasive values depending, e.g., upon the number of States that are parties to them);[21] and (b) in any event, those labour standards applicable through conventions that were originally designed for States may not necessarily apply to investors *stricto sensu*. It is imperative – through careful negotiation and drafting of treaties – to not only choose the language most suitable for application to investors, but also create different standards and burdens of proof (and perhaps reparation standards) when it comes to investors' obligations. These obligations could further be sub-categorised when it comes to violation of peremptory norms.[22]

Now, in the context of rights of indigenous peoples, when we speak of State obligations, their rights are largely governed by the ILO regime. However, there is an evident gap when it comes to their rights' regulation for investor conduct. The expansion of business activities into indigenous lands without

20 Oyster "5 Countries with the Best Employment Laws for Workers' Rights" <https://www.oysterhr.com/library/five-countries-with-the-best-labor-and-employment-laws-for-workers-rights> accessed 28 November 2024. These are Norway, Denmark, Belgium, The Netherlands, and Germany.

21 ILO, "List of Ratifications by Convention" < https://normlex.ilo.org/dyn/normlex/en/f?p=1000:12001> accessed 30 September 2024.

22 Some authors argue that certain forms of child labour are equivalent to slavery, thus making them *jus cogens* violations (Katarina Maletić, Investor Obligations under International Law to Respect Labour Rights and to Comply with International labour standards (Master's Thesis, University of Amsterdam, 2020), relying upon Federico Lenzerini, 'International Trade and Child Labour Standards' in Francesco Franconi, *Environment, Human Rights and International Trade* 308).

the Free, Prior, and Informed Consent (FPIC) of indigenous peoples increases the adverse impacts on the human rights of indigenous peoples.[23]

A toolkit published in 2023 – titled "*Respecting Indigenous Rights: An Actionable Due Diligence Toolkit for Institutional Investors*" – crucially notes:

> As investments on or near Indigenous lands increase, failing to ensure that Indigenous rights are respected means investors risk failing to deliver on their climate and environment commitments. They also risk increasingly being involved in human rights abuses through their investee companies or through the value chains of their investee companies. Investors' failure to understand Indigenous peoples' rights also ignores material business risks, which have already cost investors and companies billions in cost overruns, delays, and project cancellation, in addition to reputational damage.[24]

In light of the above, in the author's view, the following are the core selected ILO and other instruments relevant to regulate investors' conduct in this sphere.

2.1 Soft Law Tools

2.1.1 ILO Declaration on Fundamental Principles and Rights at Work (1998)

The ILO Declaration on Fundamental Principles and Rights at Work, adopted in 1998 (and amended in 2022)[25] upholds "the basic human values that are vital to our social and economic lives"; these include: (a) freedom of association;[26] (b) the elimination of all forms of forced or compulsory labour; (c) the elimination of discrimination in respect of employment and occupation; and (d) a

23 See e.g., JR Owen and others, 'Fast track to failure? Energy transition minerals and the future of consultation and consent' (2022) 89 Energy Research & Social Science 102665; Global Witness, 'Last Line of Defence: The industries causing the climate crisis and attacks against land and environmental defenders' (2021) <https://www.globalwitness.org/en/campaigns/environmental-activists/last-line-defence/> accessed 1 July 2025; A Scheidel and others, 'Environmental conflicts and defenders: A global overview' (2020) 63 Global Environmental Change 102104.

24 Amazon Watch (n 11) 6.

25 ILO, 'ILO Declaration on Fundamental Principles and Rights at Work and its Follow-Up' (18 June 1998) <https://www.ilo.org/resource/conference-paper/ilo-1998-declaration-fundamental-principles-and-rights-work-and-its-follow> accessed 30 September 2024.

26 Relatedly, the ILO Request for Advisory Opinion 2023 (n 3) asked the ICJ, and it confirmed that the right to strike is protected under the Freedom of Association and Protection of the Right to Organise Convention, 1948 (No. 87).

safe and healthy working environment. Given the nature of these topics, these are standards that should equally be applicable upon investors and States alike.

2.1.2 UN Guiding Principles on Business and Human Rights (2011)

The United Nations Guiding Principles on Business and Human Rights (UN Guiding Principles) (with commentaries)[27] are a set of 31 soft law principles adopted under the aegis of the Office of the United Nations High Commissioner for Human Rights (OHCHR), implementing the United Nations "Protect, Respect and Remedy" framework on the issue of human rights and transnational corporations and other business enterprises. Since these principles are primarily centred around corporations, they are easier to take inspiration from (in contrast to sources/instruments structured around States) – and transpose to – treaties' text governing investor obligations. In particular, Principle 12 is relevant to identifying rules governing labour standards. It notes:

> The responsibility of business enterprises to respect human rights refers to internationally recognized human rights – understood, at a minimum, as those expressed in the International Bill of Human Rights and the principles concerning fundamental rights set out in the International Labour Organization's Declaration on Fundamental Principles and Rights at Work.[28]

While elaborating the standards, the commentary to the said Principle notes that the UDHR, the International Covenant on Civil and Political Rights (ICCPR), and the International Covenant on Economic, Social and Cultural Rights (ICESCR), coupled with the principles concerning fundamental rights in the eight ILO core conventions as set out in the Declaration on Fundamental Principles and Rights at Work, are the relevant standards that business enterprises' conduct should be subject to.[29]

---

27 UN OHCHR, 'Guiding Principles on Business and Human Rights' (2011) < https://www.ohchr.org/sites/default/files/documents/publications/guidingprinciplesbusinesshr_en.pdf> accessed 29 October 2024.

28 UN Guiding Principles, principle 12.

29 Ibid., Commentary to principles 12, 14.

2.1.3 OECD Guidelines for Multinational Enterprises on Responsible Business Conduct (2023)

The OECD Guidelines for Multinational Enterprises on Responsible Business Conduct (OECD Guidelines 2023)[30] – according to their foreword – are a very recent set of "recommendations jointly addressed by governments to multinational enterprises to enhance the business contribution to sustainable development and address adverse impacts associated with business activities on people, planet, and society".[31] Since these have already been negotiated by governments, it is possible that governments will be more receptive to the standards described in them when negotiating investment treaties with investor obligations.

These Guidelines have a dedicated Chapter V on "Employment and Industrial Relations", providing robust labour standards that enterprises should be subjected to. The commentary to this chapter also crucially notes that, "[i]n accordance with the ILO Human Resources Development Recommendation 195, enterprises are also encouraged to invest, to the greatest extent practicable, in training and lifelong learning while ensuring equal opportunities to training for women and other vulnerable groups, such as youth, low-skilled people, people with disabilities, migrants, older workers, and Indigenous Peoples."[32]

According to the Guidelines, enterprises should respect the rights of workers to establish or join trade unions and representative organisations for the purpose of collective bargaining,[33] and engage in constructive negotiations.[34] The enterprises should, in particular, take efforts to abolish the worst forms of child labour.[35] They should also promote equal opportunity without discrimination on the basis of "race, colour, sex, age, religion, political opinion, national extraction or social origin" or "disabilities."[36] An endeavour should also be made to provide a safe and healthy working environment in line with the ILO Declaration on Fundamental Principles and Rights at Work,[37] and the

30 OECD, 'OECD Guidelines for Multinational Enterprises on Responsible Business Conduct' (2023) <https://doi.org/10.1787/81f92357-en> accessed 29 October 2024 (OECD Guidelines 2023).

31 OECD Guidelines 2023, p. 3.

32 Ibid., p. 32.

33 Ibid., ch V, art 1(a).

34 Ibid., art 1(b).

35 Ibid., arts 1(b), (c).

36 Ibid., art 1(e).

37 Ibid., art 1(f); see also Ibid., art 4(c).

wages "should be at least adequate to satisfy the basic needs of the workers and their families".[38] Article 3 also relates to consultation and co-operation between employers and workers and their representatives through legitimate processes. Since these processes are not yet entirely clear, the ILO regime will also benefit from the Advisory Opinion sought from the ICJ on the right to strike in international law.[39]

2.1.4 ILO Tripartite Declaration of Principles concerning Multinational Enterprises and Social Policy

This recent Declaration (ILO MNE Declaration) of 2022 offers guidelines to multinational enterprises, governments, and employers' and workers' organisations in the areas of employment, training, conditions of work and life, and industrial relations.[40] It has robust principles on: (a) "Employment promotion";[41] (b) "Social security";[42] (c) "Elimination of forced or compulsory labour";[43] (d) "Effective abolition of child labour: Minimum age and worst forms";[44] (e) "Equality of opportunity and treatment";[45] (f) "Security of

38 Ibid., art 4(b).

39 ILO Request for Advisory Opinion 2023 (n 3).

40 ILO, 'Tripartite Declaration of Principles Concerning Multinational Enterprises and Social Policy' (6th edn, 2022) 5 <https://www.ilo.org/ilo-department-sustainable-enterprises-productivity-and-just-transition/areas-work/tripartite-declaration-principles-concerning-multinational-enterprises-and> accessed 28 November 2024 (ILO MNE Declaration).

41 ILO MNE Declaration, principles 13–21 (these deal with conducive employment standards in line with national social development policies and the UN Sustainable Development Goals (SDG 8)).

42 Ibid., principle 22 (deals with promotion of progressively higher social security standards).

43 Ibid., principles 23–25 (these deal with governments developing national action plans in consultation with employers' and workers' organisations).

44 Ibid., principles 26–27 (these principles crucially note that "[m]ultinational enterprises, as well as national enterprises, should respect the minimum age for admission to employment or work in order to secure the effective abolition of child labour in their operations").

45 Ibid., principles 28–31 (these principles further crucially note that "[m]ultinational enterprises should be guided by the principle of non-discrimination throughout their operations…").

employment";[46] (g) "Training";[47] (h) "Conditions of work and life";[48] (i) "Safety and health";[49] (j) "Industrial relations";[50] (k) "Freedom of association and the right to organise";[51] (l) "Collective bargaining";[52] (m) "Consultation";[53] and (n) "Access to remedy and examination of grievances"[54] – in this context, Principle 65 imperatively notes that:

> Multinational enterprises should use their leverage to encourage their business partners to provide effective means of enabling remediation for abuses of internationally recognized human rights.[55]

46 Ibid., principles 32–36 (these principles note that "[m]ultinational enterprises as well as national enterprises, through active employment planning, should endeavour to provide stable employment for workers employed by each enterprise and should observe freely negotiated obligations concerning employment stability and social security…" Additionally, these enterprises should also provide "reasonable notice" to the employers in case of transfers or takeovers of corporate structures. They should also avoid "arbitrary dismissal procedures."

47 Ibid., principles 37–40 (these principles note that multinational enterprises should setup funds with the aim of "encouraging skill formation, lifelong learning and development as well as providing vocational guidance").

48 Ibid., principles 41–42 (these principles note that "[w]ages, benefits and conditions of work offered by multinational enterprises across their operations should be not less favourable to the workers than those offered by comparable employers in the host country").

49 Ibid., principles 43–46 (these principles note that multinational enterprises "should maintain the highest standards of safety and health, in conformity with national requirements [and international safety and health standards], bearing in mind their relevant experience within the enterprise as a whole, including any knowledge of special hazards").

50 Ibid., principle 47 (noting that "[m]ultinational enterprises should observe standards of industrial relations throughout their operations").

51 Ibid., principles 48–54 (these principles highlight that workers employed by multinational enterprises (including those established in host countries) should have the right to form associations, including, in particular, enjoyment of "adequate protection against acts of anti-union discrimination in respect of their employment").

52 Ibid., principles 55–62 (these principles relate to the workers' rights of negotiating collective bargaining agreements with employers to ensure appropriate conditions of employment reflecting balanced rights and obligations of the parties concerned). Employers should provide the workers with the information concerning local relevant laws so that it enables fair and meaningful negotiations.)

53 Ibid., principle 63, which requires regular consultation between multinational enterprises and workers "on matters of mutual concern".

54 Ibid., principles 64–66.

55 Ibid., principle 65.

Annex I of the ILO MNE Declaration can also be a very useful tool for treaty drafters when they are looking for the relevant ILO instruments as per the subject matters discussed immediately above, depending also upon which of these instruments the negotiating countries have signed and place most importance upon. An excerpt of the annexure is reproduced below:

Annex I

List of ILO Declarations, international labour Conventions and Recommendations, codes of practice, guidelines, and other guidance documents relevant to the Tripartite Declaration of Principles concerning Multinational Enterprises and Social Policy.

A. *ILO Declarations*

- ILO Declaration on Fundamental Principles and Rights at Work (1998), as amended in 2022.
- ILO Declaration on Social Justice for a Fair Globalization (2008), as amended in 2022.

TABLE 8.1 International Labour Conventions and Recommendations

Forced labour	– Forced Labour Convention, 1930 (No. 29) and its Protocol of 2014; and Forced Labour (Indirect Compulsion) Recommendation, 1930 (No. 35) – Abolition of Forced Labour Convention, 1957 (No. 105) – Forced Labour (Supplementary Measures) Recommendation, 2014 (No. 203)
Child labour	– Minimum Age Convention (No. 138) and Recommendation (No. 146), 1973 – Worst Forms of Child Labour Convention (No. 182) and Recommendation (No. 190), 1999
Non-discrimination	– Equal Remuneration Convention (No. 100) and Recommendation (No. 90), 1951 – Discrimination (Employment and Occupation) Convention (No. 111) and Recommendation (No. 111), 1958

TABLE 8.1 International Labour Conventions and Recommendations (*cont.*)

Freedom of association and collective bargaining	– Freedom of Association and Protection of the Right to Organise Convention, 1948 (No. 87) – Right to Organise and Collective Bargaining Convention, 1949 (No. 98) – Collective Bargaining Convention (No. 154) and Recommendation (No. 163), 1981
A safe and healthy working environment	– Occupational Safety and Health Convention (No. 155) and Recommendation (No. 164), 1981 – Promotional Framework for Occupational Safety and Health Convention (No. 187) and Recommendation (No. 197), 2006
Industrial relations	– Workers' Representatives Convention, 1971 (No. 135) – Voluntary Conciliation and Arbitration Recommendation, 1951 (No. 92) – Co-operation at the Level of the Undertaking Recommendation, 1952 (No. 94) – Communications within the Undertaking Recommendation, 1967 (No. 129) – Examination of Grievances Recommendation, 1967 (No. 130)
Employment promotion	– Employment Policy Convention (No. 122), and Recommendation (No. 122), 1964 – Employment Promotion and Protection against Unemployment Convention (No. 168) and Recommendation (No. 176), 1988 – Employment Policy (Supplementary Provisions) Recommendation, 1984 (No. 169) – Job Creation in Small and Medium-Sized Enterprises Recommendation, 1998 (No. 189) – Promotion of Cooperatives Recommendation, 2002 (No. 193)
Equality of treatment	– Workers with Family Responsibilities Convention (No. 156) and Recommendation (No. 165), 1981 – HIV and AIDS Recommendation, 2010 (No. 200)
Security of employment	– Termination of Employment Convention (No. 158) and Recommendation (No. 166), 1982
Training	– Human Resources Development Convention, 1975 (No. 142) – Human Resources Development Recommendation, 2004 (No. 195)
Conditions of work	– Protection of Workers' Claims (Employer's Insolvency) Convention (No. 173) and Recommendation (No. 180), 1992 – Workers' Housing Recommendation, 1961 (No. 115) – Reduction of Hours of Work Recommendation, 1962 (No. 116)

TABLE 8.1 International Labour Conventions and Recommendations (*cont.*)

Occupational safety and health	– Working Environment (Air Pollution, Noise and Vibration) Convention (No. 148) and Recommendation (No. 156), 1977 – Protocol of 2002 to the Occupational Safety and Health Convention, 1981 – Occupational Health Services Convention (No. 161) and Recommendation (No. 171), 1985 – Asbestos Convention (No. 162) and Recommendation (No. 172), 1986 – Safety and Health in Construction Convention (No. 167) and Recommendation (No. 175), 1988 – Chemicals Convention (No. 170) and Recommendation (No. 177), 1990 – Prevention of Major Industrial Accidents Convention (No. 174) and Recommendation (No. 181), 1993 – Safety and Health in Mines Convention (No. 176) and Recommendation (No. 183), 1995 – Safety and Health in Agriculture Convention (No. 184) and Recommendation (No. 192), 2001 – Radiation Protection Recommendation, 1960 (No. 114) – Guarding of Machinery Recommendation, 1963 (No. 118) – Benzene Recommendation, 1971 (No. 144) – Occupational Cancer Recommendation, 1974 (No. 147) – List of Occupational Diseases Recommendation, 2002 (No. 194)
Social protection	– Social Security (Minimum Standards) Convention, 1952 (No. 102) – Employment Injury Benefits Convention, 1964 [Schedule I amended in 1980] (No. 121) – Medical Care and Sickness Benefits Convention (No. 130) and Recommendation (No. 134), 1969 – Social Protection Floors Recommendation, 2012 (No. 202)
Governance	– Labour Inspection Convention, 1947 (No. 81) – Labour Inspection (Agriculture) Convention, 1969 (No. 129) – Tripartite Consultation (International Labour Standards) Convention, 1976 (No. 144)
Indigenous and tribal peoples	– Indigenous and Tribal Peoples Convention, 1989 (No. 169)
Particular categories of workers	– Plantations Convention (No. 110) and Recommendation (No. 110), 1958 – Maritime Labour Convention, 2006, as amended

(Reproduced from pp. 21 to 23 of the ILO MNE Declaration) (rights of the ILO are reserved)

While all of the above instruments might not be explicitly referenced in a model provision, these at least provide a template for what is on the table for negotiators (depending upon the will of the States concerned) and what are their utmost priorities for setting out precise investor obligations concerning labour standards and the protection of indigenous peoples.

2.1.5 UN Declaration on the Rights of Indigenous Peoples (UNDRIP)

In particular, for rights of indigenous peoples, the UNDRIP is a handy soft law tool to rely upon by treaty drafters and negotiators. It was passed by 143 favourable votes at the UN General Assembly. While this comes at the cost of UNGA resolutions not being binding on States, many of the contents of the UNDRIP build and elaborate on pre-existing international human rights treaties, having binding value.[56] These treaties apply to indigenous peoples, who have distinctive cultures and histories, and connection to environment and traditional lands, and a legacy of dispossession, discrimination, violation of their human rights, and the non-recognition of their own political and cultural institutions.[57]

According to the Committee on the Elimination of Discrimination against Women (Committee on EDW) and the Committee on the Elimination of Racial Discrimination (CERD), the Declaration "is a clearest articulation of Indigenous peoples' rights and is recognised by treaty bodies as an interpretive guide for core human rights treaties as they pertain to Indigenous peoples".[58] Article 43 of the Declaration, in particular, envisages the "minimum standards for the survival, dignity, and well-being of the Indigenous peoples".[59] The Declaration "also addresses both individual and collective rights of Indigenous peoples, including the right to self-determination, culture, lands, territories, and resources."[60]

2.1.6 The Ten Principles of the UN Global Compact

The UN Global Compact is a voluntary initiative based on CEO commitments – thus modelled specifically for investor obligations-related clauses – to implement universal sustainability and to take steps to support UN goals.[61] Principles 3 to 6 concern internationally recognised standards. These are:

56 See Sec II(B) infra.
57 UN OHCHR (n. 10).
58 Amazon Watch (n 11) 15. See also UN Committee on the Elimination of Discrimination against Women, 'General recommendation No. 39 (2022) on the rights of Indigenous women and Girls' (26 October 2022) UN Doc CEDAW/C/GC/39, para 12; UN Committee on the Elimination of Racial Discrimination, 'Opinion adopted by the Committee under article 14 of the Convention, concerning communication No. 54/2013' (2020) UN Doc CERD/C/102/D/54/2013, para 6.5.
59 Amazon Watch (n 11) 15.
60 Ibid.
61 UN Global Compact, 'The Ten Principles of the UN Global Compact' <https://unglobalcompact.org/about> accessed 14 November 2024 (UN Global Compact).

2.1.6.1 Principle 3: Businesses Should Uphold the Freedom of Association and the Effective Recognition of the Right to Collective Bargaining

The commentary to the Principle notes that "[f]reedom of association and the exercise of collective bargaining provides opportunities for constructive rather than confrontational dialogue."[62] Establishing "genuine dialogue" assists workers and employers each to understand the other's perspectives and find ways to resolve them.[63] To effectuate such a provision in an investment treaty, companies should mandatorily "[r]espect the right of all workers to form and join a trade union of their choice without fear of intimidation or reprisal, in accordance with national law."[64]

2.1.6.2 Principle 4: Businesses Should Uphold the Elimination of All Forms of Forced and Compulsory Labour

While large companies operating legally do not normally employ labourers through such regressive policies, forced labour can also be related to businesses through their links with others, such as contractors and third-party suppliers.[65] States also run the risk of being implicated in such situations. It is, therefore, imperative that investors beware of slavery, bonded labour or debt bondage, any sale of a person into the ownership of another, exploitative practices such as (unpaid) overtime, or deprivation of food, shelter, or other necessities.[66]

In theory, if an investor fails to abide by such standards – let us take slavery, by way of example (a *jus cogens* violation) – then a State should be able to lawfully expropriate the said investment(s) made or take other necessary actions.[67]

To contextualise, Professor Valentina Vadi has made some notable observations in her work titled "*Jus Cogens in International Investment Law and Arbitration*"[68] in the section on *jus cogens* norms put forward by host States. She elucidates, particularly in relation to indigenous peoples' rights, including

---

62 Ibid.

63 Ibid., principle 3.

64 Ibid.

65 Ibid., principle 4.

66 Ibid.

67 For a further discussion of *jus cogens* norms and their application to State claims against investors, please see Section 2.2.2.2 below on *jus cogens* as a "hard law" "customary international law" norm binding on investors and States alike.

68 V Vadi, 'Chapter 12: Jus Cogens in International Investment Law and Arbitration', in M. den Heijer and H. van der Wilt (eds.), *Netherlands Yearbook of International Law 2015*, Netherlands Yearbook of International Law 46, at p. 376.

the right to be consulted in matters affecting them, that even though States have relied upon constitutional provisions instead of *jus cogens* norms as defences,[69] the normative pre-emptive character and value of these norms has been significant in investment arbitration. As she rightly notes:

> ...[J]us cogens has played an indirect role [in investment arbitration]: when states invoke public order to justify the breach of relevant investment treaty provisions, an argument can be made that there is a link and/or partial overlap between public order and jus cogens.

The rationale behind this has also been well explained by Prof. Laurence Boisson de Chazournes. In such cases, States can validly take defences such as the existence of *jus cogens* violations by investors because "States have to guarantee certain human rights as the primary custodians of the general interest within their jurisdiction but also as primary guardians of the public order on their territory."[70]

2.1.6.3 Principle 5: Businesses Should Uphold the Effective Abolition of Child Labour

Child labour is a violation of a human right as is recognised and defined by international instruments. Generally speaking, no person under the age of 18 should be allowed to work (this number may also differ, based on the national legislation of the negotiating State). ILO conventions (the Minimum Age Convention No. 138 and Worst Forms of Child Labour Convention No. 182) also regulate this right. Companies should "[a]dhere to minimum age provisions of national labour laws and regulations and, where national law is insufficient, take account of international standards,"[71] failing which host States should be able to take any actions prescribed (in the relevant investment treaty without incurring international responsibility for their own acts under a relevant multilateral treaty).

---

69 *Glamis Gold, Ltd. v. United States of America*, ICSID/UNCITRAL, Award, 8 June 2009, 48 ILM 1038, para 654.

70 L Boisson de Chazournes, 'Fundamental rights and international arbitration: arbitral awards and constitutional law' in *ICCA Congress Series No 15: International Arbitration Conference Rio de Janeiro* (Wolters Kluwer 2011) 310.

71 UN Global Compact, principle 5.

This could take two forms:

- *First*, the more traditional form, could be the State's exercise of police powers[72] – such as those relating to public morals – to annul an investment that does not amount to indirect expropriation.[73] Thus, it is arguable that, if a host State, governed by an investment treaty – having a police powers formulation in a provision – notices that the investor employs young, 10-year-old,[74] illiterate children in inhumane conditions that are "likely to harm the health, safety, or morals of children"[75] then annulling the investment will not amount to indirect expropriation.
- *Second*, seen in the new-age investment treaties like the AfCFTA Investment Protocol,[76] is through invoking investors' obligations in relation to investors respecting the rights and obligations of indigenous and local communities under relevant domestic and international laws (such as the ILO regime discussed above).[77] Such obligations of investors would also fall within the ambit of CSR practices.[78]

2.1.6.4 Principle 6: Businesses Should Uphold the Elimination of Discrimination in Respect of Employment and Occupation

Businesses should – as per the commentaries – not discriminate against employees on the basis of race, colour, sex, religion, political opinion, national

---

72 By way of example, the AfCFTA Investment Protocol, art 20(2), reads: "Non-discriminatory regulatory actions by a State Party designed to protect legitimate public policy objectives, such as public morals, public health, prevention of diseases and pests in animals or plants, climate action, essential security interests, safety and the protection of the environment, labour rights, or to comply with other international obligations, shall not constitute indirect expropriation."

73 Scholars opine that certain formulations are considered an "[e]*xpress Drafting of the Police Powers Doctrine*"; such as:

Office of the United States Trade Representative, 2012 US Model Bilateral Investment Treaty, annex B, para 4(b):

"Except in rare circumstances, non-discriminatory regulatory actions by a Party that are designed and applied to protect legitimate public welfare objectives, such as public health, safety, and the environment, do not constitute indirect expropriations."

Discussed by Oliver Barron, 'The Police Powers Doctrine and International Investment Law: Dusting Off an Old Concept in the Pursuit of Sustainable Development' (2018), 24.

74 ILO Minimum Age Convention (1973) No 138, arts 1–2.

75 ILO Worst Forms of Child Labour Convention (1999) No 182, art 3.

76 See infra, Section 4.2 on the AfCFTA Investment Protocol.

77 AFCfTA Investment Protocol art 35(1).

78 Ibid., art 38. See also Chapter 10, Steven Finizio, *Corporate Social Responsibility Obligations for Investors in Investment Agreements*.

extraction, social origin, age, disability, HIV/AIDS status, trade union membership, or sexual orientation. However, Principle 6 allows companies to consider additional areas where discrimination in employment and occupation may occur.[79]

According to Principle 6, discrimination can arise in a variety of work-related activities. These include (but are not limited to) several terms and conditions of employment, such as: "Recruitment; Hours of work and rest/ paid holidays; Maternity protection; Security of tenure; Job assignments; Performance assessment and advancement; Training and opportunities; Job prospects; Social security; Occupational safety and health".[80]

Companies should thus respect all relevant local and national laws. They should also have internal non-discriminatory practices on recruitment and build a climate of tolerance and equal access.[81]

2.2 Hard Law Instruments: Treaties and Custom

The subject matters discussed above are issues covered in many binding international human rights treaties (or other instruments that inspired such treaties). These include:

2.2.1 Universal Declaration of Human Rights (UDHR)

Negotiated by States in 1948, it is an omnibus human rights instrument that has inspired numerous other multilateral human rights treaties enjoying universal ratifications from States. It includes: (a) the right to life, liberty, and security of a person;[82] (b) the prohibition against slavery;[83] (c) the prohibition against torture or cruel, inhuman, or degrading treatment;[84] and (d) the right to freedom of peaceful assembly and association.[85] These protections extend particularly to indigenous peoples as well.[86]

79 UN Global Compact, principle 6.
80 Ibid.
81 Ibid.
82 UDHR art 3.
83 Ibid., art 4.
84 Ibid., art 5.
85 Ibid., art 20.
86 United Nations Declaration on the Rights of Indigenous Peoples (adopted 13 September 2007), UN Doc A/RES/61/295, art 1 (UNDRIP).

2.2.2 International Covenant on Civil and Political Rights (ICCPR)

Adopted by the UN General Assembly in 1966, it is now a treaty having 174 State parties.[87] The Covenant includes, in particular, the right to self-determination[88] and the right to equal opportunity[89] as well as others mentioned and listed above, as also enshrined under the UDHR.[90]

In particular, Article 27 of the ICCPR notes that ethnic, religious, or linguistic minorities "shall not be denied the right, in community with the other members of their group, to enjoy their own culture, to profess and practice their own religion, or to use their own language". In this regard, the Committee on Civil and Political Rights (CCPR) – the treaty body of the ICCPR – considers that indigenous peoples have the right to effective participation in decision-making in matters that affect their culturally significant economic activities, "which requires not mere consultation but the free, prior, and informed consent of the members of the community".[91]

2.2.3 International Covenant on Economic, Social and Cultural Rights (ICESCR)

Also adopted by the UN General Assembly in 1966, the ICESCR now has 173 State parties.[92] This treaty is particularly relevant for investors' obligations as it has an economic nature. Article 7 of the Convention relates to just and favourable conditions at work, including: (a) fair wages and equal remuneration; (b) a decent standard of living, also for the families of workers; (c) safe and healthy working conditions; (d) equal opportunity for everyone to be promoted in employment; and (e) rest, leisure, and reasonable limitation of working hours. Further, Article 8 relates to everyone's right to form trade unions and to establish national federations or confederations. Article 15 further

87 See International Covenant on Civil and Political Rights (adopted 16 December 1966, entered into force 23 March 1976) 999 UNTS 171 (ICCPR).

88 ICCPR art 1.

89 ICCPR art 25; ICCPR, art 2 of the ICCPR notes that every citizen has the right and opportunity "without distinction of any kind, such as race, colour, sex, language, religion, political or other opinion, national or social origin, property, birth, or other status" as mentioned in art 2.

90 ICCPR art 6 (Right to life); art 7 (Prohibition against torture); art 8 (Prohibition against slavery); art 22 (Freedom of association) of the ICCPR.

91 UN HRC, 'Communication No. 1457/2006' (2009) UN Doc CCPR/C/95/D/1457/2006, para 7.6.

92 See International Covenant on Economic, Social and Cultural Rights (adopted 16 December 1966, entered into force 3 January 1976) 993 UNTS 3 (ICESCR).

relates to cultural rights. The Committee on Economic, Social, and Cultural Rights (CESCR), in its famously quoted General Comment No. 21, has also stated that "Indigenous peoples' cultural values and rights associated with their ancestral lands and their relationship with nature should be regarded with respect and protected, in order to prevent the degradation of their particular way of life, including their means of subsistence, the loss of their natural resources and, ultimately, their cultural identity."[93]

2.2.4 Convention on the Elimination of All Forms of Discrimination against Women (CEDAW)

The Convention on the Elimination of All Forms of Discrimination against Women (CEDAW)[94] having 165 State parties, notes under Article 11 that Parties shall take appropriate measures to eliminate discrimination against women in employment. Other protections also relate to partaking in economic and social life,[95] specifically including for rural women.[96] In the context of indigenous peoples too, according to a recent General Recommendation No. 39 (2022) by the Committee on the Elimination of Discrimination against Women:

> 12. The Committee acknowledges that Indigenous women and girls have struggled and continue to struggle against forced assimilation policies and other large-scale human rights violations [...]. It is critical for States parties to address the consequences of historic injustices and to provide support and reparations to the affected communities as part of the process of ensuring justice, reconciliation and the building of societies free from discrimination and gender-based violence against Indigenous women and girls. The Committee highlights, in particular, the need for States to act proactively to protect the rights of Indigenous women and girls living in urban settings, where they face racism, discrimination, assimilation policies and gender-based violence.[97]

93 UN CESCR, 'General comment No. 21: Right of everyone to take part in cultural life (art 15, para 1 (a), of the International Covenant on Economic, Social and Cultural Rights)' (21 December 2009) UN Doc E/C.12/GC/21.

94 Convention on the Elimination of All Forms of Discrimination against Women (adopted 18 December 1979, entered into force 3 September 1981) 1249 UNTS 13 (CEDAW).

95 CEDAW, art 13.

96 Ibid., art 14.

97 UN Committee on the Elimination of Discrimination against Women, 'General Recommendation No.39 (2022) on the Rights of Indigenous Women and Girls' (26 October 2022) UN Doc CEDAW/C/GC/39, para 12.

Thus, by extension, it is the host State's duty to ensure that investors in areas (such as urban areas that may attract more foreign investors) do not discriminate against indigenous women and girls employed by their facilities.

2.2.5 International Convention on the Elimination of All Forms of Racial Discrimination (ICERD)

The International Convention on the Elimination of All Forms of Racial Discrimination (ICERD)[98] – having 182 State parties – states under its Article 5 that State parties undertake to prohibit and eliminate racial discrimination in all its forms and guarantee the right of everyone (including of indigenous peoples[99]), without distinction as to race, colour, or national or ethnic origin, to equality before the law.

The Committee on the Elimination of Racial Discrimination (CERD) has also – in General Recommendation No. 23 – recognised that indigenous peoples have been discriminated against, deprived of their human rights, and have lost their lands and resources; the Committee has called upon State parties to "ensure that members of indigenous peoples have equal rights in respect of effective participation in public life and that no decisions directly relating to their rights and interests are taken without their informed consent."[100]

By way of illustration, in 2010, the Norwegian Water Resources and Energy Directorate issued licences for the Roan and Storheia wind farms (among others). Despite the indigenous Sami peoples of Norway's objection to the project, stating that it violated their cultural rights to reindeer herding, the Norwegian Ministry of Petroleum and Energy rejected the position of the Sami people and allowed construction to start.

In October 2021, the Supreme Court of Norway ruled that the project violated the rights of Sami peoples to enjoy their own culture, citing Article 27 of the ICCPR (discussed above) and Article 5(d)(v) of the ICERD, which specifies States' obligations to eliminate racial discrimination in all its forms and to

98 International Convention on the Elimination of All Forms of Racial Discrimination (adopted 21 December 1965, entered into force 4 January 1969) 660 UNTS 195 (CERD).

99 UNDRIP, art 2.

100 UN Committee on the Elimination of Racial Discrimination, 'General Recommendation No. 23: Indigenous Peoples' (18 August 1997), UN Doc A/52/18.

guarantee the right of everyone to equality before the law, in the enjoyment of the right to own property alone as well as in association with others.[101]

2.2.6 Convention on the Rights of the Child (CRC)

After the UN Framework Convention on Climate Change (198 parties), the CRC, perhaps, holds the unique distinction of being the Convention with the second-highest number of parties (196) as of date. This is important, as most States negotiating investment treaties will also be parties to the CRC. The Convention envisages a whole gamut of child rights that States ought to protect in the best interests of the child,[102] such as: non-discrimination,[103] protection from violence, abuse and neglect,[104] health and health services,[105] the right to education,[106] prohibition of child labour,[107] and knowledge regarding all these rights.[108]

While some of these relate to direct obligations of the investor, such as not employing children,[109] the other obligations, such as education, health services, et al., are indirect obligations. If investors are hiring parents of children under inhumane conditions, that also has an overall detrimental impact on the child. Thus, treaty makers are encouraged to benefit from references to this Convention in investor obligations clauses.

2.2.7 International Labour Organization Convention (ILO 169)

One of the most significant developments in relation to indigenous peoples' rights has been through this Convention. According to the ILO, "[t]he provisions of Convention No. 169 are based on respect for the cultures and ways of life of indigenous and tribal peoples [...] aim[ed] at overcoming discrimin-

101 Indigenous Peoples Rights International, 'Xanharu || Upholding Indigenous Peoples' Rights Legislation and Jurisprudence: Global, Regional, and National Developments' (July 2022) <https://iprights.org/wp-content/uploads/2025/11/Xanharu-Upholding-Indigenous-Peoples-Rights-Legislation-and-Jurisprudence.pdf> accessed 16 November 2025.

102 Convention on the Rights of the Child, 1577 UNTS 3 (20 November 1989), art 1 (CRC).

103 CRC, art 2.

104 Ibid., art 19.

105 Ibid., art 24.

106 Ibid., art 28.

107 Ibid., art 32.

108 Ibid., art 42.

109 See also certain soft law tools under Section 2.1 above discussing the prohibition of child labour.

atory practices affecting these peoples [...]. The Convention covers [...] issues [...] as regards consultation and participation, rights to land, employment and vocational training, education, health and social security, customary law, traditional institutions, and cross-border cooperation."[110] These peoples have the right to own, use, develop, and control the lands, territories, and resources that they possess by reason of traditional ownership or other traditional occupation or use.[111]

Investors ought to be cognisant of their actions when operating on or near lands owned by indigenous peoples or when employing these peoples in their companies established in the host State. While an investment tribunal has denied investors' direct obligations in relation to ILO 169,[112] there is no reason why this should not be seen as an aberration; given the ground reality the world currently faces, *jurisprudence constante* from the obverse position can and should be developed.

In this context, scholars allude that this predicament of tribunals can be alleviated. They suggest that "[i]f investor responsibility clauses are to be enforceable through a counterclaim or a defence, the treaty should establish clear links between investor obligations and substantive protections that investors are entitled to under the treaty."[113] Thus, as is the objective of this chapter, if an investment treaty were to clearly spell out an ILO Convention 169-related investor obligation, tribunals will be more amenable to hearing and arbitrating upon such crucial issues.

2.2.8 Customary International Law

Many of the principles discussed above are standalone principles of customary international law, which States (and, as a corollary, investors) are bound to respect, regardless of whether those States are parties to the treaties where these principles might be enshrined. Some (additional) principles include:

110 ILO, 'International labour standards regarding indigenous and tribal peoples' < https://www.ilo.org/resource/international-labour-standards-regarding-indigenous-and-tribal-peoples> accessed 5 July 2025.

111 ILO Convention No 169, arts 13–14.

112 *Bear Creek v. Republic of Peru*, ICSID Case No. ARB/14/21, Award (30 November 2017). See III(B) infra.

113 N Bueno, A Yilmaz Vastardis, and I Ngueuleu Djeuga (n 14), 210.

2.2.8.1 The Right to Self-Determination

This right is universally recognised – including under Article 1(2) of the UN Charter – as a foundational principle.[114] It has been declared as customary international law,[115] holding *erga omnes* nature by the ICJ,[116] and is also reflected in UNGA resolutions.[117] Many formulations of this right exist under international law. One such formulation, relevant for present purposes, is the right to economic self-determination – a choice that concerns the political and economic systems of the State and the social and cultural practices adopted by its population.[118]

Dr. Edward Guntrip has written a piece on Self-Determination and Foreign Direct Investment.[119] According to him, essentially, the population of a host State endorses its economic policies.[120] The core impetus to winning such a "vote of confidence" from the population is the host State's duty of transparency,[121] obligation of providing access to information,[122] and the duty of consultation regarding future economic policies.[123] As a result, the population has

---

114 Recently, on 26 June 2025, while giving a speech at the UN General Assembly to commemorate the 80th anniversary of the UN Charter, ICJ's President, Judge Yuji Iwasawa, noted that "[t]he Charter has also 'proved essential' in establishing the self-determination of peoples as a right under international law." <https://www.icj-cij.org/sites/default/files/press-releases/0/000-20250626-sta-01-00-en.pdf> accessed 27 June 2025.

115 *Legal Consequences for States of the Continued Presence of South Africa in Namibia (South West Africa) notwithstanding Security Council Resolution 276 (1970)* (Advisory Opinion) [1971] ICJ Rep 16, 31; *Western Sahara* (Advisory Opinion) [1975] ICJ Rep 12, 31–33; *East Timor (Portugal v. Australia)* (Judgment) [1995] ICJ Rep 90, 102; *Legal Consequences of the Construction of a Wall in the Occupied Palestinian Territory* (Advisory Opinion) [2004] ICJ Rep 136, 182–83.

116 *Case Concerning East Timor (Portugal v. Australia) (Judgment)* [1995] ICJ Rep 90, 102; *Legal Consequences of the Construction of a Wall in the Occupied Palestinian Territory (Advisory Opinion)* [2004] ICJ Rep 136, 171–72.

117 UNGA Res 1514 (XV) 'Declaration on the Granting of Independence to Colonial Countries and Peoples' (14 December 1960).

118 ICCPR, art 1; ICESCR, art 1; B Saul, D Kinley and J Mowbray, *The International Covenant on Economic, Social and Cultural Rights: Commentary, Cases and Materials* (OUP 2014) 59.

119 E Guntrip, 'Self-Determination and Foreign Direct Investment: Reimagining Sovereignty in International Investment Law' (2016) 65 ICLQ 844, 845.

120 B Manin, A Przeworski and S Stoke, "Elections and Representation" in B Manin, A Przeworski and S Stoke (eds), *Democracy, Accountability and Representation* (CUP 1999) 30.

121 B Saul, D Kinley, and J. Mowbray, *The International Covenant on Economic, Social and Cultural Rights: Commentary, Cases and Materials* (OUP 2014) 67.

122 CESCR, "Concluding Observations: Azerbaijan", E./C.12/1/Add.20 (22 December 1997) para 29.

123 C Drew, "The East Timor Story: International Law on Trial" (2001) 12 EJIL 658, 659; D Raič, *Statehood and the Law of Self-Determination* (Brill 2002) 237.

a right to express its views,[124] regarding their preferred choice of economic policy. An extension of such an economic right is the host State's obligation of inviting foreign investors that are compliant with the equilibrium of the grand scheme of obligations owed by the host State to its population. Of course, this includes adherence to humane labour standards and preserving the rights of indigenous peoples. The UNDRIP affirms indigenous peoples' right to self-determination as the "right to freely determine their political status and freely pursue their economic, social, and cultural development"[125] and "the right to autonomy or self-government in matters relating to their internal and local affairs".[126]

Particularly in the context of indigenous peoples, the FPIC notion is established within the umbrella of the right to self-determination and the need to eliminate structural discrimination against indigenous peoples. FPIC, as a tool, attempts to restore indigenous peoples' cultural integrity and pride, and to redress the power imbalance between indigenous peoples and States.[127] According to world-renowned Prof. James Anaya, the then Special Rapporteur on the rights of indigenous peoples, the rights that are connected to and can be safeguarded by the right to FPIC include:

> […] in addition to rights of participation and self-determination, rights to property, culture, religion and non-discrimination in relation to lands, territories and natural resources, including sacred places and objects; rights to health and physical well-being in relation to a clean and healthy environment; and the right of indigenous peoples to set and pursue their own priorities for development, including with regard to natural resources.[128]

Thus, for present purposes, any investor employing local populations and found not following the host State's municipal and international obligations

---

124 This can take many forms, depending upon the legal system of the State, such as: Elections, Referenda, Judicial Review, Formal and Informal Consultation Mechanisms, Petitions, Public Protests, Attendance at Public Meetings. See Oxford Pro Bono Publico, "A Comparative Survey of Public Participation in the Legislative Process - Report for the National Campaign for People's Right to Information" (2011) < https://peacemaker.un.org/sites/default/files/document/files/2022/07/oxfordcomparativesurveyofpublicparticipationinthelegislativeprocess2011_0.pdf> accessed 28 June 2025.

125 UNDRIP, art 3.

126 Ibid., art 4.

127 UN Expert Mechanism on the Rights of Indigenous Peoples, 'Free, prior, and informed consent: a human rights-based approach' (2018) UN Doc A/HRC/39/62, para 11.

128 UN HRC, 'Report of the Special Rapporteur on the Rights of Indigenous Peoples, James Anaya' (2012) UN Doc A/HRC/21/47, para 50.

runs the risk of disrupting the population's right to economic self-determination (including, crucially, FPIC) expected as an obligation from the host State. As a corollary, any silence from the host State in ambivalence to such investor's actions constitutes a violation by the host State itself. Thus, as a check and balance, the author proposes that treaty drafters and negotiators create safeguards for States against investors, such that appropriate State action can be invoked if an investor's actions are found to warrant further scrutiny.

2.2.8.2 Prohibition against Slavery, Genocide, Racial Discrimination, and Torture

In 2022, the ILC, in its "Draft conclusions on identification and legal consequences of peremptory norms of general international law (*jus cogens*)",[129] prepared for the first time, in an annex to its Conclusion 23 and after assessing international jurisprudence, a "non-exhaustive list" of *jus cogens* peremptory norms. Of the eight *jus cogens* norms identified, five could be considered as related to labour standards and rights of indigenous peoples, these being (i) slavery; (ii) genocide; (iii) racial discrimination; (iv) torture; and (v) self-determination. Any investor found culpable of promoting these prohibitive practices on its employees must face strict investor obligations (as well as non-adherence to treaty obligations by States, including the spectre of expropriation without compensation).

In this context, Prof. Vadi has discussed a 150-year-old case setting the foundation for such actions by States. Back in 1875, in the *Maria Luz* arbitration, the Czar of Russia, the sole arbitrator, declared that Japan "had not breached the general rules of the Law of the Nations" in freeing the slaves being carried on the Peruvian vessel Maria Luz and denying the subsequent demands for indemnity of the Peruvian citizens.[130] When anchored in Japan, a Chinese worker escaped and complained to the Japanese authorities of mistreatment akin to slavery and asked for the protection of all the Chinese workers aboard.[131] A domestic Japanese court held that the shipping company owning the María Luz was guilty of wrongdoing and that the workers were freed of their contract, particularly, also because the illiterate workers were previously

129 ILC, 'Yearbook of the International Law Commission, 2022, vol. II, Part Two' UN Doc A/77/10.

130 S.J. Crawford, "The 'Maria Luz' Affair." *The Historian* 46, No. 4 (1984) 583–96.

131 I Saveliev, "Rescuing the prisoners of the Maria Luz: the Meji Government and the 'Coolie Trade'" in B Edström (ed), *Turning Points in Japanese History* (Routledge Curzon 2002) 75–78.

made to sign one-sided contracts and were subjected to inhumane conditions.[132]

It is crucial that, during the course of the domestic court proceedings, the ship captain argued that involuntary servitude did not run against Japanese law, as it was, according to the captain, then practised in Japan in the form of the sale of prostitutes.[133]

However, the Japanese court emphasised that the conduct of the captain breached the law of nations (now *jus cogens*) rather than Japanese law. Accordingly, the Chinese workers were then sent home. In the arbitration before the Czar, the Peruvian government asked for compensation from the Japanese government, but that was denied based on the law of nations.

It can thus be observed, that both domestic courts and ad hoc arbitrations were cognisant of the most serious breaches of humanity, referring to them as the "general rules of the Law of Nations" even as early as in 1875. Now, with even more complex forms such as modern slavery, it is incumbent upon arbitral tribunals to address *jus cogens* violations by investors and States alike.

In the context of investment arbitration, in the string of arbitrations in the aftermath of the 2001 Argentine financial crisis, the State – albeit unsuccessfully in many cases[134] – used the *jus cogens* defence to justify the non-violation of basic human rights of the public over bilateral treaty obligations with the investor. However, the tribunals were reluctant to entertain such defences even when they sometimes agreed that such obligations, in principle, existed. They primarily followed the pattern that, while such obligations existed, the content of such obligations was not defined.

One might wonder, now since these cases have been decided, we now have the benefit of the 2022 ILC Draft conclusions to give more context to the content of these obligations (at least the undisputable ones, such as the labour rights and indigenous peoples' rights discussed above).

---

132 D Keene, *Emperor of Japan: Meiji and His World, 1852–1912* (Columbia University Press 2002) 216–218.

133 Saveliev (n 131), 75–78.

134 *EDF International, SAUR international, and Léon Participationes Argentinas v. Argentina*, ICSID Case No. ARB/03/23, Award (11 June 2012), paras 912–914; *Suez, Sociedad General de Aguas de Barcelona, S.A., and Vivendi Universal, S.A. v. Argentine Republic*, ICSID Case No. ARB/03/19, Decision on Liability (30 July 2010), para 262; *Azurix v. Argentine Republic*, ICSID Case No. ARB/01/12, Award (14 July 2006), para 261; *Siemens v. Argentina*, ICSID Case No. ARB/02/8, Award (6 February 2007), para 79; *CMS Gas Transmission Co. v. Argentina*, ICSID Case No. ARB/01/08, Award (12 May 2005), para 121.

2.2.8.3 Obligations of Conventions Reflected in Customary International Law

Certain of the subject matters discussed in relation to the conventions in the preceding section are also principles of customary international law. It is imperative to acknowledge these conventions, as many States are parties to them. Therefore, the obligations described in the sub-sections above are incumbent upon (most) host States negotiating investment treaties with other States. As a corollary – if investors are found guilty of not adhering to such obligations (especially at a mass scale) – States themselves will, in principle, be liable for breach of their obligations in international law, particularly when obligations *erga omnes partes* (under the treaties discussed), including *jus cogens* violations (such as slavery), are concerned. This is consistent with the age-old principle laid down in the ICJ's first case, *Corfu Channel*, i.e., a State should have knowledge of the internationally wrongful act being committed on its territory or in its waters.[135]

Even if there is doubt on whether States will be indirectly liable, States should, as a best practice, negotiate stricter investor obligations for acts which – if committed by those States themselves – would otherwise amount to an internationally wrongful act under the treaties discussed. States should also bear in mind that other third States, parties to these treaties, such as the ICERD, can invoke the convention (even if not directly affected) for obligations *erga omnes partes*.[136]

Let us take – as an illustration – the ongoing case of *The Gambia v. Myanmar* before the ICJ. In this case, The Gambia alleges, *inter alia*, that Myanmar has been violating the ICERD (discussed above) by racially discriminating against the Rohingyas.[137] In this case, The Gambia – being a party to the ICERD – pled before the ICJ that even though it is not directly affected, it is its obligation *erga omnes partes* under the Convention to uphold its object and purpose. The ICJ on 22 July 2022 has accepted its jurisdiction over the case and proceeded to

---

135 *Corfu Channel* (*U.K. v. Albania*) (*Merits*) [1949] ICJ Rep 4, 22. In this case, the Court, *inter alia*, held that the act of laying the minefield, which caused the explosion of the British warships, could not have happened without the knowledge of the Albanian Government.

136 Recently, many States have intervened in the ongoing The Gambia (itself a third State to the dispute) v. Myanmar case at the ICJ for an alleged violation of the CERD convention, concerning the treatment meted out to the Rohingya refugees. See *Application of the Convention on the Prevention and Punishment of the Crime of Genocide* (*The Gambia v. Myanmar: 7 States intervening*): <https://www.icj-cij.org/case/178> accessed 26 November 2024.

137 The Myanmar government considers the Rohingya as British colonial and postcolonial migrants from Chittagong in Bangladesh.

the merits, noting that "[t]he Gambia, as a State party to the Genocide Convention, has standing to invoke the responsibility of Myanmar for the alleged breaches of its obligations under Articles I, III, IV and V of the Convention."[138] This step is iconic because it is not Bangladesh (not being a party to the Convention) but The Gambia that has taken this step. This opens a wider possibility of States being sued for breaches of these international obligations.

∴

Thus, it is the author's proposal for treaty drafters to include bespoke references to *jus cogens* and the form of such potential violations in the treaty text itself, such that tribunals – for whatever reason – are neither reluctant nor uncertain about the gamut of such obligations for investors and States alike. This tool of *jus cogens* norms is very important for States to introduce in treaty text pertaining to investor obligations in the context of labour rights and rights of indigenous peoples and communities. Once this is done, tribunals will also then see it as a part of their mandate to address these intertwined issues, which are at the heart of the subject-matter of this chapter.

As will be seen in the draft clauses in Section 4 below, the importance of the sources of law above is often diluted, even in the most robust investment treaties containing labour standards and indigenous peoples' rights-related investor obligations.

3 Relevant Case Law concerning Investors' Labour Obligations and Rights of Indigenous Peoples and Local Communities

Despite the protections listed in Section 2 above, this area is still underdeveloped in practice. While jurisprudence is scant, there have been some cases that can further inform investors' obligations in the context of labour rights and the rights of indigenous peoples and local communities. Examples include:

138 *Application of the Convention on the Prevention and Punishment of the Crime of Genocide (The Gambia v. Myanmar)* (Preliminary Objections, Judgment) [2022] ICJ Rep, para 114.

3.1 *Nevsun v. Araya:* Canadian Supreme Court

This recent case of 2020[139] is very momentous in the context of investors' compliance with labour standards. In this case, the Canadian Supreme Court found that a company can be held liable for violations of customary international law norms such as slavery, forced labour and cruel and inhumane treatment.[140] The proceedings were initiated by three Eritrean workers against Nevsun Resources, alleging that they were subjected to forced labour and inhumane working conditions in a Nevsun-owned mine.[141] In its decision, the Court noted that the prohibition against slavery is a *jus cogens* norm, and the prohibition against cruel, inhumane, and degrading treatment presents "an absolute right, where no social goal or emergency can limit it".[142] Similar to the reasoning adopted in *Urbaser v. Argentina*, the Court crucially also noted:

> The context in which international human rights norms must be interpreted and applied today is one in which such norms are ***routinely applied to private actors.*** It is therefore not plain and obvious that corporations today enjoy a blanket exclusion under customary international law from ***direct liability for violations of obligatory, definable, and universal norms of international law.***[143]

3.2 Dissenting Opinion of Prof. Phillipe Sands in *Bear Creek v. Peru*

This case deals with investors' obligations in relation to indigenous peoples' rights. In this case, investment protection and the rights of indigenous communities needed to be balanced by the tribunal.[144] The tribunal found that, as per the ILO 169 Convention, only host States have the obligation to engage with local communities for consultations.[145] However, Prof. Sands dissented and crucially endorsed that, though ILO 169 does not impose direct obligations upon investors, "it does not mean that it is without significance or legal effects for them".[146] He further noted that the investor's failure to follow the

139 *Nevsun Resources v. Araya,* 2020 SCC 5.
140 Ibid., paras 113, 116, 132.
141 Ibid., paras 3–4.
142 Ibid., paras 101–03.
143 Ibid., 168 (emphasis added).
144 *Bear Creek v. Republic of Peru,* ICSID Case No. ARB/14/21, Award (30 November 2017), paras 119–216.
145 Ibid., para 664.
146 *Bear Creek v. Republic of Peru,* ICSID Case No. ARB/14/21, Partial Dissenting Opinion of Professor Philippe Sands (30 November 2017), para 10.

domestic and international standards on the rights of indigenous peoples had a significant contribution to the social unrest and ultimate collapse of the project.[147]

Thus, no investor can or should ignore the relevant ILO instruments discussed in Section 2 above, which govern labour standards and the rights of indigenous peoples.

3.3 Urbaser v. Argentina

While the Urbaser case[148] is quoted in many contexts of investor obligations, insofar as labour law standards and rights of indigenous peoples are concerned, the tribunal – by way of example – acknowledged that the UDHR is a part of customary international law.[149] The tribunal crucially also noted that:

> [...] [U]pon reading the Declaration, it is evident that obligations arising therefrom do not lie exclusively on States. [...] Article 29 sets forth that everyone has duties to the community. ***Therefore, business companies and international corporations are affected by the obligations included in international human rights law.***[150]

As a corollary, it is my view that conventions such as the ICESCR[151] and ICCPR[152] (enjoying ratification from most countries) are equally applicable and binding on investors from the countries who have ratified them.

Another important observation by the tribunal in this case was that it drew a distinction between "negative"[153] and "positive"[154] obligations upon investors. This distinction is very important in the context of labour standards and rights of indigenous peoples.[155]

This means that no investor should be elusive with the idea that just simply because it may not be actively breaching rights, it is in compliance; it should also be promoting and ensuring rights, or else it runs the risk of responsibility.

147 Ibid., paras 6, 11–14.
148 *Urbaser* (n. 15).
149 Ibid., para 1158.
150 Ibid., para 1159.
151 ICESCR arts 6–8 and 10.
152 ICCPR art 7–8.
153 *Urbaser* (n. 15), paras 1209–1210. According to the tribunal, negative obligations require investors to abstain from or not violate human rights.
154 Ibid., *para* 1210. According to the tribunal, positive obligations require investors to perform necessary steps to facilitate the local population in enjoying human rights.
155 As Sections 2.1 and 2.2 set out above.

3.4 Aven v. Costa Rica

In this case,[156] Costa Rica filed an environmental counterclaim in an investment arbitration, stating that the investor had caused environmental damages by violating the host State's environmental regulations.[157]

The tribunal began by first declaring that it had jurisdiction over the said claim and that Article 10A of the applicable DR-CAFTA *"also contains, at least implicitly, some obligations to investors, especially with respect to the environmental laws of the host State."*[158] It also noted that "[...] *environmental law is integrated in many ways into international law, including DR-CAFTA.* ***It is true that the enforcement of environmental law is primarily to the States, but it cannot be admitted that a foreign investor could not be subject to international law obligations in this field*** [...]."[159] Having admitted the counterclaim, in line with the *Urbaser* approach, the tribunal noted that, in principle, an investor cannot be immune from violations of *erga omnes* obligations such as environmental protection.[160] This rationale is then even more compelling for *jus cogens* violations relating to labour standards (including slavery).[161]

While ultimately the tribunal dismissed the counterclaim of Costa Rica,[162] that was only because, in its counterclaim, Costa Rica had not advanced "a precise statement of facts"[163] and only provided evidence such as "several photos and graphics [...] out of time [and that] [...] the Claimants had no opportunity to challenge the late assertions of Costa Rica. [...] Such delay deprive[d] the Claimants of their right to control the evidence and new reasoning submit-

156 *David R Aven v. Republic of Costa Rica,* ICSID Case No. UNCT/15/3, Award (18 September 2018).

157 Ibid., *para* 689.

158 Ibid., para 732.

159 Ibid., para 736 (emphasis added).

160 Ibid., *paras* 737–738. To emphasise, in particular, the tribunal in para 738 notes:

"What about the investor's obligations arising of the investment according to international law? This Tribunal shares the views of *Urbaser* Tribunal that it can no longer be admitted that investors operating internationally are immune from becoming subjects of international law. It is particularly convincing when it comes to rights and obligations that are the concern of all States, as it happens in the protection of the environment. It is pertinent to recall the observation of the International Court of Justice regarding this kind of obligations: 'In view of the importance of the rights involved, all States can be held to have a legal interest in their protection; they are obligations *erga omnes.*' (ICJ, Barcelona Traction, Light and Power Company, Limited, Report, 1970, ¶ 33)."

161 See Section 2.2.8.2 above.

162 *Aven* (n 156), para 747.

163 Ibid., para 745.

ted by the Respondent, according to due process in law."[164] Had it not been for such procedural impediments, this tribunal would have been open to hearing and adjudicating upon investors' obligations in international law.

4 ISDS in Relation to These Rights and Obligations

4.1 References to Labour Standards in Model and Other Investment Treaties

There are a few Model BITs that directly impose investors' labour obligations. The 2005 IISD Model International Agreement on Investment for Sustainable Development (IISD Model BIT) was the earliest one that contained such obligations. It noted that "investors should uphold human rights in the workplace".[165] However, even upon a cursory review, it can be observed that these references are not uniform. In contrast to the IISD Model BIT, the 2016 SADC Model BIT notes: "investors have [a] duty to respect" the said human rights.[166] According to both these Model BITs, investors "shall not undertake or cause to be undertaken acts that breach such human rights"[167] and "shall act in accordance with core labour standards as required by the 1998 ILO Declaration".[168] However, it has been observed that compliance by enterprises with non-binding documents, such as the 1998 ILO Declaration, is not always suitable for direct application but must firstly be transposed into domestic legislation.[169] Other BITs[170] and Model BITs[171] also call for compliance with labour standards in accordance with domestic law. However, a lot more needs to be done.

It is also important to connect investor obligations to a conducive text that supports counterclaims against investors or even unilateral claims. Else, many substantive rights may be dismissed at the stage of jurisdiction or admissibility before the tribunal.

This calls for a separate enquiry, but, in passing, to give an example, the ECOWAS Supplementary Act on Investment, in Article 18 connects the provi-

164 Ibid., para 746.
165 IISD Model BIT (2005), art 14B.
166 SADC Model BIT (2012), art 15.1.
167 IISD Model BIT, art 14B; SADC Model BIT, art 15.1.
168 IISD Model BIT, art 14C; SADC Model BIT, art 15.2.
169 Zandvliet R, 'International Investment Law and Labour' [2022] Trade, Investment and Labour 142, 204.
170 E.g., Ethiopia-Qatar BIT (signed 14 November 2017), art 14.
171 E.g., Netherlands Model Investment Agreement (22 March 2019) art 7(1).

sions on investor liability to the enforcement and interpretation of substantive protections afforded to the investor under the treaty, as well as acknowledging the right of the host State to initiate counter claims for an investor's breach of its responsibilities under the Act.

Thus, while treaty drafters take to pen to bolster substantive investor obligations in treaties (the theme of this chapter), they should also be mindful of creating procedural clauses that facilitate the bringing of counterclaims or even unilateral State claims against investors.

4.2 The AfCFTA Investment Protocol: The Game Changer of Investors' Obligations

The AfCFTA[172] and its Investment Protocol[173] have been deemed a "game changer" in promoting investment and encouraging progressive liberalisation of cross-border trade and investment policies. A hallmark of this Protocol is its robust investor obligations, including, in particular, those relating to labour standards and the protection of indigenous peoples. This is a welcome change, as most previous investment treaties have not had specific chapters on investor obligations. Chapter V of the Protocol deals with Investor Obligations. Articles 33 and 35 of the Protocol are by far the most comprehensive provisions in relation to the obligations we have been discussing in this chapter. These are:

172 World Bank, "Can African Trade Integration Be a Game Changer?" (World Bank Blogs) <https://blogs.worldbank.org/en/voices/can-african-trade-integration-be-game-changer> accessed 28 November 2024.

173 N Lamprou and E Iluezi-Ogbaudu, "The AfCFTA Investment Protocol – A Potential Game Changer for the African Continent?" (Linklaters Arbitration Links, 31 May 2023) <https://www.linklaters.com/en/insights/blogs/arbitrationlinks/2023/may/afcfta-investment-protocol> accessed 28 November 2024.

Article 33
Business Ethics, Human Rights and Labour Standards

Investors and their investments shall comply with high standards of business ethics, investment-related human rights and labour standards, and in particular shall:

a. support and respect the protection of internationally recognised human rights;

b. ensure that they are not complicit in human rights abuses;

c. comply with the International Labour Organisation (ILO) standards, including the ILO Declaration on Fundamental Principles and Rights at Work, and domestic labour legislations;

d. not use child labour or forced and compulsory labour;

e. eliminate discrimination in respect of employment and occupation;

f. refrain from discriminatory or disciplinary action against employees who submit reports to the company's board or to the competent public authorities about practices that violate domestic laws, this Protocol, or other standards of corporate governance to which the company is subject; and

g. act in accordance with fair business, marketing and advertising practices when dealing with consumers and must ensure the safety and quality of goods and services they provide.

Article 35
Indigenous Peoples and Local Communities

1. Investors and their investments shall respect the rights and dignity of indigenous peoples and local communities in accordance with relevant domestic laws and regulations, international law, norms and best practices, including the right of indigenous peoples and local communities where applicable, to free, prior and informed consent as well as to participate in the benefit of the investment.

   For greater certainty, the reference to the right to free, prior and informed consent of indigenous peoples, does not imply any obligation for investors and their investments to conclude agreements with those groups before conducting or operating their investment in the territory of State Parties which do not recognise indigenous peoples, taking into account applicable and relevant domestic laws and regulations.

2. Investors and their investments shall respect legitimate tenure rights to land, water, fisheries, and forests in accordance with relevant laws and regulations.

3. Investors, in accordance with relevant domestic law and regulations, shall submit their environmental and social impact assessments to the competent authorities and make them available and accessible to local communities and indigenous peoples and to any other stakeholder in the territory of the Host State.

Despite the AfCFTA Investment Protocol being a promising new template for new-era treaties, there is still more to be done, as I propose in the concluding section below through three key takeaway points.

5 Conclusion: Three Key Points to Drafting Strong Investor Obligations Clauses with Labour Standards and Indigenous Peoples' Rights

Having parsed through the relevant soft law tools, hard law instruments, and the relevant ISDS jurisprudence of the current regime, one thing is abundantly clear: there is room for considerable reform in how investor obligation chapters and provisions are drafted, as well as the accompanying access to arbitral remedies. They can be strengthened with clearer, specific, and pithier references to the instruments we have discussed throughout this chapter.

5.1 Primary Reliance upon Erga Omnes (including Jus Cogens) Obligations

Obligations (as discussed in Section 2) such as the prohibition of slavery, genocide, racial discrimination, and torture, as well as the right to self-determination, are incumbent upon States under customary international law, regardless of their international treaty obligations. Thus – as a corollary[174] – every State should, as a priority – when negotiating investment treaties – introduce (at least in essence and, if not verbatim, depending upon the language of the treaty) either:

- General textual reference to "norms of customary international law relevant to labour standards and indigenous peoples", and/or;
- Specific reference to "prohibition of slavery"/"self-determination"/"*erga omnes*"/"*jus cogens*" obligations et al.

These references are incumbent upon all States and – by the use of texts such as these – also upon all investors.[175]

174 And even in line with ISDS jurisprudence: See *Aven* (n 156) para 745 (and its discussion above).

175 Ibid.

5.2 Secondary Reliance upon Treaty Obligations

The treaty obligations (as discussed in Section 2.2) are incumbent differently on each State. Therefore, States should next consider introducing language such as (or similar to) the below when negotiating investment treaties with investor obligations:

- Generally, specify (at least in essence) that: "*Investors are bound by the international human rights treaties' obligations relevant to labour standards (and rights of indigenous peoples) of the States that are parties to this [investment] Treaty", or;*
- Specifically mention (at least in essence) that: "*Investors are also bound by the obligations of the States relevant to labour standards enshrined under the ICCPR, ICESCR, UDHR, ICERD, CEDAW, CRC, ILO 169*"[176], and;
- Specifically mention (at least in essence) any relevant regional treaties that the negotiating States have a special interest in.[177]

Specificity – even to the extent of referencing not just relevant instruments but also their relevant provisions – can eliminate ambiguity in the application of international treaties in investment arbitrations. Most importantly, it can also eliminate any debate around whether obligations under international human rights treaties are directly or indirectly binding on investors.[178] Once the essence of international human rights treaties is implanted in the relevant investment treaty, a tribunal needs only to conduct a plain and simple reading analysis of the "*lex specialis*" to proscribe or prescribe any investor conduct in violation of such provisions without needing to determine the (perhaps unsettled) questions regarding the extent to which such obligations are already extant upon investors as a matter of general international law.

5.3 Tertiary Reliance upon Soft Law Obligations

Soft law obligations is a term of art that is perhaps an oxymoron. Soft law instruments and other tools are optional (for inspiration or as a model) for the States negotiating the concerned investment treaties. Some of these are in the form of treaties that the States are parties to. However, it also depends

176 This will also depend upon the other human rights treaties (such as regional or bilateral) the States are parties to.

177 Taking the example of the AfCFTA Investment Protocol, the Protocol, in its chapter on investor obligations, in Article 34 on Environmental Protection, specifically notes that investors shall "respect the right to a clean, healthy and sustainable environment, as reflected in ***Article 24 of the African Charter of Human and Peoples' Rights*** [...]." (emphasis added)

178 Even though it has been accepted in *Urbaser* (n. 15), para 1193.

upon how strong and binding (or weak and aspirational) the text of the said treaty is and how it was conceived. Thus, I believe that soft law also has two distinct types:

5.3.1 Soft Law Instruments Negotiated by States

The instruments listed in Section 2.1 are instruments that States should consider introducing in the clauses relating to investor obligations, depending upon their preferences and the relevant investments and tools relating to certain selected labour standards.

Of particular importance, and those worth highlighting (though not an exhaustive list), are the following:

- ILO Declaration on Fundamental Principles and Rights at Work (1998);[179]
- ILO Tripartite Declaration of Principles Concerning Multinational Enterprises and Social Policy;
- UN Declaration on the Rights of Indigenous Peoples;
- OECD Guidelines for Multinational Enterprises on Responsible Business Conduct;
- The Ten Principles of the UN Global Compact;
- United Nations Guiding Principles on Business and Human Rights;
- Relevant domestic law standards of the negotiating States.[180]

Since soft law instruments enjoy great reception by States, States thus might be more amenable to utilising these in their drafting of new investment treaties enshrining investor obligations. More importantly, in particular, the OECD Guidelines, the UN Guiding Principles, and the Ten Principles of UN Global Compact have been drafted as such, targeted at regulating investors' conduct, thus making them ripe and readily transposable in investor obligation clauses in treaties.

5.3.2 Other Effective Soft Law Instruments

There is sometimes an unsaid hierarchy between soft law instruments. Some of these instruments could be negotiated by States themselves in the form of resolutions et al. and others could take the form of reports or decisions. The former could be more persuasive since they already have the endorsement of some States – short of them having the force of binding conventions. The latter, however, do not automatically have such endorsements.

---

179 For example, this is also referred to in Article 33 of the AfCFTA Investment Protocol.

180 See Chapter 3, Augustin Barrier, *Compliance with national law and international law.*

Soft law tools are more ad hoc (yet sometimes effective). The benefit of using these tools is that they add a layer of specificity to further contextualise the relevant obligation(s) being discussed.

Of particular importance, and those worth highlighting (though, again, not an exhaustive list), are the following:

- General Recommendations and General Comments of treaty bodies (such as those relating to ICCPR, ICESCR, CEDAW, ICERD, et al.);[181]
- Reports of UN Special Rapporteurs on these issues;[182]
- Decisions of international courts, investment tribunals, and domestic courts;[183]
- Resolutions of the United Nations or others;

To give some context to this – take, once again, for example – the AfCFTA Investment Protocol in Article 34 on Environmental Protection specifically refers to the "United Nations General Assembly A/RES/76/300 ('The human right to a clean, healthy and sustainable environment')". Now, while UN General Assembly resolutions are otherwise not binding, the text of this resolution is now within the text of a treaty as an investor obligation provision and thus can be used as *lex specialis*.

In relation to the rights and obligations that are in question in this chapter, General Recommendations and General Comments of treaty bodies, in particular, and, let us say, trend-setting sources like the *Urbaser v. Argentina* case, become crucial for drafting stronger investor obligation related clauses.

Thus, treaty negotiators might consider generally, specifying (at least in essence) that:

> Investor conduct is guided by decisions of international courts and tribunals and national courts and General Recommendations and General Comments of international human rights treaty bodies and UN Special Rapporteurs' reports on the questions of labour standards and indigenous peoples' rights by obtaining and respecting their Free, Prior, and Informed Consent in any of its activities.

Or treaty drafters and negotiators may specify some tools and their articles to emphasise considerations that are a priority for them.[184] It is important to introduce "guided by" like phrases (aspirational text) rather than the "shall" (binding) language because it is possible that else such clauses based on soft

181 See Section 2.2 supra.

182 E.g., UN HRC (n. 128).

183 See Section 3 supra.

184 Such as CEDAW General Recommendation No 39 (n 94); CERD General Recommendation No 23; CESCR General Comment No 21 (n 93) et al.

law instruments (different from the soft law instruments negotiated by States above that have more persuasive values) will not see the light of day. A self-conscious exercise and check of the three key points mentioned above (in chronology) can highly assist investment treaty drafters and negotiators to draft stronger and well-reasoned investor obligations reflecting the prevalent labour standards of the current international labour law order aligned with the realities of the twenty-first century's socio-political, economic, and legal landscape.

While it may not always be possible to adopt this gold standard, any selections of the instruments and tools discussed will augment the current weaker regime of investor obligations in treaties. The more States are interested in protecting labour standards and rights of indigenous peoples, the stronger investor obligations in new-age investment treaties we shall have. As practitioners and academics, we can only layout the gold standards and suggest drafting exercises.

> **Ultimately, it is upon the socio-political and socio-economic will of the States negotiating investor obligations in treaties – and how far they are willing to go – to protect the will of the people.**

∴

As a practical matter and caveat, while this might call for a separate analysis, however, in passing, all of the above can only be fully and truly effectuated in practice when there are also bespoke reparations standards prescribed for the investors, so that adequate compensation can be awarded to the (counter) claiming States.[185]

∴

185 For instance, on the calculation of damages, the Netherlands Model BIT, in Article 23, expects tribunals to reduce damages for investors' failure to comply with the UNGPs and OECD Guidelines.

CHAPTER 9

Investor Obligations: Corporate Governance

Mathias Wolkewitz[1]

Investor obligations is a topic that is discussed controversially as the "Great Debate" reflected at the beginning of this publication shows.[2] This chapter explores the topic of international investor obligations from the very specific angle of corporate governance. It will seek to develop a state-of-play in three steps. First, it is important to clearly define corporate governance for the purposes of this analysis as its definition can be very broad and almost always depends on the context in which it is used (**Section 1**). Second, it is necessary to have a cursory glance at the international framework relating to corporate governance in general as it seems appropriate to identify whether international investor obligations relating to corporate governance can be established at this point in time (**Section 2**)[3] (here it might be helpful to refer also to

1 The views expressed in my speech at the symposium in Geneva as well as in this chapter are my own and cannot be attributed to any organisation I am affiliated with.

2 Patrick Abel, 'International Investor Obligations – Towards Individual International Responsibility for the Public Interest' in International Investment Law, Beiträge zum ausländischen öffentlichen Recht und Völkerrecht vol 315, Anne Peters and Armin von Bogdandy (eds), (Max Planck Society for the Advancement of Science, Heidelberg 2022); Ibazatunde Fagbohunlu and Ilyne Mevorach, 'Standards of Protection and the Obligations of the Investor' GAR Global Arbitration Review (17 October 2022); Ted Gleason, 'Examining Host-State Counterclaims for Environmental Damage in Investor-State Dispute Settlement from Human Rights and Transnational Public Policy Perspectives' (2021) 22 International Environmental Agreements 447; Alice Ischano, Lisa E Sachs and Jesse Coleman, 'International Investment Agreements: A Review of Trends and New Approaches (2015–2016)' (2017) 18 Yearbook on International Investment Law and Policy; Alice De Jonge, Transnational Corporations and International Law: Accountability in the Global Business Environment (Edward Elgar Publishing 2011); Peter T Muchlinski, 'Regulating Multinationals: Foreign Investment, Development, and the Balance of Corporate and Home Country Rights and Responsibilities in a Globalizing World' in Jose E Alvarez and others (eds), The Evolving International Investment Regime: Expectations, Realities, Options (Oxford 2011); Todd Weiler, 'Balancing Human Rights and Investor Protection: A New Approach for a Different Legal Order' (2004) 27 Boston College International and Comparative Law Review 432, 432–433.

3 The focus of this chapter is on direct investor obligations. Requirements for investors to comply with the national law of the host State, also named indirect investor obligations, are occasionally mentioned but are not in focus.

 | HTTPS://DOI.ORG/10.1163/9789004769854-010

certain topics addressed in other chapters within this book). Third, a look will be taken at the Protocol on Investment to the Agreement Establishing the African Continental Free Trade Area more specifically and its Article on Corporate Governance will be analysed and compared to the state-of-play sketched out in Section 2 (**Section 3**).

1 Definitions of Corporate Governance

Corporate governance can be defined, described, or delineated in various ways depending on the purpose for, or context in which, the term is used.

Broader definitions are typically used when discussing regulatory policy in relation to corporate governance practices, for example in the 1992 Cadbury Report, which identifies corporate governance very generally as "the system by which companies are directed and controlled".[4]

The OECD seems to take a more relational-structural and thus broader view according to which "[c]orporate governance involves a set of relationships between a company's management, board, shareholders and stakeholders".[5] Corporate governance according to the OECD – and quite similar to the Cadbury Report – also includes "the structure and systems through which the company is directed and its objectives are set, and the means of attaining those objectives and monitoring performance are determined".[6]

Other components of such broad definitions include that corporate governance involves balancing the interests of a company's many stakeholders, which can include shareholders, senior management, customers, suppliers, lenders, the government, and the community. In such definitions, corporate governance encompasses practically every sphere of management, from action plans to performance measurement and corporate disclosure.[7]

Other definitions often found in scholarly writings and literature on corporate management seem to be more process oriented and see corporate governance as "processes, both formal and informal, through which a corporation is

4 Report of the Committee on the Financial Aspects of Corporate Governance, (See a division of Professional Publishing Ltd.) London 1992, para. 2.5, 15.

5 OECD, G20/OECD Principles of Corporate Governance 2023 (OECD Publishing 2023) <https://doi.org/10.1787/ed750b30-en> accessed 16 April 2025.

6 Ibid.

7 Cf. Kaspar Müller, 'Corporate Governance and Globalization: The Role and Responsibilities of Investors, in Selected Issues in Corporate Governance: Regional and Country Experiences' (United Nations Conference on Trade and Environment, Geneva 2003) 21–25.

administered and managed".[8] Corporate governance in that sense also "involves the legal requirements imposed upon the corporation, the policies adopted by such corporation, and the informal customs within the corporation".[9] The concept of corporate governance in such definitions also embodies the interactions between the many parties that can be viewed as stakeholders in the corporation such as directors, managers, shareholders, employees, customers, banks, and regulators.[10]

A broad definition that combines many adopted definitions is that "corporate governance" describes the processes, structures, and mechanisms that influence the control and direction of corporations. In this context, "control" is about how stakeholders and other agencies external to a corporation control or influence those responsible for directing and managing the affairs of the corporation, and "direction" is about the strategic guidance and management of the corporation. A broad interpretation of "control and direction" encompasses the roles and influences of governments and regulatory agencies, capital market participants and existing shareholders and debtholders, managerial labour markets, suppliers and customers, community and special interest groups, and internal participants (directors, executive managers, and other employees).[11]

Narrower definitions usually focus on a disciplinary interest or context such as accounting, finance, law, or management that appears purpose-specific. Examples of narrower definitions in particular contexts include "a system of law and sound approaches by which corporations are directed and controlled focusing on the internal and external corporate structures with the intention

8 Oxford Reference, 'Quick reference "corporate governance"' (Oxford University Press 2024) <https://www.oxfordreference.com/display/10.1093/oi/authority.20110803100456449> accessed 16 April 2025; see also The Corporate Governance Institute, 'What is Corporate Governance?' <https://www.thecorporategovernanceinstitute.com/insights/lexicon/what-is-corporate-governance/> accessed 16 April 2025. "The term corporate governance refers to how companies are run and for what purpose. Corporate governance also defines an organization's power structure, accountability structure, and decision-making process. It is essentially a set of tools that enables management and the board to run an organization more efficiently and effectively. Environmental awareness, ethical behaviour, corporate strategy, compensation, and risk management are all aspects of corporate governance."

9 Ibid.

10 Ibid.

11 Greg Shailer, 'Corporate Governance' in D C Poff and A C Michalos (eds), *Encyclopedia of Business and Professional Ethics* (Springer International Publishing AG 2018).

of monitoring the actions of management and directors and thereby, mitigating risks which may stem from the misdeeds of corporate officers".[12]

For the purposes of this chapter, such narrower definitions in the sense of corporate law, corporate structures, and related topics such as accounting are used.[13] This allows one to focus on these specific aspects and differentiates the topic of this chapter from other specific aspects such as corporate social responsibility, human and labour rights and environmental protection, which are covered by broader definitions and have been addressed by other chapters in this book.

2 International Framework for Corporate Governance

This chapter will focus on identifying certain elements of the current international framework for corporate governance. I will analyse whether a rule of public international law exists that could submit companies to international investor obligations regarding corporate governance in the areas of corporate and accounting laws. In this analysis, general means of interpreting laws such as the wording of provisions and systematic interpretation will be used, but also Article 38 of the Statute of the International Court of Justice (ICJ Statute)[14] will, *inter alia*, be considered to analyse if elements of the framework would qualify as law or even a rule of international law.[15] In addition, bilateral international agreements will be considered which may constitute international law between the parties, but may not necessarily qualify as a more general rule of international law.[16] Whether elements of the framework would be appropriate to be considered in any proceedings before international courts or tribunals when interpreting rules of international law is outside the scope of this chapter and may deserve separate attention.

12 Anazett Pacy Sifuna, 'Disclose or Abstain: The Prohibition of Insider Trading on Trial' (2012) 27 Journal of International Banking Law and Regulation 9.

13 If in the following text, where the term "Corporate Governance" is used, it has the meaning as defined in this Chapter; see also Müller (n 7) 23–24.

14 Statute of the International Court of Justice, 26 June 1945 (UNCIO XV, 355).

15 See also Abel (n 2) 44.

16 This article does not analyse the capacity of an entity to have rights and obligations under international law, also referred to as international subjectivity or international personality and takes the notion that non-State actors have international subjectivity for the sake of argument as given; for this discussion see Abel (n 2) 39–41 with further reference and stating that the particular rights and obligations the respective entity with an acknowledged international legal subjectivity has, if any, remains a separate question, at 39.

2.1 The UN Guiding Principles on Business and Human Rights

Regarding corporate governance in the international context the UN Guiding Principles on Business and Human Rights (UN Guiding Principles) are often referred to first.[17] Potentially this is due to the fact that they are the result of a discussion in the United Nations including in the UN Economic and Social Council and other UN bodies that existed for decades. The UN Guiding Principles were finally adopted by the UN Human Rights Council in 2011.[18]

When analysing the UN Guiding Principles, the first observation is that the term "corporate governance" as such does not appear in the document although certain aspects in the broader corporate governance definitions mentioned above are of course addressed in various areas of the document. However, in the sense of the narrower definition that has been chosen for this chapter, Chapter I, Section B entitled "Operational Principles" stipulates that States should "ensure that other laws and policies governing the creation and ongoing operation of business enterprises, such as corporate law, do not constrain but enable business respect for human rights".[19] Thus, the UN Guiding Principles indeed reflect on corporate governance. However, Chapter I deals with the principles relating to States, not non-State actors such as companies. The commentary expands to explain that laws and policies that govern the creation and ongoing operation of business enterprises, such as corporate and securities laws, directly shape business behaviour.[20] The conclusion is that while States bear the responsibility to set the legal framework within their territory, the behaviour of businesses is just a reflection of such national legislation.

Furthermore, it is noteworthy that the General Principles set out at the beginning of the UN Guiding Principles state:

> Nothing in these Guiding Principles should be read as creating new international law obligations, or as limiting or undermining any legal obligations a

---

17 David Gaukrodger, 'Business responsibilities and investment treaties' OECD Working Papers on International Investment 2021/02, Paris 2021, 23–24 <https://www.oecd-library.org/finance-and-investment/business-responsibilities-and-investment-treaties_4a6f4f17-en> accessed 16 April 2025.

18 Ibid., 24–29.

19 United Nations Human Rights Council, 'Guiding Principles on Business and Human Rights' (2011) 4 <https://www.ohchr.org/sites/default/files/documents/publications/guidingprinciplesbusinesshr_en.pdf> accessed 16 April 2025.

20 Ibid., 5.

> State may have undertaken or be subject to under international law with regard to human rights.[21]

This statement certainly includes national laws addressing corporate structures and indeed legal obligations of such corporate structures as well as roles and responsibilities of corporate bodies. It does, however, clearly articulate that the UN Guiding Principles do not stipulate international law, let alone for companies.[22] This is confirmed by the presentation of the UN Guiding Principles by the Special Rapporteur John Ruggie to the UN Human Rights Council on 30 May 2011 when he stated:

> The Guiding Principles' normative contribution lies not in the creation of new international law obligations but in elaborating the implications of existing standards and practices for states and businesses [...].[23]

Therefore, applying the relevant sources of international law as stipulated by Article 38 of the ICJ Statute, the UN Guiding Principles are not an international convention establishing rules expressly recognised by any contesting States (para. 1 lit. a)).[24] The principles relating to corporate governance also do not qualify as customary international law in accordance with Article 38 para. 1 lit. b) of the ICJ Statute. Customary international law requires a general practice of the States (State practice) accepted as law (*opinio iuris*).[25] Against the background of the UN Guiding Principles, at least regarding business responsibilities, these principles lack acceptance as law and thus do not qualify as customary international law. The same conclusion can be drawn looking at business responsibilities under the rubric of general principles of law in accordance with Article 38 para. 1 lit. c) of the ICJ Statute.[26]

---

21 Ibid., 1.

22 See also Abel (n 2) 46.

23 John G Ruggie, Presentation of Report to United Nations Human Rights Council, Special Representative of the Secretary-General for Business and Human Rights (Geneva, 30 May 2011) <https://www.ohchr.org/sites/default/files/Documents/Issues/TransCorporations/HRC_2011_Remarks_Final_JR.pdf> accessed 17 April 2025, 2.

24 Cf. Gaukrodger (n 17) 23.

25 James Leslie Brierly, *The Law of Nations: An Introduction to the Law in International Relations* (7th edn, OUP 2012); James Crawford, *Brownlie's Principles of Public International Law* (9th edn, OUP 2019).

26 This argument is clearly limited to business responsibilities. State responsibilities, in particular the obligations to protect human rights are not only documented in various international conventions but also in large parts reflect customary international law.

The conclusion from this analysis clearly indicates that the provisions of the UN Guiding Principles do not even create a rule of international law regarding corporate governance for States. Equally they do not form a foundation for a rule of international law for companies or create respective investor obligations.

2.2 International Investment Law

Considering international investment law as a possible basis for a rule of international law on corporate governance for businesses, two aspects shall be addressed. First, it is posited that certain bilateral investment treaties which are often regarded as "new generation international investment agreements" include binding obligations on investors pertaining to corporate social responsibility, human and labour rights, anti-corruption, corporate governance and the environment.[27] Such obligations are also characterised as direct obligations of conduct for foreign investors.[28] Second, some awards of arbitral tribunals are referred to when it comes to investor obligations in international law.[29] The former could qualify as sources of international law as international conventions in accordance with Article 38 para. 1 lit. a) of the ICJ Statute, the

27 Barnali Choudhury, 'Investor Obligations for Human Rights' (2020) 35 ICSID Review – Foreign Investment Law Journal, Issue 1–2, 84–104.

28 Kristina Hellwig and Karsten Nowrot, 'Towards Investors' Responsibilities in International Investment Agreements – A Path for China?' (Rechtswissenschaftliche Beiträge der Hamburger Sozialökonomie, vol 46, Hamburg 2021) 12–17, referring also to the Community Investment Code of the Economic Community of the Great Lakes Countries, signed 31 January 1982 (see UNCTAD, International Investment Instruments: A Compendium, vol II, 1996, 251 ff); The Charter on a Regime of Multinational Industrial Enterprises in the Preferential Trade Area for Eastern and Southern African States, 21 November 1990 (see UNCTAD, International Investment Instruments: A Compendium, vol II, 1996, 427 ff); the Investment Agreement for the Common Market for Eastern and Southern Africa (COMESA) <https://www.comesa.int/wp-content/uploads/2020/10/English-Revised-Investment-agreement-for-the-CCIA-28.09.17-FINAL-after-Adoption-for-signing.pdf> accessed 17 April 2025; The Economic Community of West African States (ECOWAS) Supplementary Act A/SA.3/12/08 Adopting Community Rules on Investment and the Modalities for their Implementation, in force since 19 January 2009 <https://investmentpolicy.unctad.org/international-investment-agreements/treaties/treaties-with-investment-provisions/3547/ecowas-supplementary-act-on-investments-2008> accessed 17 April 2025.

29 Markus Krajewski, 'A Nightmare or a Noble Dream? Establishing Investor Obligations Through Treaty Making and Treaty Application' (2020) 5 Business and Human Rights Journal, Volume 1, 105–129.

latter as subsidiary means for the determination of rules of international law in accordance with Article 38 para. 1 lit. d) of the ICJ Statute.[30]

2.2.1 Bilateral Investment Treaties

With respect to bilateral investment treaties, certain of the treaties most frequently mentioned in relation to corporate governance have been entered into by Brazil,[31] namely the Investment Cooperation and Facilitation Agreement between the Federative Republic of Brazil and the Republic of India signed on 25 January 2020 (Brazil–India BIT)[32] or the Investment Cooperation and Facilitation Agreement between the Federative Republic of Brazil and the Republic of Malawi signed on 25 June 2015 (Brazil–Malawi BIT).[33] However, according to the UNCTAD International Investment Agreements Navigator, only one of them is in force.[34] Therefore, only the Brazil-India BIT can qualify as an international convention in accordance with Article 38 para. 1 lit. a) of the ICJ Statute, or be relied on as compelling evidence of *opinio iuris* or a general principle.

Ignoring for the sake of argument that one of these two Brazilian BITs is not in force, a closer look shall be taken at these two examples focusing on the provisions relating to corporate governance in the two BITs.

Regarding the Brazil–India BIT,[35] Part III is entitled "Investor Obligations and Responsibilities". It contains two articles, one about "Compliance with laws" (Article 11) and the other about "Corporate Social Responsibilities" (Article 12).

---

30 See International Law Commission, 'Draft Report of the International Law Commission on the Work of its 75th Session' (28 May 2024) UN Doc A/CN.4/L.999, draft conclusions 6 and 7 and commentary 7 to draft conclusion 2 as adopted by the International Law Commission (ILC) on first reading.

31 Babatunde Fagbohunlu and Inyene Robert, Standards of Protection and the Obligations of the Investor Global Arbitration Review (17 October 2023).

32 UNCTAD, 'Brazil–India BIT (2020)' <https://investmentpolicy.unctad.org/international-investment-agreements/treaties/bilateral-investment-treaties/4910/brazil—india-bit-2020> accessed 30 June 2026.

33 UNCTAD, 'Brazil–Malawi BIT (2015)' <https://investmentpolicy.unctad.org/international-investment-agreements/treaties/bilateral-investment-treaties/3663/brazil—malawi-bit-2015> accessed 17 April 2025.

34 UNCTAD, 'Brazil: International Investment Agreements' <https://investmentpolicy.unctad.org/international-investment-agreements/countries/27/brazil> accessed 17 April 2025.

35 Brazil-India BIT, (n 32).

Article 11 stipulates in essence compliance obligations ("shall comply"; "shall not"; "shall provide") for investors with national laws of a contracting party of the BIT. While being stipulated in an international treaty, this may not add anything to the scope of obligations an investor would be submitted to with respect to his investment in the host State (in this case either Brazil or India) anyway. The application of national laws to an investment in the host State derives from the sovereignty of the host State over its territory.

Looking at Article 12 ("Corporate Social Responsibilities") the language already indicates a difference. In this provision "[i]nvestors and their investments shall strive to achieve" (Article 12.1) or "[t]he Investors and their investments shall endeavour to comply" (Article 12.2). This wording clearly expresses that the provisions do not stipulate obligations of result for investors. This is further underlined in Article 12.2 by the fact that it only lists "voluntary principles". Finally, these voluntary principles are characterised by rather unspecific wording. On Corporate Governance, Article 12.2 f) of the Brazil–India BIT reads that the investor shall "support and advocate for good corporate governance principles, and develop and apply good corporate governance practices, including anti-corruption measures". Nowhere in the Brazil–India BIT are these principles and practices defined more specifically, despite the anti-corruption measures mentioned. Thus, even assuming the Brazil–India BIT to be an international convention, the drafting of Article 12 clearly indicates that the parties to this BIT did not want to create binding obligations. This persists even if the UN Guiding Principles would be considered for interpretation of the rather unspecific provision of Article 12.2 f of the Brazil–India BIT. Therefore, this article does not qualify to establish an obligation due to its non-binding character,[36] let alone a rule of international law regarding corporate governance or respective investor obligations.

The relevant provisions of the Brazil–Malawi BIT[37] (not in force) in its Article 9 on "Corporate Social Responsibility" are worded very similarly. First, no provision comparable to Article 11 of the Brazil–India BIT exists in this treaty. Second, Article 9 uses similar soft language ("shall strive to the highest possible level" and "shall develop their best efforts to comply"). Also, this provision stipulates "voluntary principles". Thus, the analysis of the Brazil–Malawi

36 Hellwig and Nowrot (n 28) 15–16.

37 Brazil-Malawi BIT, (n 33).

BIT is no different from the Brazil–India BIT. No hard international investor obligation relating to corporate governance may be said to exist.[38]

Even looking at one of the other Brazil BITs already in force, namely the Cooperation and Facilitation of Investments Agreement between the Federative Republic of Brazil and the United Arab Emirates of 15 March 2019,[39] the concepts of Articles 14 ("Compliance with Domestic legislation") and 15 ("Corporate Social Responsibility") are identical and the wording in Article 15 is similarly non-binding as in the other Brazilian BITs. Thus, the Brazil–India BIT, while stipulating in individual cases the obligation of a foreign investor to comply with national laws of the host State and thus stating the obvious, does not create *inter partes* international investor obligations on corporate governance.

Besides the Brazil–India BIT, the Nigeria–Morocco BIT of 2016[40] (also not yet in force) is often mentioned in the context of investor obligations. It seems in Article 18 to provide clear investor obligations post-establishment of an investment. However, looking more closely at the wording, not only do such obligations relate to matters outside corporate governance but also apart from the obligation to maintain an ISO 14001 or equivalent environmental standard certification, the obligations stipulated are quite unspecific. This might tend to suggest that the provisions relating to one or more of the above aspects are non-binding provisions.[41]

The BITs mentioned above only represent individual bilateral treaties which would not be capable to establish a broader rule of international law on corporate governance on their own. However, an analysis by the OECD demonstrates that legality requirements are being used extensively in BITs around the globe, as evidenced by a mapping conducted by UNCTAD resulting for the time period until 2014 in 1,620 out of 2,527 and between 2015 and 2020 in 28 out of 49 treaties.[42] While this again is an obvious reflection of the general principle of sovereignty of a State, similar soft and non-binding provisions in such BITs, even if they demonstrate that such provisions are used to a

---

38 A different view regarding environmental and social impact assessment is taken by Hellwig and Nowrot (n 28) 14 also referring to Articles 17 to 19 of the BIT.

39 UNCTAD, 'Brazil–UAE BIT (2009)' <https://investmentpolicy.unctad.org/international-investment-agreements/treaty-files/5855/download> accessed 17 April 2025.

40 UNCTAD, 'Morocco–Nigeria BIT (2016)' <https://investmentpolicy.unctad.org/international-investment-agreements/treaty-files/5409/download> accessed 17 April 2025.

41 C Nyombi, T Mortimer and N Ramsundar, 'The Morocco-Nigeria BIT: Towards a New Generation of Intra-African BITs' (2018) 29(2) International Company and Commercial Law Review 69.

42 See Gaukrodger (n 17) 100 for further reference.

large extent,[43] do not create a direct obligation under international law for investors regarding corporate governance.[44]

Neither do the legality requirements in the BITs internationalise domestic law. The language of such provisions is usually very general referring to the laws (sometimes all laws) of the host State. Thus, the BITs do not modify or interpret the domestic law. They just state a compliance requirement. Such an obligation itself, being isolated without expanding on specific rules, seems not to elevate domestic law obligations to the status of international investor obligations through a BIT. A different question would be what the effect may be of investment tribunals interpreting and applying (on the basis of the legality requirement) domestic law.[45] However, this is not the place to further expand on the topic of internationalising domestic law.

The conclusion of the above analysis is that the provisions of treaties relating to corporate governance, to the extent stipulating obligations referring to the national laws of the parties only, are stating the obvious. Other provisions that are indicated as investor obligations in such treaties do have a soft or non-binding character only. Such provisions in BITs are by far too general and vague to create international investor obligations or to make any meaningful difference.[46] Legally, they do not qualify as binding rules of international law in accordance with the criteria of Article 38 of the ICJ Statute and are thus not international investor obligations.

2.2.2 Awards of Investment Arbitration Tribunals

Second, a number investment arbitration awards which discuss potential international investor obligations are cited in the context of analysis on international investor obligations. While all these cases focus on potential human rights obligations of companies or businesses, they have been addressed in some cases in the context of potential corporate social responsibility obligations of companies. As corporate social responsibility may include corporate governance, it is worth looking at an example.

43 Ibid., 85–86.

44 It may, however, create an indirect obligation for investors under international law; see Abel (n 2) 217–221.

45 For the potential internationalization of domestic legislation through investment tribunals see Abel (n 2) 101–107.

46 In the OECD Working Papers on International Investment 2021/02 they are named "hortatory clauses", Gaukrodger (n 17) 103–108 citing in addition to the Brazilian Model and the Morocco–Nigeria BIT further examples.

In the 2016 case of *Urbaser and others v. the Republic of Argentina*,[47] the claimants operated water and sewage services in the area of Greater Buenos Aires. They alleged a violation of various rights under the Spain–Argentina BIT of 1991[48] caused by the conduct of the host State government in the Argentinean economic crisis of 2001. The tribunal in its award held that by and large investors have no binding human rights obligations.[49] But the tribunal elaborated in its decision that corporations may have negative human rights obligations, i.e. obligations to refrain from certain proscribed conduct. More specifically, the tribunal found as follows:

> The Tribunal may mention in this respect that international law accepts corporate social responsibility as a standard of crucial importance for companies operating in the field of international commerce. This standard includes commitments to comply with human rights in the framework of those entities' operations conducted in countries other than the country of their seat or incorporation. In light of this more recent development, it can no longer be admitted that companies operating internationally are immune from becoming subjects of international law. On the other hand, even though several initiatives undertaken at the international scene are seriously targeting corporations [sic] human rights conduct, they are not, on their own, sufficient to oblige corporations to put their policies in line with human rights law. The focus must be, therefore, on contextualizing a corporation's specific activities as they relate to the human right at issue in order to determine whether any international law obligations attach to the non-State individual.[50]

The exact scope of such negative obligation, however, remains blurry in the decision.[51] Moreover, the decision raises fundamental concerns regarding the legal basis for such potential international obligations. The tribunal refers in its reasoning for example to the Universal Declaration of Human Rights[52] and

---

47 *Urbaser S.A. and Consorcio de Aguas Bilbao Bizkaia, Bilbao Biskaia Ur Partzuergoa v. The Argentine Republic*, ICSID Case No. ARB/07/26, Award (8 December 2016) (*Urbaser v. Argentina*).

48 Acuerdo para la Prohocion y la Proteccion Reciproca de Inversiones entre el Reino de España y La República Argentina (1991) <https://investmentpolicy.unctad.org/international-investment-agreements/treaty-files/119/download> accessed 17 April 2025.

49 Urbaser v. Argentina (n 47) cf. para 1209 with specific reference to the human right to water which was relevant in this case.

50 Ibid., para. 1195.

51 Abel (n 2) 59–61.

52 *Urbaser v. Argentina* (n 47) para. 1196.

the ILO Tripartite Declaration,[53] but opinion is not unanimous that the first instrument reflects or has attained the status of international law, and this is even less so in the case of the second instrument, being mere declarations as they are. None of these instruments has the status of a binding source of international law in accordance with Article 38 para. 1 of the ICJ Statute. Likewise, the States explicitly intended not to produce legally binding effects on companies through these instruments.[54]

Furthermore, decisions like in the *Urbaser* case addressing (but not finally establishing) positive investor obligations seem to be few so far. Other cases mentioned in this context are two further decisions by ICSID tribunals in *Burlington v. Ecuador*[55] and *Perenco v. Ecuador*[56] as well as two decisions by UNCITRAL tribunals in *Al-Warraq v. Indonesia*[57] and *Aven v. Costa Rica*.[58] Thus, it seems not appropriate to argue that these decisions be considered as a subsidiary means for the determination of the rules of international law in accordance with Article 38 para. 1 lit. d) of the ICJ Statute. This would require not only a broader recognition of this topic by international courts and tribunals[59] but also the identification of clear obligations on investors, including on corporate governance, which is not the case so far.

Despite the fact that the legal discussions that have developed in these proceedings and are reflected in the mentioned awards relate to international human rights and not corporate governance *per se*, the awards show that even for international human rights (let alone for corporate governance) international investor obligations have not crystallised so far.

2.2.3 Conclusion

The state-of-play on international investor obligations in corporate governance and even beyond in international investment law is that such obligations so far do not exist. BITs remain vague in provisions covering the broader

53 Ibid., para. 1198.

54 Abel (n 2) 59–61.

55 *Burlington Resources Inc. v. Republic of Ecuador*, ICSID Case No. ARB/08/5, Decision on Counterclaims (7 February 2017).

56 *Perenco Ecuador Ltd. v. The Republic of Ecuador*, ICSID Case No. ARB/08/6, Interim Decision on the Environmental Counterclaim (11 August 2015).

57 *Hesham Talaat M. Al-Warraq v. The Republic of Indonesia*, UNCITRAL, Final Award (15 December 2014) (*Al-Warraq v. Indonesia*).

58 *David Aven et al. v. The Republic of Costa Rica*, UNCITRAL, Case No. UNCT/15/3, Final Award (18 September 2018) (*Aven v. Costa Rica*).

59 Andreas Zimmermann, Christian J Tams, Karin Oellers-Frahm and Christian Tomuschat (eds), *The Statute of the International Court of Justice: A Commentary* (3rd edn, OUP 2019).

aspect of corporate social responsibility even if they do sometimes mention corporate governance. Thus, they cannot even be interpreted generally in the way of constituting legal obligations of companies at all. This conclusion is confirmed by the results that can be taken from individual decisions by investment tribunals. Also, considering the sources of international law in accordance with Article 38 of the ICJ Statute, a rule of international law regarding an international investor obligation cannot be established to date. To the extent that BITs stipulate the obligation to comply with the national law of the host State, these obligations merely state the obvious fact that such obligations are already embodied in the sovereignty a State exercises over its territory.

3 Protocol on Investment to the Agreement Establishing the African Continental Free Trade Area

Finally, in this section, focus shall be put on the draft Protocol on Investment to the Agreement Establishing the African Continental Free Trade Area (the AfCFTA Investment Protocol).[60] This instrument has been, since its adoption in February 2023, reflected in some literature but a closer analysis is outstanding.[61] Despite its relatively recent adoption, the AfCFTA Investment Protocol is an interesting case study as many of the bilateral and multilateral instruments addressing investor obligations are also between African States or cover African regional organisations such as ECOWAS or COMESA.[62]

In particular, Article 39 of the AfCFTA Investment Protocol (entitled "Corporate Governance") will be addressed which stipulates as follows:

> 1. Investors and their investments **shall meet national, regional and internationally accepted standards of corporate governance**, in particular in respect of transparency and accounting practices.
> 2. **Investors** and their investments shall, in accordance with domestic laws and regulations:

60 Only available in draft form African Union, Draft AfCFTA Investment Protocol (STC/Legal/Exp, January 2023).

61 Fagbohunlu and Robert (n 31).

62 ECOWAS, Supplementary Act A/SA.3/12/08 Adopting Community Rules on Investment and the Modalities for their Implementation (adopted on 19 December 2008, entered into force on 19 January 2009); Investment Agreement for the COMESA Common Investment Area (adopted on 23 May 2007).

a. **ensure the equitable treatment of all** shareholders;

b. **encourage active cooperation with their stakeholders** to create wealth, jobs, and sustainable financial management;

c. **make timely and accurate disclosure on all material matters regarding an enterprise or company**, including the financial situation, performance, ownership, and governance of the enterprise or company, risks related to environmental liabilities, and any other matters relating to the enterprise and company in accordance with the relevant and applicable regulations and requirements; and

d. **comply with national policies on human resource development** and to the extent possible invest in training, capacity building, and knowledge transfer through programmes for human resource development.

3. **State parties are encouraged to improve their regulatory and institutional framework for corporate governance** in support of the requirements of this article.

4. **State parties shall put in place measures enhancing transparency in financial reporting**, disclosure, accounting, and audit practices in support of the requirements of this article, in accordance with domestic laws, regulations and applicable international standards, and obligations.

There are two general observations to begin with. First, the language within the AfCFTA Investment Protocol addressing investors seems significantly more concrete than the wording used in the BITs mentioned in the previous section and in the regional African instruments. That may indicate that the provisions could already have a legally binding effect applying general means of interpreting law and also that they may be much more operational. Second, it is noteworthy that Article 39 of the AfCFTA Investment Protocol does not only address investors but likewise States, both in encouraging (para. 3) and obliging (para. 4) terms. In the following sections, certain elements of the provision will be discussed.

3.1 The AfCFTA as a Source of International Law

As in the previous chapter it is considered first whether the AfCFTA Investment Protocol qualifies as a source of international law in general in accordance with Article 38 of the ICJ Statute before coming back to Article 39 of the protocol and its individual provisions.

The AfCFTA Investment Protocol has been adopted by the Assembly of the Heads of State and Government of the then 54 Member States of the African Union.[63] Once ratified, the AfCFTA Investment Protocol would have regional coverage throughout the entire African continent. Once it enters into force, the AfCFTA Investment Protocol could be considered to be a particular international convention in accordance with Article 38 para. 1 lit a) of the ICJ Statute. This conclusion is drawn based on stronger arguments than in the case of the bilateral investment treaties referenced in the previous section. It rests on the observation that while BITs by definition are international treaties between two sovereign States only, the AfCFTA Investment Protocol, if in force, with its 54 member States and its regional coverage of the African continent represents a much broader consensus amongst the contracting parties. It seems, however, too far reaching to interpret such regional consensus to the effect that the protocol would constitute a general international convention in the sense of Article 38 para. 1 lit a) of the ICJ Statute,[64] which would rather require a global convention or at least a consensus reaching beyond a regional agreement.

However, despite the notion that the AfCFTA Investment Protocol could be considered upon its entry into force as international law in the sense of Article 38 of the ICJ Statute, a closer look needs to be taken at the wording of the Investment Protocol's provisions and in particular at its Article 39 regarding "Corporate Governance".

3.1.1 "[N]ational, Regional and Internationally Accepted Standards of Corporate Governance" (Article 39 Para. 1)

In analysing the provision, the first observation is that the wording clearly stipulates that investors "shall meet" these standards, thus indicating a clear obligation. However, even assuming that national, regional, and internationally accepted standards would be sufficiently defined, the provision may create problems regarding legal certainty for investors,[65] as the wording clearly

63 Linklaters, 'The AfCFTA Investment Protocol – A potential game changer for the African continent?' (May 2023) <https://www.linklaters.com/insights/blogs/arbitrationlinks/2023/may/afcfta-investment-protocol> accessed 17 April 2025.

64 Cf. *Al-Warraq v. Indonesia* (n 57).

65 Legal certainty is considered one of the fundamental principles of the rule of law. The principle that "[t]he law must be accessible and so far as possible intelligible, clear and predictable" is one of the eight fundamental principles of the rule of law identified by Tom Bingham, *The Rule of Law* (Penguin Books 2011); see also referring to Bingham, this principle has also been emphasised by the European Commission for Democracy

stipulates that the investor shall comply with *all* such standards thus taking a cumulative approach.

In any case national and regional standards may differ, and they may even involve different legal concepts. For example, German corporate law provides for a so-called two-tier internal structure of corporate bodies containing a management board exclusively responsible for day-to-day-business[66] and a supervisory board limited to control and supervision but being prohibited to interfere into the day-to-day-business.[67] Showcasing the extent of variation, this national German concept of organising its corporate bodies is far from representing a uniform regional concept even within the European Union.[68] Internationally, Anglo-American corporate law systems also operate differently with a one-tier system with one board containing both executive and non-executive directors.[69]

Thus, the legal question is simply whether national, regional, and internationally accepted systems exist, how are they discerned, and how do they relate to each other? Is one prevailing? While Article 39 para. 1 of the AfCFTA Investment Protocol may therefore, considering its wording, create an international investor obligation,[70] it lacks legal certainty, with the practical consequence for a foreign investor that it may be unclear about the nature and extent of such obligation. Interesting, but beyond the scope of this chapter, is the question whether such obligation with all its attendant uncertainty would be in line with the general principles of the rule of law. At very least it creates a fundamental dilemma for investors in seeking to comply with the obligation.

3.1.2 "[E]quitable Treatment of All Shareholders" (Article 39 Para. 2 Lit. a))

Investors and their investments shall treat all shareholders equally. The wording of the provision using "shall" clearly indicates an obligation. Thus, it may be well argued that Article 39 para. 2 lit a) of the AfCFTA Investment Protocol establishes on this subject matter an international investor obligation.

---

through Law (Venice Commission), Report on the Rule of Law (Council of Europe Doc CDL-AD(2011)003rev, 4 April 2011).

66 Section 76 para. 1 German Stock Corporation Act.

67 Section 111 para. 4 1st sentence German Stock Corporation Act.

68 Carsten Jungmann, 'The Effectiveness of Corporate Governance in One-Tier and Two-Tier Board Systems – Evidence from the UK and Germany' (2006) 3 European Company and Financial Law Review 426.

69 Ibid.

70 As such the AfrCFTA Investment Protocol is thus comparable with the African Charter on Human and Peoples' Rights (adopted on 27 June 1981, entered into force on 21 October 1986) 1520 UNTS 217; for the latter see Abel (n 2) 47.

Without here engaging in a comparative study on the national laws of the member States of the African Union, the question is whether it is necessary to establish such international investor obligation, as such an obligation is often well established in national laws. For example, Section 53a of the German Stock Corporation Act (*Aktiengesetz*) stipulates: "Subject to the same prerequisites being given, stockholders are to be treated equal".[71] This provision was incorporated into the law in 1978 and is based on European law, in particular Article 50 para. 2 lit. g) of the Treaty on the Functioning of the European Union.[72] Thus, at least in the European Union such equal treatment can be considered to be a common principle reflected in respective obligations in the national corporate laws of the EU member States.

However, it seems surprising that a corporate law obligation normally stipulated in national law is included in an international treaty. This is even more the case where Article 32 of the AfCFTA Investment Protocol provides that investors and their investments shall carry out their obligations in compliance with all relevant domestic laws and regulations.[73] This creates the impression that not all parties to the AfCFTA Investment Protocol have implemented this obligation in their national laws which is underpinned by the encouragement of the State Parties, in Article 39 para. 3 of the Protocol, to improve *inter alia* their regulatory framework for corporate governance.[74]

This leads practically to two consequences that Article 39 para. 2 lit. a) of the AfCFTA Investment Protocol may have upon investors. Either the provision is redundant to equivalent national law provisions which may exist in member States, or the provision covers regulatory gaps in such member States and puts an international obligation on the investor as substitute. The first consequence can be considered a systemic inconsistency. The second again submits the foreign investor to uncertainty regarding the legal requirements it has to comply with.

---

71 Aktiengesetz of 6 September 1965 (BGBl I, 1089), as amended by Article 18 of the Law of 23 October 2024 (BGBl 2024, No. 323).

72 Uwe Hüffer and Jens Koch, Aktiengesetz (18th edn, CH Beck 2024) § 53a para 1; see also Directive (EU) 2017/1132 of the European Parliament and of the Council of 14 June 2017 relating to certain aspects of company law [2017] OJ L169/46, 46–127.

73 This illustrates the asymmetry which has been attributed to investment law that only States have obligations towards investors and not vice versa; see Abel (n 2), 48–49 with further reference.

74 Cf. UNCTAD, Report of the Expert Meeting on Good Governance in Investment Promotion (17 November 2004) UN Doc TD/B/COM.2/EM.15/3, para 4; Abel (n 2) 38; Anne Peters, *Beyond Human Rights: The Legal Status of the Individual in International Law* (Cambridge University Press 2016) 76–78.

3.1.3 "[T]imely and Accurate Disclosure on All Material Matters regarding an Enterprise or Company" (Article 39 Para. 2 Lit. c))

Investors and their investments shall make timely and accurate disclosure including regarding the financial situation of the company in accordance with the relevant and applicable regulations. In interpreting this rule and the attendant questions as to what the relevant and applicable regulations are, it seems most reasonable from a perspective of systematic interpretation to refer back to Article 39 para. 1 of the AfCFTA Investment Protocol requiring investors and their investments to meet national, regional, and internationally accepted standards. Notably, this provision refers to accounting practices which are certainly relevant to describe the financial situation of a company.

When taking recourse to Article 39 para. 1 of the AfCFTA Investment Protocol for interpreting para. 2 lit. c), the dilemma mentioned above stemming from the cumulative concept of this provision gains further practical relevance. It shall be illustrated by a further example relating to national and international generally accepted accounting practices. The overarching concept under the German Commercial Code remains, also after its last revision, the protection of *creditors*. The International Financial Reporting Standards (IFRS) on the other hand focus on the protection of *investors* in the company.[75] This divergence nonetheless results in some similarities despite other notable differences.[76]

Without describing the details of the differences, it is obvious that different requirements apply to which investors would apparently have to comply given the cumulative concept of Article 39 para. 1 of the AfCFTA Investment Protocol. It has, however, to be considered that also in other countries, by existing law, one company may have to comply with both IFRS and national generally accepted accounting principles (GAAP).[77] This is the case if, for example, a company is listed at a stock exchange which typically requires IFRS accounting but also needs to provide accounts in accordance with

75 See Manfred Godek, 'Was IFRS vom HGB unterscheidet und was bei der Umstellung auf IFRS zu beachten ist' (29 September 2022) Haufe.de <https://www.haufe.de/finance/buchfuehrung-kontierung/ifrs-oder-hgb-eine-entscheidungshilfe/unterschied-zwischen-ifrs-und-hgb-umstellung-auf-ifrs_186_448526.html> accessed 17 April 2025.

76 For an overview, see PricewaterhouseCoopers (ed), *IFRS versus German GAAP – Summary of Similarities and Differences* (February 2010) <https://www.pwc.com/gx/en/ifrs-reporting/pdf/ifrs-vs-german-gaap-similarities-and-differences_final2.pdf> accessed 17 April 2025.

77 Zehra G Kavame Eroglu, 'Global Adoption of IFRS as an Example of International Financial Law Making' (2021) 53 George Washington International Law Review 239–320.

national GAAP (for example for dividend distribution to its shareholders). Thus, both standards serve different purposes. Still, this parallel application for different purposes requires firstly clear national accounting standards providing also for a clear purpose; secondly clear definition of the respective scope; and thirdly an established practice of handling both standards by the statutory auditor of a company.

This example again demonstrates that, while the provision analysed could well be characterised as an international investor obligation, its application faces considerable challenges for foreign investors but also for the host State.

3.1.4 Measures to Improve the "Regulatory and Institutional Framework for Corporate Governance" and "Enhancing Transparency in Financial Reporting" (Article 39 Paras. 3 and 4)

Article 39 para. 3 of the AfCFTA Investment Protocol encourages State parties to improve their regulatory and institutional framework for corporate governance. Its vagueness demonstrates how difficult it seems to be to reach agreement between the State Parties to establish obligations on each of them to implement a regulatory and institutional framework on corporate governance. Article 39 para. 4 further requires State parties to put measures in place enhancing transparency in financial reporting, disclosure, accounting, and audit practices. It thus stipulates an express State obligation to ensure transparency in financial reporting. However, it remains to be seen if and to what extent the State parties will comply with this obligation.

Given the legal uncertainties illustrated above, it seems necessary for the State parties to take charge in implementing such framework of corporate governance regulation in order to mitigate or remove these uncertainties. Otherwise, the lack of a regulatory and institutional framework, as well as the existence of less developed national laws on financial reporting in certain jurisdictions, increases the legal uncertainty even further for investors. At the same time, this uncertainty will restrict host States from effectively monitoring compliance with the obligations of investors.

4 Conclusion

Where does this all leave us with international investor obligations and corporate governance?

In essence, corporate governance still seems to be almost entirely a matter of national laws. On the international level, the *status quo* clearly indicates that the provisions of the UN Guiding Principles do not even create a rule of international law regarding corporate governance for States. Equally they do not form a foundation for a rule of international law on corporate governance for companies or create respective investor obligations.

BITs, regional investment instruments and investment tribunals have not changed this *status quo* regarding corporate governance. The state-of-play on international investor obligations on corporate governance in and even beyond international investment law shows that such obligations so far do not exist.[78] BITs remain vague in provisions covering the broader aspect of corporate social responsibility (even if they do sometimes mention corporate governance). Thus they cannot even be interpreted generally in the manner of constituting legal obligations on companies at all. This conclusion is confirmed by the results that can be taken from individual decisions by investment tribunals. Also, considering the sources of international law in accordance with Article 38 of the ICJ Statute, a rule of international law regarding an international investor obligation cannot be established. To the extent BITs stipulate the obligation to comply with the national laws of the host State, these obligations merely recognise the obvious fact that such an obligation is already embodied in the sovereignty a State exercises over its territory.

Article 39 of the AfCFTA Investment Protocol, however, seems to set a different trend. It seems to be the first investment instrument that affords specific focus to corporate governance, while corporate social responsibility and other aspects included in the broader definition of corporate governance are addressed in separate articles of the Protocol. It is also significantly more concrete in its wording. It still contains other legal challenges; namely regarding legal certainty and clarifying the legal relationship between the different standards mentioned in respect of the corporate governance obligation.

In general, there seems to be a trend to create international investor obligations including for the matter of corporate governance. However, the fundamental question remains, considering, in particular, the requirements to comply with national laws, whether international investor obligations are needed for matters that are typically regulated in those very national laws. Some jurisdictions may be confronted with governance challenges in developing, adapting and implementing robust rules at the national level which reflect best practices already common in other jurisdictions, both on the Afri-

---

78 In literature a trend is apostrophized as "[a] nascent doctrine of direct obligations" Abel (n 2) 108–118 or "Towards Investors' Responsibilities in International Investment Agreements" Hellwig and Nowrot (n 28). Still the state-of-play remains that such direct investor obligations have not yet been constituted.

can continent and elsewhere around the globe. And it may be reasonable to assume that such challenges are sometimes manifold. However, the solution of establishing international investor obligations on corporate governance to compensate possible gaps in the national legislations or enforcement machineries of the States could very well create the above-mentioned uncertainties. Such uncertainties may pose considerable challenges not only for foreign investors but also potentially for the respective host States.

CHAPTER 10

Corporate Social Responsibility Obligations for Investors in Investment Agreements

Steven Finizio[1]

1 Introduction

An ongoing discussion with regard to investment treaties has concerned how to strike an effective balance between the rights and obligations of investors, on the one hand, and States on the other; and how to make that balance robust and enforceable, including with regard to placing affirmative obligations on investors. This chapter discusses developments with regard to one area of investor obligations – those concerning corporate social responsibility (CSR), although some of the discussion is applicable to other investor obligations, particularly, investor obligations relating to social development and human rights.

States are increasingly including affirmative investor obligations in bilateral and multilateral investment treaties, including CSR or similar provisions. This chapter discusses the evolution of CSR provisions, including changes in how they are drafted. As such clauses have evolved, they have increasingly been drafted in more mandatory language rather than in voluntary or aspirational terms, and some investment agreements now include more detailed requirements, including some that are more measurable. This has potentially significant consequences in terms of both investor conduct and effective enforcement of such obligations, including enforcement through international arbitration. In that regard, this chapter discusses how increased clarity with regard to such clauses can increase their relevance if a dispute arises between an investor and a State, including with regard to jurisdictional and admissibility issues, merits defenses, and potential counterclaims by the State.

1 The author thanks Mr. Jacob Omorodion, formerly a senior associate at WilmerHale for his assistance towards the preparation of this chapter.

This chapter is organised as follows: **Section 2** describes understandings of CSR; **Section 3** describes how CSR provisions in investment treaties have been drafted, and the evolution of those provisions, including with regard to whether they are mandatory and the specificity of their obligations; and **Section 4** describes how investors' CSR obligations can be enforced in disputes relating to investment agreements, including through jurisdictional and admissibility objections, defenses to claims by investors, and counterclaims.

2 What Is Corporate Social Responsibility?

Corporate social responsibility is often described in broad terms, and can be defined differently across industries, geographies, and disciplines. Even within the context of international law, there are different understandings of the scope and meaning of CSR. The scope of CSR concerns also arguably overlaps with the scope of other investor obligations that are also increasingly incorporated into investment treaties, such as environmental, social, and governance (ESG), labour, corporate governance, and similar obligations. For purposes of this chapter, it is not important to settle on a specific definition of CSR, although some of the ways that CSR has been described are highlighted below.

One potential starting point in defining CSR is the definition used in the European Commission's "Green Paper on Promoting a European Framework for Corporate Social Responsibility", which describes CSR as "a concept whereby companies integrate social and environmental concerns in their business operations in their interaction with their stakeholders on a voluntary basis".[2] That Green Paper also notes that CSR "should nevertheless not be seen as a substitute to regulation concerning social rights or environmental standards, including the development of new appropriate legislation".[3] This underscores that there are different sources of CSR commitments: CSR requirements may be voluntary, they may be found in contracts, they may be imposed through regulation or legislation, and they may be referred to in investment agreements.

There are many other descriptions of CSR. As Professor Nitish Monebhurrun has explained:

2 Commission of the European Communities, *Promoting a European Framework for Corporate Social Responsibility* (Green Paper, 18 July 2001), 8.

3 Ibid.

> The understanding of what is corporate social responsibility has changed over time. If part of the liberal doctrine initially considered that the only social responsibility which companies had was to make profits, the scope of corporate social responsibility has been widened with the aim of mitigating and preventing the negative social externalities which can be related to business conduct. Corporations are, accordingly, not expected to act solely for their own benefits or for those of their shareholders. If they do not always have a legal duty to make their host States and host societies more prosperous, they do have a duty – a corporate social responsibility – not to conduct their business to the detriment of the local population. By the means of this duty of care, the business sphere has thus been enlarged to include social, environmental and human rights considerations.[4]

Other commentators have described CSR as encompassing "integration of economic, governance, social, and environmental concerns; strong stakeholder engagement; voluntary [in] nature, [and] exceeding [the] law's requirements".[5] Still others have described CSR as:

> generally embod[ying] the notion that a corporation must act in a responsible manner with regard to the environment, community and broader society in which it operates. In its most basic form, CSR emphasizes an approach to corporate governance and operations that integrates and balances the self-interest of the corporation, and those of its investors, with the concerns and interests of the public.[6]

What emerges from these different descriptions is that the goal of CSR is to ensure that businesses – and, by extension, investors – have responsibilities that go beyond the maximisation of profits, and which encompass social well-being, including with regard to the environment, labour, sustainability, and human rights. While a goal for those promoting CSR is for businesses them-

4 Nitish Monebhurrun, 'The Corporate Duty to Contribute to Sustainable Development from the Perspective of International Arbitration' in Lawrence Boo and Gary B. Born (eds), *Asian Arbitration Journal* (2021) 17(2) 84–85.

5 Kabir Duggal and Marta Piazza, 'Corporate Social Responsibility (CSR)' (*Jus Mundi*, 6 May 2024), para 1 <https://jusmundi.com/en/document/publication/en-csr> accessed 27 February 2025.

6 Jarrod Hepburn and Vuyelwa Kuuya, Corporate Social Responsibility and Investment Treaties' in MarieClaire Cordonier Segger, Markus W. Gehring, and Andrew Newcombe (eds), *Sustainable Development in World Investment Law* (Kluwer Law International 2011), 589–590.

selves to voluntarily enact CSR policies, States may require CSR commitments in both agreements and through investment treaties, and are increasingly doing so, as discussed below.

3 How Have CSR Provisions in Investment Treaties Evolved?

There has been a notable evolution in the approach to including investor obligations in investment treaties, which can be seen in how CSR obligations have been included in such instruments. Historically, many investment treaties have only referred to CSR or similar obligations with regard to the conduct of the contracting parties to the instrument – in other words, the States entering into the investment treaties – and not as obligations for investors at all. However, as discussed below, as reflected in more recent treaties and model agreements, it appears that investor obligations with regard to CSR or similar concerns will increasingly be included in investment treaties going forward.

This section discusses the introduction of references to CSR in investment agreements and how those provisions have changed over time, including with regard to whether they apply to the investor, rather than the State parties to the treaty, whether they are voluntary or obligatory, and the degree of specificity of the obligations. These drafting choices have direct consequences for the relevance of such provisions to disputes between investors and States.

In addition to historically referring to CSR commitments with regard to the contracting parties to an investment treaty – i.e. the States – the practice has been to refer to CSR commitments as voluntary.[7] This dovetails with older understandings of CSR, as described above, which emphasise the voluntary nature of CSR, and the notion that CSR may go beyond what actually is required by applicable laws. While this may appear toothless from the perspective of enforceability, the reasoning behind including voluntary CSR provisions in investment agreements is that doing so may have an institutional cultural and policy impact in encouraging CSR.[8] That said, this "soft CSR"

7 See, e.g. Crina Baltag, Riddhi Joshi, and Kabir Duggal, 'Recent Trends in Investment Arbitration on the Right to Regulate, Environment, Health and Corporate Social Responsibility: Too Much or Too Little?' in Meg Kinnear and Campbell McLachLan (eds), *ICSID Review – Foreign Investment Law Journal* 38(2), 20 ("CSR provisions have yet to gain traction among States as binding obligations. Currently, the soft-law form of provision is favoured."); Hepburn and Kuuya (n 6).

8 Monebhurrun (n 4), 89–90 ("[I]f the patterns of expected corporate social behavior entrenched in international investment agreements do not bind the investors, they do (at

approach is subject to criticisms that such provisions are "tantamount to window dressing" and/or a "mere illusion".[9]

Although references to CSR commitments are often still couched in voluntary or aspirational language, this approach is starting to change, as described below. Section 3.1 describes how the CSR obligations of contracting parties (i.e. States) to investment treaties have been addressed; Section 3.2 describes the increasing inclusion of CSR and similar obligations for investors, as well as the increasing reference to more mandatory and detailed obligations.

3.1 CSR Clauses Directed at Contracting Parties

There are a number of ways in which CSR and similar commitments for the contracting parties, i.e. the State parties to treaties, that are voluntary – or at least non-mandatory – have been incorporated into investment treaties. These include (1) preambulatory clauses, encouraging the contracting parties to fulfil or consider CSR goals in their conduct; (2) operative clauses with permissive language with regard to CSR goals; and (3) operative clauses that include voluntary language bundled within obligatory language. A number of investment treaties contain combinations of the abovementioned ways.

3.1.1 References to CSR in Preambulatory Clauses

At the lightest and most high-level, investment treaties will sometimes include specific CSR or CSR-related language in the preamble or preambulatory clauses to indicate that the obligations within the agreement should be fulfilled with a "spirit" of CSR, if not a specific obligation. A number of investment treaties have included this kind of language. An early example is the Organization of the Islamic Conference's 1981 Agreement on Promotion, Protection, and Guarantee of Investments, in which the preambulatory clauses refer to investments as vehicles for "economic and social development", with reference to the "common interest and mutual benefit", and "development and rais[ing] the standard of living".[10]

---

least) have a policy function which aims at fostering the adherence to a culture of corporate social responsibility.").

9 Ibid., 90 ("Some authors posit that non-binding CSR is tantamount to window dressing and only serves the interests of the market.").

10 Hepburn and Kuuya (n 6), 599; General Secretariat of the Organisation of the Islamic Conference, *Agreement on Promotion, Protection and Guarantee of General Secretariat of the Organisation of Islamic Conference* (1981), Preamble, 241–242 ("Convinced that relations among the Islamic States in the field of investment are one of the major areas of

This approach is also seen, for example, in the Netherlands 2019 Model Investment Agreement, that includes references in its preamble to the State parties "reaffirming their commitment to sustainable development and to enhancing the contribution of international trade and investment to sustainable development".[11]

Similarly, Canada's 2021 Model Foreign Investment Protection and Promotion Act (FIPA) refers to CSR-type interests, without using the term directly, in its preambulatory clauses. The FIPA notes that it is "[r]ecognizing that the promotion and protection of investments of investors ... will be conducive to the stimulation of mutually beneficial business activity ... and to the promotion of sustainable development."[12] It also "[r]eaffirm[s] the importance of promoting responsible business conduct, cultural identity and diversity, environmental protection and conservation, gender equality, the rights of Indigenous peoples, labour rights, inclusive trade, sustainable development, and traditional knowledge, as well as the importance of preserving the Party's right to regulate in the public interest."[13] As noted, however, these are drafted as considerations for the State parties, and not as obligations for investors.

3.1.2 References to CSR in Operative Clauses Directed at States

In addition to preambulatory language, some treaties also include non-mandatory references to CSR commitments by the contracting parties (again, rather than investors) in operative clauses directed at the State parties. As discussed below, these clauses often are written using aspirational language, using phrases such as "shall endeavour" or "strive"; others are written as requiring the States to "encourage" investors to operate in ways that respect CSR considerations.

3.1.2.1 Obligations to "Endeavour" or "Strive"

Even where these provisions directed at the contracting parties are part of the operative clauses in an investment agreement, they are often limited in impact because the content of the obligations is articulated in either aspir-

---

economic cooperation among these states through which economic and social development therein can be fostered on the basis of common interest and mutual benefit ... Anxious to provide and develop a favourable climate for investments, in which the economic resources of the Islamic countries could circulate between them so that optimum utilization could be made of the resources in a way that will serve their development raise the standard of living of their peoples.").

11 Netherlands 2019 Model Investment Agreement, Preamble.

12 Canada 2021 Model Foreign Investment Protection and Promotion Act (FIPA), Preamble.

13 FIPA, Preamble.

ational or broad terms. This is done, for example, through the use of language such as "should" rather than "shall", or by using language to describe the obligation so it may be either easy to comply with or difficult to show it has not been.

This is seen for example in the OIC investment agreement, in which Article 3 sets out an obligation to pursue investment opportunities in a way that fosters social development:

> The contracting parties ***shall endeavour*** to open up various fields and investment opportunities to the capital on the widest possible scale, in such a way that may suit their economic conditions and on the basis of achieving mutual benefits for the parties to the investment in a way that will foster the social and economic development of the host state in accordance with its set objectives and plans while, at the same time, achieving a profitable investment return for the capital.[14]

Similarly, the Netherlands 2019 Model Investment Agreement has a number of such references, including Article 3(4), which refers to an obligation on "[t]he Contracting Parties" to "***strive*** to strengthen the promotion and facilitation of investments that contribute to sustainable development ...."[15] Similarly, Article 6(6), on "Sustainable Development", refers to the contracting parties "reaffirm[ing] their obligations under the multilateral agreements in the field of environmental protection, labour standards and the protection of human rights to which they are party, such as the Paris Agreement, the fundamental International Labour Organization (ILO) Conventions, and the Universal Declaration of Human Rights."[16]

3.1.2.2 Obligations to "Encourage"

Some investment agreements go further and refer to a State's obligations with regard to its investors' compliance with CSR, but nonetheless are drafted in ways that are vague and difficult to enforce, and, importantly, do not create obligations for the investors themselves. For example, Article 7(2) of the Netherlands Model BIT provides that "the Contracting Parties ***reaffirm the importance*** of each Contracting Party ***to encourage investors*** operating within its territory or subject to its jurisdiction ***to voluntarily incorporate*** into their internal polices those inter-

14 Agreement on Promotion, Protection and Guarantee of Investments Among Member States of the Organisation of the Islamic Conference, at art 3 (emphasis added).
15 Netherlands 2019 Model Investment Agreement, art 3(4) (emphasis added).
16 Ibid., art 6(6).

nationally recognised standards, guidelines, and principles of corporate social responsibility that have been endorsed or are supported by that Party."[17]

Thus, even where investment treaties have more extensive CSR provisions directed at the contracting parties, like those in Article 7 of the 2019 Netherlands Model BIT, the impact of those provisions is often limited because the references are to commitments by the State parties and not investors, and the commitments are often non-mandatory or, when written as obligations, the scope of the obligation is often vague and aspirational, and therefore almost impossible to enforce.

3.1.2.3 Right to Regulate

There is another way that CSR considerations are sometimes addressed in the operative clauses in investment treaties. CSR obligations may be addressed by way of "right to regulate" clauses. While such clauses do not encourage or obligate investors to maintain certain CSR standards, such clauses may give the State the ability to regulate conduct that relates to CSR considerations. For example, Article 3 of Canada's Model FIPA provides:

> The ***Parties reaffirm the right*** of each Party ***to regulate*** within its territory ***to achieve legitimate policy objectives***, such as with respect to the protection of the environment and addressing climate change; social or consumer protection; or the promotion and protection of health, safety, rights of Indigenous peoples, gender equality, and cultural diversity.[18]

Similar provisions, emphasising States' right to regulate with regard to such policy objectives, including some that relate to CSR concerns, are increasingly common in investment treaties, as discussed below.

3.2 CSR Clauses Directed at Investors

A more notable development has been an increase in model investment agreements as well as some more recent treaties that provide for CSR and other obligations for investors. Some of those agreements are drafted in terms that are voluntary or aspirational, but there are an increasing number of model agreements and treaties that include mandatory CSR and similar obligations for investors, and those obligations are increasingly drafted to include specific and even measurable obligations. The shift to more manda-

17 Ibid., art 7(2) (emphasis added).
18 FIPA, art 3 (emphasis added).

tory CSR provisions – and provisions directed at investors – in international investment agreements tracks the trend in domestic law, where many States have adopted laws requiring businesses to observe minimum CSR and/or ESG standards.[19]

As described below, States have taken different approaches to both whether investor obligations are mandatory (and, if so, how mandatory) and how detailed (and measurable) such obligations are, with the recent Protocol on Investment to the Agreement Establishing the African Continental Free Trade Area (AfCFTA) arguably going farthest. The subsections below discuss the approaches taken (1) in the Draft Pan-African Investment Code and the Nigeria-Morocco BIT, (2) by Brazil in a number of recent bilateral investment treaties, and (3) in the AfCFTA Protocol.

3.2.1 The Investor Obligations in the PAIC and the Nigeria–Morocco BIT

The Draft Pan-African Investment Code (PAIC), published by the African Union Commission in 2016, and the Nigeria–Morocco BIT, also from 2016, were notable developments with regard to introducing CSR obligations for investors and in making those obligations more detailed.

Article 22 of the Pan-African Investment Code, on "Corporate Social Responsibility", contains firm obligations for investors, although these are not set out in detail. Article 22 establishes the following requirements for investors:

> (1) Investors ***shall*** abide by the laws, regulations, administrative guidelines, and policies of the host State.
>
> (2) Investors ***shall***, in pursuit of their economic objectives, ensure that they do not conflict with the social and economic development objectives of host States and shall be sensitive to such objectives.
>
> (3) Investors ***shall*** contribute to the economic, social, and environmental progress with a view to achieving sustainable development of the host State.[20]

19 Hepburn and Kuuya (n 6), 594 ("There is now a significant amount of domestic law governing the wider relations between corporations and society. It covers areas such as the environment, corporate governance, transparency and information disclosure, labour standards, and consumer protection. This reflects an increasing reliance on the law – rather than the market – to regulate these areas.").

20 Pan-African Investment Code (PAIC), art 22 (emphasis added).

While a step forward in terms of providing mandatory CSR obligations for investors, the obligations are expansively worded and not specific. Article 22(2) broadly obligates investors to not conflict with States' "social and economic development objectives", while Article 22(3) broadly obligates investors to "contribute to the economic, social and environmental progress", without indicating how "contribute" and "progress" are to be measured. The PAIC approach therefore clearly creates an obligation, but the content of that obligation is vague in a way that could complicate a State's ability to rely on that obligation or to establish that an investor has violated that obligation. As commentators have noted, ambiguity can lead to the terms being more perfunctory than consequential, as there are no clear standards against which to assess investor conduct.[21]

The 2016 Nigeria–Morocco BIT goes further than the PAIC approach in a number of ways. First, while it uses some aspirational language, it makes clear that investors have affirmative obligations, including CSR requirements. Article 24, on "Corporate Social Responsibility", provides:

> (1) In addition to the obligation to comply with all applicable laws and regulations of the Host State and the obligations in this Agreement, and in accordance with the size, capacities and nature of an investments [sic], and taking into account the development plans and priorities of the Host State and the Sustainable Development Goals of the United Nations, ***investors and their investments should strive to make the maximum feasible contributions*** to the sustainable development of the Host State and local community ***through high levels of social responsible practices.***
>
> [...]
>
> (3) Where standards of corporate social responsibility increase, investors should strive to apply and achieve the higher level standards.[22]

Second, in Article 22(1), the Nigeria–Morocco BIT refers to international standards (i.e. the UN Sustainable Development Goals), and Article 22(3)

21 Baltag, Joshi, and Duggal (n 7), 19 ("The ambiguous language fails to clearly inform investors of the extent of their obligations, thereby rendering these provisions aspirational.").

22 Reciprocal Investment Promotion and Protection Agreement Between the Government of the Kingdom of Morocco and the Government of the Federal Republic of Nigeria, 3 December 2016, art 24 (emphasis added).

incorporates forward-looking language to take into account future changes to international standards.

Third, the Nigeria–Morocco BIT has additional provisions that go further to create a mandatory set of measurable obligations for investors. Article 18 ("Post-Establishment Obligations") sets out a list of obligations that investors/investments "shall" fulfil:

> Investments ***shall***, in keeping with good practice requirement relating to the size and nature of the investment, ***maintain an environmental management system.*** Companies in areas of resource exploitation and high-risk industrial enterprises shall ***maintain a current certification to ISO 14001 or an equivalent*** environmental management standard.
>
> Investors and investments ***shall uphold*** human rights in the host state.
>
> Investors and investments ***shall act*** in accordance with core labour standards required by the ***ILO Declaration on Fundamental Principles and Rights of Work, 1998.***
>
> Investors and investments ***shall not manage or operate*** the investments in a manner that circumvents international environmental, labour, and human rights obligations to which the host state and/or home state are Parties.[23]

These obligations are written in mandatory terms and, while some are vaguely worded, such as "uphold[ing] human rights", others are more specific and refer to international instruments and standards, such as the ISO 4001 environmental management standard and the ILO Declaration on Fundamental Principles and Rights at Work.

3.2.2 The Investor Obligations in Brazil's Recent BITs

Brazil has also addressed CSR in a number of recent investment agreements, although Brazil's approach arguably is less mandatory than the approach in the Nigeria–Morocco BIT. Brazil has entered into several bilateral investment

23 Ibid., art 18 (emphasis added).

treaties – including its BITs with Guyana in 2018,[24] Morocco in 2019,[25] and India in 2020[26] – that combine "right to regulate" provisions that exclude certain liabilities with express and detailed investor obligations for CSR.

An example of Brazil's approach can be seen in its BIT with India. Article 12 of the BIT, on "Corporate Social Responsibility", provides that investors "shall strive to achieve … sustainable development", before setting out a list of "voluntary principles and standards" relating to the environment, human rights, local capacity, and corporate governance, among others, that investors "shall endeavour to comply with".[27] Although it uses "shall strive" and "shall endeavour" language and refers to "voluntary" standards, the CSR clause is relatively detailed (it provides a list of eleven CSR goals).[28]

---

24 See Cooperation and Investment Facilitation Agreement Between the Federative Republic of Brazil and the Co-operative Republic of Guyana (Brazil–Guyana BIT), art 15.

25 See Investment Cooperation and Facilitation Treaty between the Federative Republic of Brazil and the Kingdom of Morocco (Brazil–Morocco BIT), art 13.

26 See Investment Cooperation and Facilitation Treaty between the Federative Republic of Brazil and the Republic of India (Brazil–India BIT), art 12.

27 Brazil–India BIT, art 12.

28 Brazil-India BIT, article 12.1 provides that "Investors and their investments shall strive to achieve the highest possible level of contribution to the sustainable development of the Host State and the local community, through the adoption of a high degree of socially responsible practices, based on the voluntary principles and standards set out in this Article and internal policies, such as statements of principle that have been endorsed or are supported by the Parties." Article 12.2 then contains a list of 11 "voluntary principles and standards for a responsible business conduct and consistent with the laws adopted by the Host State" that "investors and their investments shall endeavour to comply with": "a) contribute to the economic, social and environmental progress, aiming at achieving sustainable development; b) respect the internationally recognized human rights of those involved in the companies' activities; c) encourage local capacity building through close cooperation with the local community; d) encourage the creation of human capital, especially by creating employment opportunities and offering professional training to workers; e) refrain from seeking or accepting exemptions that are not established in the legal or regulatory framework relating to human rights, environment, health, security, work, tax system, financial incentives, or other issues; f) support and advocate for good corporate governance principles, and develop and apply good corporate governance practices, including anti-corruption measures; g) develop and implement effective self-regulatory practices and management systems that foster a relationship of mutual trust between the companies and the societies in which their operations are conducted; h) promote the knowledge of and the adherence, by workers, to the corporate policy, through appropriate dissemination of this policy, including professional training programs; i) refrain from discriminatory or disciplinary action against employees who submit grave reports to the board or, whenever appropriate, to the competent public authorities, about practices that violate the law or corporate policy; j) encourage, whenever possible, business associates, including service providers and outsources, to apply the principles of business conduct consistent with

The same BIT also provides that certain CSR-related claims are excluded from some of the protections for investors provided through the BIT.[29] In particular, the Brazil–India BIT expressly carves out certain public health, safety, and environmental measures from claims of expropriation, stating that "[n]on-discriminatory regulatory ***measures*** by a Party or measures or awards by judicial bodies of a Party that are ***designed and applied to protect legitimate public interest or public purpose objectives such as public health, safety and the environment shall not constitute expropriation*** under this Article."[30]

3.2.3 The Investor Obligations in the AfCFTA Protocol for Investment

The most comprehensive recent model investment agreement to impose investor obligations with regard to CSR and similar concerns is the Protocol for Investment of the African Continental Free Trade Agreement, adopted in 2023. There are a number of provisions addressing CSR in the Protocol. In addition to narrowing protections available to investors (for example, by not providing an FET obligation) and limiting potentially recoverable damages for expropriation (particularly with regard to consequential damages), the Protocol addresses CSR and sustainable development in a number of different ways, including by addressing expressly the right to regulate in Article 24.

Of particular relevance, Chapter 5 of the Protocol sets out affirmative and often detailed obligations for investors. A number of the articles in Chapter 5 relate to subjects that are similar to or even arguably fall within the concept of corporate social responsibility – in addition to the obligation to adhere to

---

the principles provided for in this Article; and k) refrain from any undue interference in local political activities."

29 The Brazil–India BIT, and other recent Brazil BITs, depart from most other investment agreements in not providing investors with an enforceable dispute resolution mechanism, such as international arbitration, if an investor alleges that a protection provided to it by the BIT has been breached. Instead, Article 18, on "Dispute Prevention Procedure", provides a mechanism through which a State party can raise the alleged breach to a Joint Committee (established pursuant to Article 13), which will issue a report with findings with regard to the alleged breach. See Investment Cooperation and Facilitation Treaty between the Federative Republic of Brazil and the Republic of India, Articles 13 ("Joint Committee for the Administration of the Treaty") and 18 ("Dispute Prevention Procedure"). Article 14 also requires the State parties to establish "a single National Focal Point, or Ombudsman, whose main responsibility shall be to support investors from the other Party in its territory" which will "[f]ollow up on requests and enquiries of the other Party or of investors of the other Party with the competent authorities" and report to the Joint Committee. See Brazil–India BIT, art 14.

30 See Brazil-India BIT, art 6.4 (emphasis added).

international and domestic laws (Article 32), Chapter 5 includes provisions addressing "Business Ethics, Human Rights and Labour Standards" (Article 33), "Environmental Protection" (Article 34), "Indigenous Peoples and Local Communities" (Article 35), "Socio-Political Obligations" (Article 36), "Anti-Corruption" (Article 37), "Corporate Social Responsibility" (Article 38), and "Corporate Governance" (Article 39). Chapter 5 is notable for the level of detail in many of the articles, including references in some articles to applicable standards[31] or to creating affirmative and measurable obligations (e.g., to conduct assessments).[32]

Article 38, on "Corporate Social Responsibility", includes language that is not as expressly mandatory and is more aspirational (e.g. "shall endeavour", "encourage", "promote", and "foster") than some of the other investor obligation provisions in Chapter 5. At the same time, Article 38 goes much further than many other CSR provisions in its detailed discussion of various actions to be taken by investors. In full, Article 38 provides:

> 1. Investors and their investments shall endeavour to achieve the highest possible level of contribution to the sustainable development of the Host State and the local community, through the adoption of a high degree of socially responsible practices, in accordance with the principles and standards set out in Paragraph 2 of this Article.
> 2. Investors and their investments shall endeavour to:
>   a. stimulate economic, social, and environmental progress, aiming at achieving sustainable development;
>   b. encourage the strengthening of local capacities through close cooperation with the local community;
>   c. encourage the development of human capital, especially by creating employment opportunities and facilitating access of workers to professional training;
>   d. promote gender equality and inclusiveness in their activities;

31 For example, Article 35(c), on Business Ethics, Human Rights and Labour Standards states that investors "shall comply with the International Labour Organisation (ILO) standards, including the ILO Declaration on Fundamental Principles and Rights at Work, and domestic labour legislations".

32 For example, Article 34(c), on Environmental Protection, states that investors shall "carry out an environmental impact assessment, in accordance with the best international standards and practices and as required by domestic law carry out an environmental impact assessment, in accordance with the best international standards and practices and as required by domestic law".

e. refrain from seeking exemptions that are not established in the legislation of the Host State, relating to environment, health, security, work or financial incentives, or other issues;
f. develop and apply effective self-regulatory practices and management systems that foster a relationship of mutual trust between the companies and the community in which the operations are conducted;
g. promote the knowledge of workers about corporate policies, through appropriate dissemination of these policies, including programmes for professional training;
h. encourage, whenever possible the business associates, including service providers and sub-contractors, to apply the principles of corporate social responsibility provided for in this Article; and
i. foster the benefit sharing arising from an investment with the local communities concerned based on mutually agreed terms to facilitate access to an adequate standard of living.

3. State Parties undertake to encourage investors operating within their territories or subject to their jurisdiction to incorporate into their internal policies internationally recognized standards, guidelines, and principles of corporate social responsibility including those set out in Paragraph 2 of this Article.[33]

Despite using the phrase "shall endeavour" to characterise the obligations, by setting out a detailed list of specific actions expected of investors with regard to CSR, Article 38 should help clarify expectations about investor conduct, while also creating ways to potentially assess compliance if a dispute arises.

As noted above, in addition to the lengthy lists of specific investor obligations in Chapter 5, the Protocol also has a "right to regulate" provision that refers to CSR and similar objectives and states that regulations intended to implement the referenced goals and principles are not breaches of the Protocol and do not give rise to claims by investors. In particular, Article 24 ("Right to Regulate") provides that:

1. In accordance with customary international law and other general principles of international law, ***each State Party has the right to regulate***, including to take measures to ensure that investment in its territory is consistent with the ***goals and principles of sustainable development***, and

33 Protocol for Investment of the African Continental Free Trade Agreement, art 38.

with ***other national environmental, health, climate action, social, and economic policy objectives*** and essential security interests.

2. For greater certainty, measures taken by a State Party to comply with its international obligations under other relevant treaties shall not constitute a breach of this Protocol.
3. For avoidance of doubt, ***the exercise of the right to regulate under Paragraphs 1 and 2 cannot give rise to any claim by an investor for compensation.***[34]

3.3 Specificity of Obligations

Chapter 5 of the Protocol for Investment in the AfCTA reflects one way to create specific and obligatory investor obligations. The length and detail of the Protocol overall, and the provisions in Chapter 5 in particular, are a departure from the approach in many investment agreements. This reflects a drafting dilemma with regard to investor obligations. Vaguer provisions may give less guidance to investors and may be harder to enforce; however, more specific provisions will need to be lengthy and harder to draft, and investors may be able to argue that any omitted items cannot be considered obligations. Moreover, detailed provisions may become outdated and referenced standards may no longer be relevant or otherwise optimal.

One potential approach to providing more specificity and to making obligations more measurable, and therefore compliance easier to assess, is to refer to or incorporate existing international instruments. This approach is seen in some of the investment treaties discussed above. One option, used in several of the investment agreements discussed above, is to refer to the ILO standards, including the ILO Declaration on Fundamental Principles and Rights at Work.

Another CSR standard that potentially can be referred to is the United Nations Guiding Principles on Business and Human Rights (UNGP).[35] The UNGP sets out specific standards intended to ensure that businesses respect human rights, including operational principles relating to policy statements,

---

34 Ibid., art 24 (emphasis added). Other protections in the Protocol are similarly limited. See, e.g. art 13 relating to National Treatment.

35 Article 7 of the Netherlands 2019 Model Investment Agreement, on "Corporate Social Responsibility", makes multiple references to the UNGP as one of the "internationally recognized standards, guidelines and principles of corporate social responsibility".

human rights due diligence, remediation, and legal compliance.[36] The UNGP also provides operational principles for States, such as Article 3, on "General State Regulatory and Policy Functions".[37] These and the other principles in the UNGP could be referred to in an investment agreement to help clarify the responsibilities of both the State and the investor with regard to CSR.[38]

Another potential approach to detailing specific CSR and other investor obligations is through the use of annexes. Thus, such obligations can be set out in an operative clause, and that clause can be supplemented by reference to accompanying annexes that provide more detailed metrics, thresholds, and descriptions related to those obligations.[39] Baltag, Joshi, and Duggal propose that such annexes could be tailored by industry, scale of business activity, and other metrics and could also have the added benefit of avoiding

---

36 For example, with respect to policy statements, Article 16 of the UNGP provides: "As the basis for embedding their responsibility to respect human rights, business enterprises should express their commitment to meet this responsibility through a statement of policy that: (a) Is approved at the most senior level of the business enterprise;

(b) Is informed by relevant internal and/or external expertise; (c) Stipulates the enterprise's human rights expectations of personnel, business partners and other parties directly linked to its operations, products or services;

(d) Is publicly available and communicated internally and externally to all personnel, business partners, and other relevant parties; (e) Is reflected in operational policies and procedures necessary to embed it throughout the business enterprise."

37 Article 3 of the UNGP provides: "In meeting their duty to protect, State should: (a) Enforce laws that are aimed, or have the effect of, requiring business enterprises to respect human rights, and periodically to assess the adequacy of such laws and address any gaps; (b) ensure that other laws and policies governing the creation and ongoing operation of business enterprises, such as corporate law, do not constrain but enable business respect for human rights; (c) Provide effective guidance to business enterprises on how to respect human rights throughout their operations; (d) Encourage, and where appropriate require, business enterprises to communicate how they address their human rights impacts."

38 Although outside the scope of this chapter, the 2019 Hague Rules on Business and Human Rights Arbitration (the "Hague Rules") are designed with the purpose of, *inter alia*. giving effect to the UNGP. The Hague Rules provide "the possibility of a remedy for those affected by the human rights impact of business activities, as set forth in Pillar III of the [UNGP]" and provide "[b]usinesses with a mechanism for addressing human rights impact with which they are involved, as set forth in Pillar II and Principles 11 and 13 of the [UNGP]." 2019 Hague Rules on Business and Human Rights Arbitration, at Preamble. More generally, the Hague Rules "provide a set of procedures for the arbitration of disputes related to human rights impact of business activities." *Id.*

39 Baltag, Joshi, and Duggal (n 7), 19 ("States may also formulate detailed requirements in the annexes to the IIAs that would specify further requirements based on the size and business activities of the industry.").

"claims of discrimination, unfair treatment, etc." as the result of such measures.[40]

In any event, the more the obligations are clear and measurable, the greater the likelihood that the State can demonstrate that the investor has failed to comply with the CSR obligations in the investment agreement. More detailed and measurable obligations therefore may enhance the possibility of meeting the burden of proving such objections if a dispute arises.

4 How Can Investors' CSR and Similar Obligations be Enforced in Investment Arbitration?

Most investment agreements provide for international arbitration as the mechanism for enforcing obligations under the agreement.[41] Under current investment agreements, only investors can commence claims. Thus, even if an investor violates a mandatory CSR obligation in an investment agreement, the host State cannot initiate a claim against the investor.[42] This raises the practical question as to the effect of an investor obligation to comply with a CSR or a similar requirement in an investment agreement. Where a State can argue that an investor has breached a CSR or a similar investor obligation in an investment agreement, there are several potential consequences when a dispute arises. The effectiveness of the States' reliance on the breach of such an obligation will depend on how mandatory the obligation is and how clearly it is defined.

First, if the State can show that an investor has failed to comply with an express obligation, the State may be able to argue that the investor or the investment does not qualify for protection under the investment agreement because of an alleged failure to comply with CSR or similar obligations. To the extent such obligations are mandatory, that may allow the State to argue as a preliminary matter that there is no jurisdiction for a tribunal to consider

40 Baltag, Joshi, and Duggal (n 7), 19.

41 Some investment treaties, such as those entered into by Brazil as discussed above, do not provide international arbitration as an option for resolving disputes between investors and States. Some recent treaties anticipate the potential use of a multilateral court mechanism. See, e.g. EU-Canada Comprehensive Economic and Trade Agreement (CETA), section F.

42 This is the case unless and until reforms are made that would create reciprocity in the obligations in investment treaties, as discussed in Jose Daniel Amado, Jackson Shaw Kern and Martin Doe Rodriguez, *Arbitrating the Conduct of International Investors* (CUP 2018).

claims or that such claims are not admissible because the investor or the investment have not complied with the express prerequisites to claiming protection under the investment agreement. Whether such an objection is well-grounded will depend on how the treaty is drafted and when the investor or investment must qualify for protection under the treaty. While the force of such arguments about post-investment conduct may be subject to debate, the State may argue that, even if the breach of an affirmative obligation does not mean the investor or investment did not initially qualify for protection (e.g. at the time of investment), the subsequent breach means that the investor's claim is inadmissible or otherwise invalid.

Second, even if compliance with the obligation is not considered relevant to jurisdiction or the admissibility of the investor's claim, the investor's failure to comply with its obligations may be a defense to the investor's claims both on the facts and the law. The State may also argue, for example, that the measures it took that have been challenged by the investor do not constitute violations of the investment agreement because of the investor's own breaches.

In addition, clearly drafted "right to regulate" provisions or carve-outs for CSR-related policies will also potentially provide defenses to investor claims. Moreover, references to CSR and similar policy objectives in the operative clauses in an investment agreement may help persuade a tribunal that the substantive protections afforded to investors must be understood in light of – and may be limited by – those policy commitments by the State parties.

Third, in some instances, investor obligations may potentially provide the State with the opportunity to bring counterclaims against the investor after the investor commences an arbitration under an investment agreement. Although counterclaims in investment arbitrations remain relatively rare, there have been several notable recent cases in which a State has successfully pursued counterclaims against investors who had commenced investment treaty arbitrations against that State.

The ICSID Convention,[43] the ICSID Arbitration Rules,[44] and the UNCITRAL Arbitration Rules[45] all recognise the possibility of counterclaims by States in investment treaty cases. In considering whether to allow counterclaims by States, investment tribunals generally look, first, to whether the investment agreement can be interpreted to provide for consent by the investor and the State to counterclaims; and, second, to whether the proposed counterclaims are sufficiently connected to the investor's claims to be admissible.[46]

Tribunals have admitted counterclaims against investors for breaches of environmental obligations in several recent cases, including *Perenco v. Ecuador* and *Burlington Resources v. Ecuador*.[47] Assuming the test for consent can be met, there should be an even stronger basis for finding a sufficient connection where the counterclaim arises in connection with an express investor obligation in the investment agreement.

43 Article 46 of the ICSID Convention gives tribunals jurisdiction to determine "counterclaims arising directly out of the subject matter of the dispute". Article 46 of the ICSID Convention and Rule 40 of the ICSID Arbitration Rules set out three conditions for a counterclaim (except where otherwise expressly agreed by the parties): the counterclaim must be connected with the subject matter of the claim; the counterclaim must be within the consent of the parties to the dispute, as is necessary under Article 25 of the Convention for any primary claim; and the counterclaim is subject to the general jurisdictional requirements of ICSID. In other words, a counterclaim that meets the other requirements, but does not arise out of an investment or is not lodged between an investor and a State party to the Convention may be outside the tribunal's jurisdiction.

44 ICSID Arbitration Rules, Rule 40 ("Except as the parties otherwise agree, a party may present an incidental or additional claim or counter-claim arising directly out of the subject-matter of the dispute, provided that such ancillary claim is within the scope of the consent of the parties and is otherwise within the jurisdiction of the Centre").

45 UNCITRAL Arbitration Rules, Article 21(3) ("the respondent may make a counterclaim or rely on a claim for the purpose of a set-off provided that the arbitral tribunal has jurisdiction over it").

46 In *Urbaser v. Argentina*, the tribunal found that a factual link between the investor's claim and the State's counterclaim satisfied Article 46 of the ICSID Convention. See *Urbaser SA and Consorcio de Aguas Bilbao Bizkaia, Bilbao Biskaia Ur Partzuergoa v. The Argentine Republic*, ICSID Case No. ARB/07/26, Award dated 8 December 2016.

47 *Perenco Ecuador Ltd v. Republic of Ecuador*, ICSID Case No. ARB/08/6 (awarding Ecuador US$54 million in damages for a counterclaim for environmental damage by the investor); *Burlington Resources Inc v. Republic of Ecuador*, ICSID Case No. ARB/08/5 (awarding Ecuador US$41 million in damages for a counterclaim for environmental damage by the investor). See also *Urbaser SA and Consorcio de Aguas Bilbao Bizkaia, Bilbao Biskaia Ur Partzuergoa v. The Argentine Republic*, ICSID Case No. ARB/07/26 (finding that the tribunal had jurisdiction over Argentina's counterclaim alleging that the investor had violated its commitments and its obligations under international law based on the human right to water); *David R Aven and Others v. Republic of Costa Rica*, ICSID Case No. UNCT/15/3 (finding that the tribunal had jurisdiction over Costa Rica's counterclaims on the basis that an investor has obligations under international law to protect the environment, which could be enforced under the treaty).

One consideration with potential counterclaims is whether the State believes it will be more effective and efficient to pursue claims for breaches by the investor in an investment arbitration rather than through local regulatory, civil, and/or criminal proceedings. There are reasons why a State may want to pursue a counterclaim in an investment arbitration relating to CSR and similar obligations. These include that the CSR obligations that arise from the text of the investment agreement may not be found in local law or other contractual agreements with the investor. There may therefore be no other legal basis for these particular claims by the State. The State may also be interested in setting off the claims made by the investor in the investment arbitration. The State may also be mindful of the international enforceability of an investment treaty award in its favour.

For the reasons discussed above, meeting the burden of showing the breach of an investor's CSR obligation should be easier if the obligations are clear and measurable. In the context of counterclaims, the State will also need to consider whether it can show it was damaged by the investor's breach of its obligations, which may be harder to do with certain CSR obligations than it may be with regard to, e.g. the environmental damages which resulted in successful counterclaims by Ecuador in the *Perenco* and *Burlington Resources* cases discussed above.

5 Conclusion

As more recent investment agreements show, CSR obligations have a growing role to play in international investment agreements – and therefore in investment treaty disputes. More recent model investment agreements and a number of recent treaties have incorporated increasingly mandatory and detailed clauses providing for affirmative investor CSR obligations. Such an approach not only provides greater clarity to investors about their expected conduct but also can provide States with a wider and more reliable set of options with regard to enforcing such obligations, and may make the consequences of breaches of CSR obligations more significant in the event an investment dispute arises.

CHAPTER 11

Responsible Business Conduct Meets Profit Shifting: Tax Compliance as Investor Obligations

Vincent Beyer[1]

1 Introduction

In the business world, tax and investment are inextricably linked. For international lawyers, the two are rigidly divided. Although issues related to international tax are slowly beginning to appear within the collective consciousness of international investment lawyers, the knowledge gap between the two legal communities is wide.[2] Nevertheless, in recent years investment practitioners and policymakers have started to pay closer attention to developments in the international tax arena.

This slowly growing connection takes place against the background of a stable number of tax-related cases in investor–State dispute settlement (ISDS). Over the past two decades, approximately 15 percent of all treaty-based cases implicated some sort of tax measure.[3] In total, at least 165 cases challenging tax measures have been brought by investors.[4] These tax-related cases involve a wide range of measures, including windfall profits taxes, capital gains taxes, the withdrawal of incentives, and the conduct of tax-related investigations. Often tax and non-tax-related elements of State conduct are

---

1 I would like to thank the editors of this volume as well as the participants of the symposium on investor obligations in international law (Geneva, May 2024) for their helpful comments and feedback.

2 For recent attempts to bridge the gap UNCTAD, *International Investment Agreements and Their Implications for Tax Measures: What Tax Policymakers Need to Know* (United Nations 2021) <https://unctad.org/system/files/official-document/diaepcbinf2021d3_en.pdf> accessed 14 August 2023; UNCTAD, *Double Taxation Treaties and Their Implications for Investment: What Investment Policymakers Need to Know* (United Nations 2024) <https://unctad.org/system/files/official-document/diaepcb2024d1_en.pdf> accessed 14 August 2024.

3 UNCTAD, 'Facts on Investor–State Arbitrations in 2021: With a Special Focus on Tax-Related ISDS Cases' (UNCTAD 2022) IIA Issues Note No. 15 <https://unctad.org/system/files/official-document/diaepcbinf2022d4_en.pdf> accessed 18 November 2022.

4 Ibid.

intertwined and many of these cases do not present themselves as pure tax disputes.

More recently ISDS has seen a number of cases that more closely involve the native domain of international tax lawyers, base erosion and profit shifting (BEPS) by large multinational enterprises (MNEs). The *Lone Star v. Korea* case, for example, considered issues relating to the investor's access to the benefits of a double tax treaty (DTT), tax planning, and the use by Korean authorities of domestic rules to fight the abuse of DTTs.[5] One of the main issues at stake related to the imposition of capital gains taxes on the sale of shares held by Lone Star's Belgian entity. Under the Belgium–Korea DTT, Korea was not entitled to impose capital gains tax. As Korean authorities considered Lone Star's business structure to serve the sole purpose of improperly availing itself of DTT benefits, the tax authorities denied access to said treaty.

Tax measures do not only make an appearance in dispute settlement. To some extent, they have always been addressed in international investment agreements (IIAs). The vast majority of IIAs provide, for example, for a carve-out for the benefits arising from DTTs from the scope of the most-favoured-nation (MFN) provision of IIAs.[6] More wide-ranging carve-outs – often partial rather than absolute – can be found in the vast majority of modern IIAs.[7] Furthermore, an increasing number of tax-related provisions in IIAs are beginning to focus on the collection of taxes. Some treaties now contain clauses that exempt measures taken for the effective and equitable collection of taxes – trade lawyers will recognise this GATS Article XIV(d)-style language – and others explicitly clarify that, for example, "internationally recognized tax policies, principles, and practices should not constitute an expropriation".[8]

These developments in ISDS and IIAs take place against the background of a rapidly changing international tax environment. The OECD/G20 BEPS Action Plan, published in 2013,[9] led to the development of 15 actions on various issues related to tax evasion and avoidance. The project has now grown into the BEPS Inclusive Framework, with almost 150 participating jurisdic-

5 *LSF-KEB Holdings SCA and others v. Republic of Korea* ICSID Case No. ARB/12/37 (Award, 30 August 2022).

6 UNCTAD, 'Mapping of IIA Content' (*UNCTAD Investment Policy Hub*) <https://tinyurl.com/a4mtpwf7> accessed 7 August 2023.

7 Vincent Beyer, 'International Investment Agreements and the Global Minimum Tax: Of Treaty Troubles and Investment Incentives' (2024) 27 Journal of International Economic Law 241, 245–47.

8 United States–Korea Free Trade Agreement [hereinafter: US Korea FTA] (adopted on 30 June 2007, entered into force on 15 March 2012) Annex 11-F.

9 OECD, *Action Plan on Base Erosion and Profit Shifting* (OECD Publishing 2013).

tions.[10] Work on BEPS continues, including with the implementation of a global minimum tax of 15 percent on the profits of large MNEs.

Briefly put, the international tax and investment landscapes are changing, with investment policymakers taking note of developments in the tax arena and vice versa. Both fields are on a trajectory of closer entwinement. Now, there is a new frontier on this path: direct investor obligations on tax and tax avoidance.

Exemplary of such obligations is Article 40 of the African Continental Free Trade Area (AfCFTA) Protocol on Investment (PoI) entitled "Taxation and Transfer Pricing". Given the provision's centrality to the subsequent discussion, paragraph 1 is reproduced in its entirety:

1. Investors and their investments shall:
   a. ensure that all transactions with related or affiliated companies are arm's length transactions at fair market price in accordance with the domestic regulations of the Host State and relevant international best practices;
   b. conduct their operations in a manner that fully complies with all applicable domestic tax laws and international rules and principles relating to base erosion and profit shifting practices; and
   c. provide all information required by the Host State to ensure compliance with the applicable laws relating to taxation.

Paragraph 2 of Article 40 additionally obliges State Parties to "cooperate in the detection and prevention of transfer pricing manipulation by investors", including through the provision of information and the conduct of joint tax audits. Since paragraph 2 concerns obligations of States, rather than investors, it will not be further considered here.

As it will be explained below, direct tax-related investor obligations are not entirely new on the international plane. However, given the reach of the AfCFTA PoI, with over 50 participating countries, the text of the Protocol will be taken as a model to set out the detailed content of the obligation (Section 2), its origins, prevalence and importance, particularly to African economies (Section 3), as well as the value added and challenges arising from this novel investor obligation (Section 4).

---

10 OECD, 'Members of the OECD/G20 Inclusive Framework on BEPS - Updated May 2024' (7 December 2022) <https://www.oecd.org/tax/beps/inclusive-framework-on-beps-composition.pdf> accessed 2 July 2026.

2 The Scope of Tax-Related Investor Obligations: Related Party Transactions and BEPS Rules and Principles

For investment lawyers who are not necessarily familiar with the intricacies of international tax avoidance and evasion, Article 40 of the AfCFTA PoI may appear somewhat cryptic. The following subsections set out what related party transactions, transfer pricing, and the arm's length standard are, addressed in paragraph (1)(a). It then provides background on "international rules and principles" relating to BEPS, the focus of paragraph (1)(b).

2.1 Related Party Transactions, Transfer Pricing, and the Arm's Length Standard in a Nutshell

Related party transactions involve exchanges of goods, services, or funds between entities that are under common control, typically sharing ownership, management, or financial interests. For example, the different subsidiaries of an MNE group routinely engage in related party transactions as part of their normal business. Examples include the sale of goods for further processing, the payment of royalties for the use of trademarks, or interest payments on intra-group loans. No problems arise as long as the prices and terms in transactions between related parties – so-called transfer prices – are comparable to those independent parties would have negotiated.

The potential problem with related parties is that any profits of the group's individual subsidiaries ultimately accrue to the entire group. Hence, transfer prices can be set arbitrarily, without any connection to the economic interests of individual entities. Abusive or aggressive transfer pricing practices occur when transactions are strategically mispriced to move profits from high-tax jurisdictions to low-tax ones, thereby eroding the tax base in the higher-tax countries.

To illustrate, a mining subsidiary in a high-tax jurisdiction may rent equipment from another subsidiary of the same group, located in a low-tax jurisdiction, at inflated rates. Alternatively, it may pay excessive fees for specialised services. Another common technique is the mispricing of loans between related parties, leading to excessive interest payments that reduce taxable profits in the high-tax jurisdiction. The European Commission quotes an estimate that "corporate tax evasion makes up 60% to 65% of illicit financial flows".[11] Information asymmetries make it often difficult to detect and prevent

11 Directorate-General for International Cooperation and Development (European Commission), 'Collect More – Spend Better: Achieving Development in an Inclusive and

such illicit financial flows.[12] Staying with the example of the mining sector, throughout its entire value chain – from exploration, development, and production to processing – related party transactions are prevalent, involving specialised equipment, technical services, and financing, all of which can be mispriced to shift profits.

The so-called arm's length standard exists to respond to such practices. Any transfer price should be comparable to what independent parties would have agreed upon if negotiating at arm's length, thereby preventing MNEs from manipulating prices to shift profits across borders. The standard is prominently codified in Article 9 of both the OECD and UN Model Tax Conventions and contained in virtually all of the approximately 3,500 DTTs that are currently in force.

The implementation of the arm's length standard is typically carried out through detailed transfer pricing regulations enforced by national revenue authorities. However, not all countries have adopted domestic legislation or detailed regulations.[13] When adopted, national transfer pricing regulations often align closely with the guidelines developed by the Organisation for Economic Co-operation and Development (OECD). The OECD Transfer Pricing Guidelines, born out of the 1979 Report on Transfer Pricing and Multinational Enterprises and most recently updated in 2022,[14] serve as a non-binding, yet, highly influential framework for applying the arm's length standard. Although the guidelines are a non-binding recommendation under Article 5(b) of the OECD Convention, compliance with them is considered an international best practice, and many jurisdictions around the world use them as a reference point.[15]

In addition to the OECD guidelines, the United Nations has developed the UN Practical Manual on Transfer Pricing for Developing Countries, with its

---

Sustainable Way' 7 <https://op.europa.eu/en/publication-%20detail/-/publication/7914c998-ecd6-11e5-8a81-01aa75ed71a1/language-en> accessed 9 September 2024.

12 United Nations, 'Tackling Illicit Financial Flows in Africa Arising from Taxation and Illegal Commercial Practices' (2022) 13 <https://www.un.org/osaa/sites/www.un.org.osaa/files/tackling_iffs_in_tax_reform_and_illegal_commercial_practices_-_nov_2022.pdf> accessed 9 September 2024.

13 See the discussion *infra* surrounding footnotes 57–59.

14 OECD, *OECD Transfer Pricing Guidelines for Multinational Enterprises and Tax Administrations 2022* (OECD Publishing 2022).

15 Alberto Vega, 'International Governance through Soft Law: The Case of the OECD Transfer Pricing Guidelines' (2012) Max Planck Institute for Tax Law and Public Finance Working Paper 2012 – 05.

latest version published in 2021.[16] This manual, equally extensive as the OECD Guidelines and spanning over 650 pages, offers detailed guidance and similarly outlines use of the five generally accepted methods for determining an arm's length price. All five methods do so, in very simplified terms, by either comparing transfer prices to uncontrolled transactions or by establishing what a reasonable profit would have been.[17] The UN manual aims to address the unique challenges faced by developing countries, which often struggle with limited resources and expertise.[18]

One of the significant challenges in implementing the arm's length standard is the need for commercially sensitive information, such as contracts with unrelated parties, to make accurate comparisons. This information asymmetry often puts tax authorities at a disadvantage, especially in developing countries. To address this, various global, regional, and sectoral initiatives have been established with the aim of increasing tax transparency and information sharing.[19] Additionally, several of the Actions of the G20/OECD BEPS Project, address questions of global tax transparency, including Action 13 which requires large MNEs to file Country-by-Country reports on their income and taxes paid.[20]

Despite these efforts, implementing the arm's length standard remains complex and resource intensive. The OECD's framework, while comprehensive, is often criticised for lacking inclusiveness, particularly in addressing the concerns of developing economies at the agenda setting stage, instead of only with respect to the implementation of fully formulated rules.[21] The United Nations, though more inclusive, lacks the resources and long-standing expertise of the OECD. As a result, regional initiatives such as the African Tax

16 United Nations, *United Nations Practical Manual on Transfer Pricing for Developing Countries* (3rd edn, United Nations 2021).

17 Ibid., 128–198; OECD, *OECD Transfer Pricing Guidelines for Multinational Enterprises and Tax Administrations 2022* (n 14), 97–148.

18 United Nations Manual (n 16), xi.

19 See, for example, the Extractive Industries Transparency Initiative <https://eiti.org> accessed 12 September 2024; Global Forum on Transparency and Exchange of Information for Tax Purposes <https://www.oecd-ilibrary.org/taxation/global-forum-on-transparency-and-exchange-of-information-for-tax-purposes-peer-reviews_2219469x> accessed on 12 September 2024.

20 OECD, 'Transfer Pricing Documentation and Country-by-Country Reporting, Action 13–2015 Final Report' (OECD 2015) 13 <https://www.oecd.org/tax/transfer-pricing-documentation-and-country-by-country-reporting-action-13-2015-final-report-9789264241480-en.htm> accessed 11 November 2023.

21 Irma Johanna Mosquera Valderrama, 'The Study of the BEPS 4 Minimum Standards as A Legal Transplant: A Methodological Framework' (2020) 48 Intertax 719, 730.

Administration Forum may play a crucial role in bridging the gap and ensuring that the arm's length standard is effectively applied in all jurisdictions.[22]

2.2 Other Means of Base Erosion and Profit Shifting

The manipulation of transfer prices is but one means of BEPS. A range of other practices exist. Those are summarily addressed in Article 40(1)(b) AfCFTA PoI by requiring investors to comply with "domestic tax laws and international rules and principles relating to [BEPS]". The focus of the subsequent discussion will be on international rules and principles rather than domestic tax laws. Two principal problems arise in this respect. First, a wide range of tax practices by MNEs fall into a grey area where a range of outcomes can be justified, and practices are neither clearly permitted nor clearly abusive. Second, whereas paragraph 1(a) on transfer pricing references "best practices", a term that would include non-binding or informal rules such as, guidelines, codes, and standards, paragraph 1(b) refers to "international rules and principles". The different language here could be interpreted to refer to, at least implicitly, formally binding rules in the latter provision.

These two problems can be illustrated by reference to intra-group loans and so-called thin capitalisation rules. One can imagine the simple scenario where an entity within an MNE group, located in a low-tax jurisdiction, provides a loan to another entity, located in a high-tax jurisdiction. If the interest rate is higher than for a commercially comparable loan, this is an issue of transfer mispricing, addressed in the previous section. However, even if the interest terms are at arm's length, such intra-group financing can still be used to shift profits. The reason is that interest payments are generally tax deductible. Thus, the more interest is being paid by the company in the high-tax jurisdiction, the lower its profits (and the lower its resulting tax burden). Once received by the related entity in the low-tax jurisdiction, these payments are subject to tax. However, as the tax rate of the related entity is much lower (or even zero), the overall tax burden of the MNE group decreases. Consequently, there is an incentive to leverage subsidiaries in high-tax jurisdictions with large amounts of debt.

Debt financing is a business reality and cannot simply be prohibited. At the same time, it is an extremely simple way of shifting profits. The G20/OECD BEPS Project recognised the importance of tackling this issue in its 2013

22 See generally, the work of the African Tax Administration Forum <https://ataftax.org/> accessed on 15 September 2024.

Action Plan.[23] It proposed the development of so-called thin capitalisation rules that limit the amount of tax-deductible interest. Subsequently, in 2015, the final report on Action 4 – "Limiting Base Erosion Involving Interest Deductions and Other Financial Payments" recommended a best practice approach. In simplified terms, if the interest payments of an entity are higher than a certain percentage of its income,[24] any deduction for interest in excess of this percentage will not be allowed.[25] One of the issues is that not all countries are similarly situated. The OECD Report, thus, proposes for this percentage to be "within a best practice range or 'corridor'",[26] somewhere between 10 and 30 percent.[27]

This is the first problem set out above, i.e. the fact that many tax practices fall within grey areas. BEPS is not always an exact science. There is a range of permissible outcomes, and "international rules and principles" are not always clear-cut. Based on the Report for BEPS Action 4, one could argue that a general principle exists that disallows excessive interest deductions. However, unless countries adopt national laws that specify a percentage, it is difficult to draw the line given the OECD's explicit acknowledgement that a range of permissible outcomes exists. A requirement to comply with "international rules and principles" as specified in Article 40(1)(b) of the AfCFTA PoI quickly becomes difficult in practice. At the same time, one should, however, acknowledge that there is a great number of practices that certainly fall outside the grey area. Given the OECD's proposed "corridor" of 10–30 percent, interest deductions that amount to 50 percent of an entity's earnings would appear to fail to comply with international rules and principles.

Equally problematic, and relating to the second problem identified above, international tax governance is notorious for the promulgation of informal rules. Staying with the example of interest payments, BEPS Action 4 can be

---

23 OECD, *Action Plan on Base Erosion and Profit Shifting* (n 9), 17.

24 In reality it is an entity's earnings before interest, taxes, depreciation, and amortization (EBITDA), see, OECD, 'Limiting Base Erosion Involving Interest Deductions and Other Financial Payments, Action 4–2015 Final Report' (OECD 2015) 25 <https://www.oecd.org/en/publications/limiting-base-erosion-involving-interest-deductions-and-other-financial-payments-action-4-2015-final-report_9789264241176-en.html> accessed 9 September 2024.

25 Put differently, one determines an entity's earnings before interest, taxes, depreciation and amortization. Second, this amount is multiplied by the specified maximum percentage of allowed deductions. Third, if the actual interest expense of the entity exceeds the sum calculated in the second step, the excess cannot be deducted for tax purposes.

26 OECD 2015 Final Report (n 24), 49.

27 Ibid., 50.

described as a recommendation of a best practice that requires its adoption in national law. Even the almost 150 members of the BEPS Inclusive Framework are not formally, as a matter of public international law, obliged to implement any of the recommendations developed in the BEPS Actions. More generally, the identification of international tax rules that are formally binding on the international plane, outside of DTTs, is difficult.[28] General principles of law, as referenced in Article 38(1)(c) of the Statute of the International Court of Justice may more readily exist but their identification and delimitation is not straightforward either. One could, alternatively, read the term "principles" as used in Article 40(1)(b) of the AfCFTA PoI somewhat more widely to include, for example, non-binding principles. It would then encompass informal rules, allowing for a wider range of BEPS practices to be captured by the provision.

To summarise, the undefined scope of "international rules and principles" on BEPS in Article 40(1)(b) raises a number of difficulties. The provision is likely able to address the most egregious practices by MNEs. However, given the proliferation of informal tax rules on the international plane, the most straightforward way for governments to safeguard their domestic tax base is to adopt binding rules on the national plane. Those are, without doubt, captured by Article 40(1)(b).

3 Investor Obligations on Tax: Origin, Prevalence, and Importance

3.1 Origin and Prevalence

Tax-related investor obligations did not appear out of nowhere. The arm's length standard has a long history, including outside of the approximately 3,500 DTTs that explicitly prescribe it. Trade rules such as, the *Customs Valuation Agreement* and the *SCM Agreement* include it.[29] It is widespread in

28 For an attempt to explore the existence of international customary law from tax practices, see, Reuven S Avi-Yonah, *International Tax as International Law: An Analysis of the International Tax Regime* (Cambridge University Press 2007); raising a word of caution with respect to the identification of customary international rules on tax, especially as crystallised from treaty practice, see Céline Braumann, 'Taxes and Custom: Tax Treaties as Evidence for Customary International Law' (2020) 23 Journal of International Economic Law 747.

29 Agreement on Implementation of Article VII of the General Agreement on Tariffs and Trade 1994 (entered into force on 1 January 1995) art 1(2); Agreement on Subsidies and Countervailing Measures [hereinafter: SCM Agreement] (entered into force on 1 January 1995) 1869 UNTS 14, fn 59.

domestic laws and sometimes even contained in contracts such as mining contracts.[30] Other measures to tackle BEPS have a long history as well. Thin capitalisation legislation (described in the preceding section) was first introduced in 1972 in Canada and other early adopters.[31] The OECD has dealt with the topic at least as far back as 1986.[32] Similarly, limitation of benefits provisions to restrict access to DTT benefits have long existed around the globe.[33] That IIAs, including broader economic cooperation agreements directly address transfer pricing and BEPS is, however, a relatively recent phenomenon.

References to "BEPS" as a State obligation to implement minimum standards made their first appearance in IIAs only in 2020, with none of these treaties that include the term being pure investment protection treaties but rather broader economic framework agreements.[34] The concept of "transfer pricing" was included somewhat earlier, already in the EU-Cameroon Economic Partnership Agreement from 2009 under the heading of customs valuation as well as the 2021 rollover agreement concluded between the UK and Cameroon.[35]

30 UNCTAD, 'Tackling Illicit Financial Flows for Sustainable Development in Africa' (United Nations 2020) 109.

31 Jennifer Blouin and others, 'Thin Capitalization Rules and Multinational Firm Capital Structure' [2014] IMF Working Paper WP/14/12 <https://www.imf.org/external/pubs/ft/wp/2014/wp1412.pdf> accessed 22 November 2022.

32 See the report 'Thin Capitalisation' issued by the OECD Committee on Fiscal Affairs. Contained in OECD, *Model Tax Convention on Income and on Capital: Full Version 2017* (OECD Publishing 2017) R(4).

33 The first such clause was reportedly contained in a 1962 DTT, see William P Streng, 'Treaty Shopping: Tax Treaty Limitation of Benefits Issues' (1992) 15 Houston Journal of International Law 1, 10, fn 27.

34 See the following three agreements where the parties agree to implement minimum standards against BEPS: Political, Free trade and Strategic Partnership Agreement between Ukraine and the United Kingdom of Great Britain and Northern Ireland (entered into force on 1 January 2021) art 330; ibid 5.1; Partnership Agreement between the European Union and its Member States, of the one part, and the Members of the Organisation of the African, Carribean and Pacific States, of the other part (adopted on 15 November 2023, pending entry into force) art 12(6); see also the following treaty referencing capacity building with respect to the two-pillar solution for taxing the digital economy, Indo-Pacific Economic Framework for Prosperity Agreement Relating to a Fair Economy (entered into force on 12 October 2024) 18.

35 Interim Agreement with a view to an Economic Partnership Agreement between the European Community and its Member States, of the one part, and the Central Africa Party, of the other part (entered into force on 4 August 2014) art 38(2); Interim Agreement establishing an Economic Partnership Agreement between the United Kingdom of Great Britain and Northern Ireland, of the one part and the Republic of Cameroon, of the other part (entered into force on 19 July 2021) art 38(2).

As a more general concept, references to transfer pricing can also be found in the Armenia–EU Comprehensive and Enhanced Partnership Agreement from 2017.[36] This extreme rarity and relative novelty of explicitly including core tax concepts in economic cooperation agreements somewhat underlines the divide between the regulation of tax and investment/trade issues on the international plane. From this perspective, direct investor obligations on these issues appear even more striking.

Surprisingly, as a direct obligation on investors, the inclusion of BEPS and transfer pricing has a relatively long, albeit limited, history in IIAs and Model IIAs. A 1998 Model BIT developed by the Consumer Unity and Trust Society (now known as CUTS International) covered a number of investor obligations, including a requirement to comply with "internationally agreed guidelines or standards relating to transfer pricing".[37] The first reference in an inter-State Model is contained in the 2012 Southern African Development Community (SADC) Model BIT, referencing the investor obligation to comply with the arm's length standard.[38] Article 10 of the Democratic Republic of the Congo–Rwanda BIT (2021) directly adopts the SADC model clause.[39] The Economic Community Of West African States Common Investment Code (ECOWIC), Articles 41–44, in force since 2019, provide for differently worded but substantively similar obligations to those contained in Article 40 of the AfCFTA PoI. Notably, unlike the AfCFTA PoI, the ECOWIC designates the OECD Transfer Pricing Guidelines as the relevant international standard with which investors are required to comply.[40]

As the AfCFTA builds on regional economic communities,[41] it is explicable that the PoI incorporates substantively similar obligations as contained in the ECOWIC. However, as this section shows, direct tax-related investor obliga-

36 Comprehensive and enhanced partnership agreement between the European Union and the European Atomic Energy Community and their Member States of the one part, and the Republic of Armenia, of the other part (entered into force on 1 March 2021) art 27.

37 CUTS, 'International Investment Instruments: A Compendium: Model International Agreement on Investment (Consumer Unity and Trust Society)' (1998) art 1J.

38 "Southern African Development Community (SADC) Model Bilateral Investment Treaty with Commentary" (2012) art 16.

39 Democratic Republic of the Congo–Rwanda Bilateral Investment Treaty (adopted on 26 June 2021, not in force) art 10.

40 ECOWAS Common Investment Code (ECOWIC) (entered into force on 22 December 2019) art 41(2).

41 Agreement Establishing the African Continental Free Trade Area [hereinafter: AfCFTA] (entered into force on 30 May 2019) preamble.

tions in IIAs currently constitute an exclusively African phenomenon. Given the rarity and novelty of any references to transfer pricing and BEPS in investment treaties, this is unsurprising. It may well be that the African continent is simply ahead of the curve in this respect. At the same time, as discussed in the following section, transfer pricing is a topic of particular relevance to African countries. This may at least partially explain these countries' early sensitisation on the subject.

3.2 The Importance of Transfer Pricing to African Countries

Arm's length transfer prices are far more important than the uninitiated reader might assume. Establishing concrete data as to how much trade takes place between related entities is somewhat difficult but relatively reliable estimates exist that provide a hint as to the magnitude of the issue. In 2002, the OECD estimated that "more than 60% of world trade takes place within multinational enterprises".[42] This number has been repeatedly invoked over the past two decades.

More recent – and probably more accurate – estimates are lower but remain significant. The World Bank, for example, found in 2017 that above 30 percent of trade takes place within MNE groups.[43] Similarly, country-by-country reporting data published by the US Internal Revenue Service suggests that intra-group transactions account for approximately 30 percent of total MNE revenue.[44] Thus, it is relatively safe to assume that at least one third of world trade (by transaction value) takes place between related parties.[45] Put differently, one in every three dollars in international trade is exchanged

42 John Neighbour, 'Transfer Pricing: Keeping It at Arm's Length' (2002) 230 OECD Observer 29, 29.

43 Csilla Lakatos and Franziska Ohnsorge, 'Arm's-Length Trade A Source of Post-Crisis Trade Weakness' [2017] World Bank Group Policy Research Working Paper 8144 6 <https://documents1.worldbank.org/curated/en/659891499793795498/pdf/WPS8144.pdf> accessed 9 September 2024.

44 Internal Revenue Service, 'SOI Tax Stats - Country by Country Report' <https://www.irs.gov/statistics/soi-tax-stats-country-by-country-report> accessed 17 September 2024. See, Table 1A. Country-by-Country Report (Form 8975): Tax Jurisdiction Information (Schedule A: Part I) by Major Geographic Region and Selected Tax Jurisdiction; The data provides a total MNE revenue (from 1,791 MNE groups) of USD 27.38 trillion of which USD 8.13 trillion arose between related parties.

45 See also Nick Shaxson, 'Over a Third of World Trade Happens inside Multinational Corporations' (*Tax Justice Network*, 9 April 2019) <https://taxjustice.net/2019/04/09/over-a-third-or-more-of-world-trade-happens-inside-multinational-corporations/> accessed 17 September 2024.

between related entities, making such transactions susceptible to manipulation for the purposes of shifting profits and reducing the overall tax burden of MNEs.

Not all intra-group transactions are, however, manipulated. Given the difficulty to establish an estimate for intra-MNE trade in general, to reliably approximate the amount of illicit financial flows, including as a result of abusive transfer pricing practices, is even more challenging. Focusing on the African continent, on an extremely general level, any number of tax revenue that is lost annually is, with certainty, in the billions. A 2007 newspaper report referenced USD 150 billion in annual illicit financial flows.[46] The United Nations Economic Commission for Africa estimated that annual illicit financial outflows from Africa due to mispricing stood at USD 50 billion between 2010 and 2015.[47] The United Nations Conference on Trade and Development (UNCTAD) found in its 2020 Economic Development in Africa Report that overall illicit financial flows, including abusive transfer pricing, amount to USD 88.6 billion on average per year.[48] Work on refining the measurement of illicit tax and commercial financial flows continues within international organisations.[49]

Focusing on country-specific estimates paints an equally bleak picture. Approximately USD 8.8 billion are calculated to have left Zambia during the decade from 2001 to 2010.[50] Sharife and Grobler described the case of illicit diamond trades where under-invoicing contributed to billions in lost government revenue.[51] More generally, the African Development Bank identified "inefficient taxation of extractive activities and the inability to fight abuses

46 Nick Mathiason, 'Western Bankers and Lawyers "Rob Africa of $150bn Every Year"' (*The Observer* 21 January 2007) <https://www.theguardian.com/money/2007/jan/21/business.theobserver2> accessed 17 September 2024.

47 United Nations Economic Commission for Africa, 'Pressure on Governments, Critical in Probing Africa's Stolen Funds' <https://repository.uneca.org/handle/10855/36009> accessed 17 September 2024.

48 UNCTAD, 'Tackling Illicit Financial Flows for Sustainable Development in Africa' (n 30).

49 UNCTAD, 'Towards a Statistical Framework for the Measurement of Tax and Commercial Illicit Financial Flows' (United Nations 2024).

50 ATAF, 'Illicit Financial Flows and Domestic Resource Mobilisation in the Extractives: Proposals for African Resource-Rich Countries' (ATAF 2021) <https://au.int/sites/default/files/newsevents/workingdocuments/42690-wd-ATAF-IFFs_and_DRM_in_Extractive_Industries_2021.pdf> accessed 9 September 2024.

51 Khadija Sharife and John Grobler, 'Kimberley's Illicit Process' (2013) 30 World Policy Journal 65.

of TP [transfer pricing] by multinational enterprises" as a sizeable cause of BEPS.[52]

This ultimately contributes to the problem that around half of the world's developing economies struggle to achieve tax to GDP ratios above 15 percent.[53] In OECD countries this ratio is notably higher at 30–45 percent.[54] Moreover, taxation of corporate revenue is a comparatively important share of tax revenue in Africa, including due to practical limitations in collecting personal income taxes. Illicit financial outflows, with abusive transfer mispricing accounting for a large share, exceed official development assistance received by the continent as well as inflows of foreign direct investment.[55] Consequently, massive amounts of wealth are leaving Africa, unduly reducing government revenue and impairing the ability to provide public services. Abusive transfer pricing and BEPS are, thus, as serious a concern as more commonly quoted problems relating to certain investors' undue harm of the environment or their failure to comply with basic labour standards or to respect human rights.[56]

4 Opportunities and Challenges Arising from Tax-Related Investor Obligations

4.1 Opportunities: The Value Added of Direct Tax Obligations

There are at least four principal avenues through which the inclusion of tax-related investor obligations adds value to the AfCFTA PoI. They reinforce

52 African Development Bank Group, 'Domestic Resource Mobilization across Africa: Trends, Challenges and Policy Options' (African Development Bank Group 2010) 4 <https://www.afdb.org/en/documents/document/policy-brief-domestic-resource-mobilization-across-africa-trends-challenges-and-policy-options-21932> accessed 9 September 2024.

53 Directorate-General for International Cooperation and Development (European Commission) (n 11), 6.

54 Ibid., 6.

55 UNCTAD, 'Tackling Illicit Financial Flows for Sustainable Development in Africa' (n 30), 25, 155, 181.

56 See supra, Chapter 5, Jackson Shaw Kern and Mohit Khubchandani, "Enforcing International Environmental and Climate Change Law on Investors: Reflections on the Investment Protocol to the African Continental Free Trade Area and Beyond"; Chapter 8, Mohit Khubchandani, "Soft Law or Hard Law? Selected International Labour and Indigenous Peoples' Rights Standards Transposable to Investor Obligations in New-Age Investment Treaties".

existing rules on the international plane, mitigate gaps in domestic regulatory frameworks, can create the necessary impetus for tax-related technical assistance and capacity building, and create a degree of certainty for investors and States alike with respect to the compliance of domestic tax measures with the AfCFTA PoI.

First, with respect to the reinforcement of existing rules, as set out, rules and principles relating to transfer pricing and BEPS have a long-established history and are, nowadays, well-anchored on the international plane. Nevertheless, in many respects they consist of informal international law, which lacks a forum for direct enforcement against private entities. Depending on how investor obligations can be enforced under the AfCFTA PoI,[57] States, including their revenue authorities, may have the possibility to bring direct legal actions against foreign investors on the international plane. Importantly, this may allow for the nearly world-wide enforcement of any award in favour of the State. This matters especially with respect to tax-related investor obligations as, by its very nature, base erosion and profit shifting may lead to empty corporate shells in the host State that are stripped of any financial assets against which an award could be enforced.

Additionally, under Article 47 of the PoI, States are required to create procedures to bring civil actions against investors in their home States. Although the scope of this obligation, and notably the question whether it applies to the tax-related investor obligations, will depend on the domestic implementation by individual States, it at least appears to open an additional avenue for enforcement. Thus, rather than having to bring tax enforcement actions against domestic entities that are unable to fulfill any resulting financial liabilities, the Protocol might allow States to directly pursue investors in the courts of their home States.

The last point concerning the reinforcement of existing rules on the international plane relates to the capacity of individual countries to comply with existing recommendations and the development of bespoke approaches to implementation. The PoI's relatively vague language, referencing "relevant international best practices" relating to transfer pricing and "international rules and principles" on BEPS, leaves room to develop African approaches on these issues. As set out above, the ECOWIC directly referred to the OECD Transfer Pricing Guidelines as the relevant international standard. While the OECD Guidelines are of significant importance for determining appropriate transfer prices, and will likely continue to do so, they are also not necessarily

57 Negotiations on the dispute settlement annex have not been formally concluded at the time of writing.

suited to the capacities and specific needs of all African economies, including least developed countries. The reinforcement of existing rules may, thus, take the additional dimension of developing regional approaches for implementation, ultimately enhancing compliance with international rules.

Second, Article 40 on taxation and transfer pricing may mitigate domestic regulatory gaps. Not all (African) countries have explicitly incorporated the arm's length standard into their domestic laws.[58] In addition, the standard requires detailed rules for implementation. Many African countries do not have the appropriate regulatory frameworks in place.[59] As of 2019 "about half of the countries in sub-Saharan Africa still did not have any form of domestic transfer pricing rules".[60] Consequently, it is almost impossible to challenge the practices of MNEs through local authorities.

Article 40(1) may help to counter this problem. Its reference to international best practices in subparagraph (a) opens the door to supplement inadequate domestic regulatory frameworks. Thus, in countries that lack domestic rules, the provision would enable local authorities to directly rely on the OECD Transfer Pricing Guidelines or the UN Practical Manual as spelling out international best practices. Some doubts may be raised whether domestic courts would allow for the assessment of tax liabilities directly by reference to informal international rules. However, with the entry into force of the PoI, governments would gain another tool to bolster their legal argument that direct reliance on international best practice is appropriate.

Concerning BEPS more broadly, as referenced in Article 40(1)(b) of the PoI, a similar argument could be made. Although it may be more difficult to identify "international rules and principles", they do exist. For example, some of the outcomes of the 2015 G20/OECD BEPS Project were directly implemented through the Commentaries to the UN and OECD Model Conventions. The Commentaries provide detailed guidance for the interpretation and application of DTT provisions. As BEPS practices change over time, so do the Commentaries' interpretations of existing treaty provisions, an informal means of keeping a decentralised system of thousands of DTTs adaptable to current circumstances. Some of the interpretations developed as a consequence of the BEPS Project may become relevant to the extent that African countries

58 See, for example, Alexandra Readhead, 'Transfer Pricing in the Mining Sector in Guinea: Case Study' (Natural Resource Governance Institute 2016) 3 <https://resourcegovernance.org/sites/default/files/documents/nrgi_guinea_transfer-pricing-study.pdf> accessed 9 September 2024.

59 UNCTAD, 'Tackling Illicit Financial Flows for Sustainable Development in Africa' (n 30), 105.

60 Ibid., 114.

have adopted DTTs. In combination with Article 40(1)(b), such new interpretations may be directly applicable to investor practices, mitigating domestic regulatory gaps.

Third, tax-related investor obligations may create the necessary impetus for the provision of related technical assistance and capacity building. In the context of the AfCFTA PoI, Article 43 provides for technical assistance, capacity building and cooperation to "further the implementation" of the Protocol. With respect to BEPS, and transfer pricing in particular, one of the main concerns is the lack of capacity to effectively audit the practices of MNEs.[61] This is even the case where robust domestic legislation is in place. The differences in economic development on the continent, thus, translate into opportunities for cooperation, exchange of best practices and technical assistance. Some African countries have, for example, established highly trained transfer pricing and international tax units in their domestic revenue authorities. Other jurisdictions may be able to learn from these experiences.

More broadly, tax-related investor obligations help raise awareness among investment policymakers and practitioners of the importance of domestic revenue mobilisation. The challenge is, thus, no longer to attract investment but rather to attract investment that contributes to raising government revenue. By integrating transfer pricing and BEPS issues into investment policy frameworks, those responsible for the oversight of investors are directly alerted to the relevance of investor compliance with tax obligations. This may help remedy a lack of political will, largely caused by lack of awareness, to bolster domestic capacities in this area.

Fourth, the inclusion of tax-related investor obligations in IIAs can help create a degree of certainty for investors and States alike with respect to the compliance of domestic tax measures with the investment treaty in question. For investors, the reference to international best practices on transfer pricing and international rules and principles relating to BEPS ensures a degree of certainty. Linking expectations of investor behaviour to international rules, principles, and best practices ensures consistency in these expectations. MNEs will be required to adopt largely similar practices regardless of where they invest. Furthermore, the stability that arises from aligning expected behavior with international standards ensures a degree of continuity in the treatment of investors. Their compliance with best practices in the first place

61 Pietro Guj, Stephanie Martin and Alexandra Readhead, 'Transfer Pricing in Mining with a Focus on Africa: A Briefing Note' (World Bank Group 2017) vi <https://documents.worldbank.org/en/publication/documents-reports/documentdetail/213881485941701316/transfer-pricing-in-mining-with-a-focus-on-africa-a-briefing-note> accessed 9 September 2024.

makes MNEs somewhat immune to having to comply with radical regulatory changes as a consequence of changing political whims.

For States, tax-related investor obligations equally create a degree of certainty. Measures adopted in pursuance of international rules and principles relating to BEPS or implementing best practices on transfer pricing should largely be shielded from challenge under the investment protection standards of the treaty. Investors, which are obliged by Article 40(1) to already comply with such rules, principles, and best practices in the first place, are unlikely to be able to successfully claim that domestic tax measures violate the PoI's investment protection standards when they simply seek alignment with such international standards. This is not entirely irrelevant as the exception for tax measures from the PoI's scope under Article 3(4)(e) only applies to "measures taken in accordance with the applicable laws and regulations of a State Party", not any tax measures. This exception can be interpreted to be broad, but it is not unlimited. In particular, it is unclear to what extent it covers the enactment of new tax laws. Arguably, the requirement to comply with "applicable laws and regulations of a State Party" does not exclusively refer to the procedural requirements for the enactment of new tax measures. The reference to "applicable laws and regulations" could potentially still leave room for scrutiny over whether the tax measure might be discriminatory or arbitrary. Tax measures adopted in pursuance of international rules and principles relating to BEPS or implementing best practices on transfer pricing should, in any case, be difficult to challenge under the PoI's investment protection standards, given the investor obligation to comply with such rules, principles, and best practices regardless of domestic laws.

The Lone Star case, referenced in the introduction to this chapter, serves to illustrate this last point. To recall, Korean tax authorities disallowed reliance on the DTT exception for taxing capital gains under the Korea–Belgium DTT. The way in which Lone Star had structured its Korean investment, routing a US investment through Belgium, was solely to avail itself of tax treaty benefits according to Korean authorities. It did not serve any other rational economic purpose.[62] One of the reasons why the arbitral tribunal sided with Korea on this point was the long-standing history of the Korean anti-treaty-abuse rule as a matter of domestic law as well as in the international tax regime.[63] If the same or similar facts were to arise in a case involving a party to the AfCFTA PoI, the country may be able to argue that, even in the absence of a long-standing domestic practice, investors are already required to comply with

62 *Lone Star v. Korea* (n 5), paras 389–397.

63 Ibid., 405–410.

international principles on BEPS by virtue of Article 40(1), arguably prohibiting them from structuring investments for the sole purpose of unduly availing themselves of DTT benefits in inappropriate circumstances.[64] This is regardless of the existence of domestic rules on the matter. For States, the investor obligation contained in Article 40(1), therefore, operates as much as a shield as it is a sword.

5 Challenges Relating to the Inclusion of Tax-Related Investor Obligations

The point of this brief section is not to discuss the merits (or lack thereof) of including investor obligations in IIAs.[65] Instead, the focus is briefly on two issues that arise in particular with respect to tax-related obligations, relating to questions of implementation and the suitability of ISDS to deal with tax-related disputes. First, one of the main challenges relating to Article 40(1) of the AfCFTA PoI is inextricably linked to the issue of technical assistance and capacity building, discussed above. To be fully effective, some of the investor obligations, including those on tax, require domestic implementation or the adoption of adequate domestic regulatory frameworks. While the references to international best practices, rules, and principles are helpful, the provision becomes far more effective if domestic transfer pricing regulations and adequate domestic laws are adopted. Moreover, even existing laws can suffer from insufficient enforcement.[66] The inclusion of tax-related investor obligations on its own, thus, does little to build domestic capacity. Ultimately, the provision is far from self-executing and requires a significant investment in domestic capacities relating to tax regulation and enforcement.

Second, one may wonder whether ISDS - not necessarily arbitration but ISDS writ large - is the right place to deal with transfer pricing and BEPS-related disputes. The tax community has previously displayed a strong preference for non-adversarial dispute settlement.[67] There is now a discernible shift

64 See generally, OECD, 'Preventing the Granting of Treaty Benefits in Inappropriate Circumstances, Action 6–2015 Final Report' (OECD 2015) 6 <https://www.oecd.org/ctp/preventing-the-granting-of-treaty-benefits-in-inappropriate-circumstances-action-6-2015-final-report-9789264241695-en.htm> accessed 11 November 2022.

65 See generally, Chapters 1 to 3 of this volume.

66 See Guj, Martin and Readhead (n 60), vi.

67 See generally, Robert Green, 'Antilegalistic Approaches to Resolving Disputes Between Governments: A Comparison of the International Tax and Trade Regimes' (1998) 23 Yale Journal of International Law 79.

in the attitude towards binding tax arbitration. This is, for example, evidenced by its increasing adoption in DTTs as well as the multilateral instrument on BEPS.[68] Tax arbitration is, however, very different from ISDS, most prominently in its limited involvement of private parties, making the procedure largely an inter-State affair. Given the outright adversarial nature of ISDS and the lack of tax expertise among investment arbitrators, one may seriously doubt that the investment arena provides the right forum to adjudicate issues such as transfer pricing disputes. As observed by tax experts, national courts at times make fundamental errors in the interpretation of tax obligations.[69] There is no reason to believe that investment arbitrators would fare any better. The existence of such challenges should not, however, be taken as detracting from the fundamental advantage that the inclusion of tax-related investor obligations, particularly in the African context, provides.

6 Conclusion

To summarise and conclude, this chapter explored the evolving relationship between international tax measures and investor obligations. It highlights the increasing intersection of tax and investment law and examines Article 40(1) of the AfCFTA Protocol on Investment, detailing investor obligations on related party transactions and BEPS. Section 2 aimed to provide background on basic tax concepts addressed in the provision, including their meaning and origin. Subsequently, the chapter traced the pedigree and prevalence of tax-related investor obligations, with a focus on Africa's heightened vulnerability to transfer pricing abuse. The final section discussed the opportunities and difficulties of including tax-related investor obligations in IIAs, underscoring their potential to reinforce international norms and bridge gaps in domestic regulatory frameworks, while also recognising the challenges tax-related investor obligations entail.

68 Multilateral Convention to Implement Tax Treaty Related Measures to Prevent Base Erosion and Profit Shifting (entered into force on 1 July 2018) arts 18–26.

69 Brian J Arnold, 'The Interpretation of Tax Treaties: Looking to the Future' (2021) 75 Bulletin for International Taxation 665, 668.

www.ingramcontent.com/pod-product-compliance
Lightning Source LLC
LaVergne TN
LVHW080800161026
850117LV00043B/20

* 9 7 8 9 0 0 4 7 6 9 8 4 7 *